A GEEK IN CHINA

DISCOVERING THE LAND OF BULLET TRAINS, ALIBABA AND DIM SUM

MATTHEW CHRISTENSEN

Content Advisor: **MICHAEL A. PAUL**

TUTTLE Publishing

Tokyo | Rutland, Vermont | Singapore

Contents

THE CHINA FEW PEOPLE SEE

In a single generation, China has evolved from an ancient civilization into a modern nation. Reminders of the past are everywhere, from the Great Wall to the deference and respect with which people treat their elders. China has now stepped onto the world stage as a great power, but for a long time we knew next to nothing about it. And practically everything that we now touch in our daily lives comes from China, from the clothes we wear to the iPhones we carry.

China formally introduced itself to the world in 2008 when Beijing hosted the Summer Olympic Games. For many people, this was their first close look at China. Before this, their vision of the country centered around ping-pong, panda bears, kung-fu and tea. In the past two decades, the West has witnessed an emerging world power that in some ways looks like any other modern nation but in others looks awfully foreign.

Since I first visited China in the early 1980s, things have changed dramatically. At that time, China was emerging from a xenophobic period when it cut itself off from the rest of the world and was deeply entrenched in Communist ideology. With Mao Zedong's death and Deng Xiaoping's economic reforms of the early 1980s, China began a slow transformation from a society where the central government owned and operated literally everything to a new hybrid society, the likes of which the world has never seen.

I have been traveling to China for almost 30 years now, and have spent many of these years training students to travel, work and study in China. Although China today looks superficially like a modern, Westernized country, under the surface it is very different. This includes things like humor, television and movies, cultural values, how the Chinese perceive and interact with the media, their history and daily practices, the kind of literature they value, social rules of conduct, what, how and where they eat, and so on. This book attempts to expose you, the reader, to the various things in China that make it quintessentially China. These are the things that all Chinese know and have grown up with. Understanding them will help to make your own experience of China much richer because you will understand why people do the things they do and think the way they think.

Opposite top A PLA soldier at the entrance to the Forbidden City. **Opposite below** Old and new. **Left** Nanjing Road, Shanghai, during the May 1st holiday. **Below** Chen Tianshu painting and calligraphy exhibition, Liuzhou.

WHY IS CHINA DIFFERENT?

For much of China's long history, it was largely cut off from the outside world and developed independently of the West. This was partly due to geography. High mountains and harsh deserts formed a natural barrier to the west and a large ocean to the east made it difficult to go in that direction. As a result, China has developed its own internal set of values and social structures:

1. Society in China is based on a set of Confucian principles that emphasize the importance of relationships and hierarchy.

2. In Chinese society, the group is the most important unit whereas in the West we emphasize the importance of the individual. In China, being part of a group or organization and maintaining harmony within the group, even being dependent on that group, is valued highly. In the West, we teach young people to think independently, to stand out and make a name for themselves. In China, parents teach their children to fit in and to avoid anything that might isolate them.

3. The Chinese written language is based on a set of characters or symbols that are not alphabetic and must be painstakingly memorized, which is a difficult task for every Chinese student. This presents a significant barrier for many individuals from other parts of the world.

4. China is one of the world's oldest nations and has always placed great value on its history. Change comes very slowly here. Political and social structures developed 3,000 years ago still remain intact today. A change from autocratic rule to democracy is unlikely in the near future.

5. China has always been inward-looking. It has rarely been a conqueror or colonizing power. The Chinese name for China, Zhong-guo, means 'central kingdom'. Outsiders were considered barbarians and the Chinese never had much desire to leave their borders or to learn from anyone else. There was very little contact with the West until the mid-1800s, and thus China stayed unique.

WHY CHINA IS SPECIAL TO ME

I'm fascinated by antiquity and China is the ideal place to experience it. To walk a cobbled pathway along a stone city wall constructed a thousand years ago fills me with wonder. Who else has walked this same path? Reading poetry written 2,500 years ago gives me a glimpse into the lives of an ancient people, how they lived, their emotions and what they cared about.

Modern China is a wonderful mix of old and new where you find ancient Buddhist monasteries alongside gleaming high-rise buildings, glitzy multistoried restaurants next to dingy noodle shops right out of the Qing Dynasty, and high-fashion shoppers passing old men doing taichi in the park.

One of the things that continually draws me to China is its vast and varied cuisine. A fantastic meal is just around the corner no matter where you are in China.

A couple and their child on a scooter. Until recently, urban couples could officially have only one child.

MY INITIAL CULTURE SHOCK

My first exposure to Chinese culture was in Hong Kong where I lived for a year and a half. Being a British colony, Hong Kong is much more Westernized than the rest of China. But when I first boarded a plane to Shanghai, I could see immediately that things were going to be very different. The plane was full of Chinese men all wearing similar dark blue or green trousers and jackets and all smoking hand-rolled cigarettes. They all wore white shirts. Every single one of them.

The first thing you notice when you leave the airport in China in summer is the intense heat, the ear-splitting noise and the strange smells. These sensations can be overwhelming for a first-timer to China, like a hard slap in the face. The air and noise pollution are certainly more than you ever expected. In large cities, you seldom see the sun and the sky is usually gray or yellow.

You may also feel overwhelmed by the crowds. People are always 'in your face' in China, and you rarely find yourself alone. Streets are packed with people jostling one another, which can be irritating. They often stare at foreigners, making you feel awkward. But many Chinese are friendly and will go out of their way to help you. Traffic is completely chaotic. Be very cautious when crossing the street as cars will very rarely stop for you.

Everything feels different and foreign. This is normal. Even if you expect it, it can still be a bit overwhelming the first few days. Initially, the food may make your stomach churn. And you may feel unnerved to see people spitting in the streets, or so many people smoking, including young women.

But don't despair. Keep an open mind and a willingness to learn, and you will adapt quickly and enjoy your new environment. Many things that seem totally foreign at first quickly become part of the everyday reality of life. Each time

you go back to China, the transition is smoother until you get to the point that when you step off the plane a 'China' switch is thrown and you are 'back home' again.

LOOKS CAN BE DECEPTIVE

China's big cities don't look much different from any other big modern city in the world. Towering steel and glass skyscrapers, upscale shopping centers, young people dressed in designer fashions, modern subway systems and countless restaurants and clubs are all part of the new China. But you

MY FIRST EXPERIENCE IN CHINA

I first went to China in 1985 as a college student to study Chinese. Before that, I had lived in Hong Kong, which whetted my appetite to see the real China. After a long flight from San Francisco, full of Chinese men smoking hand-rolled cigarettes, we landed in Shanghai, spent the night there, then boarded the train the next morning for Nanjing where I would be studying at Nanjing University. It was immediately apparent that this was not the Westernized Hong Kong I knew. Back then, China had a raw, rough quality about it. At the same time, it had an aura of deep history and cultural richness that immediately attracted me. The streets were teeming with bicycles and people but very few cars, and everyone was dressed in dark blue or green Mao outfits. Although I was expecting a dour, downtrodden people who had just a few years earlier survived the Cultural Revolution, the Chinese were happy, open and generous. I felt at home.

Relaxing in a traditional garden in Suzhou, spring 1985.

Above A cheerful taxi driver plying his trade.
Right The glass and steel skyscraper-studded Shanghai skyline.

may be surprised by the astonishing bling factor seen in big cities. Urban Chinese are obsessed with Western fashion and luxury goods. Jack Ma, the chairman of the Alibaba Group, is the richest person in China with an estimated worth of US$30 billion. His group of companies has transformed Internet shopping in China.

But get off the main thoroughfares, into the side streets and the back alleys, and you'll see a very different China. Behind the glitzy façade, most Chinese remain a conservative people governed by Confucian values and thousands of years of history. You'll see peasants carrying shoulder poles with baskets of fruit alongside businesswomen with iPhones, old Chinese men dressed in traditional padded jackets and black cotton-soled shoes with pet birds in bamboo cages in the same park where young men dressed like NBA stars are playing basketball, a back alley in Beijing where people still burn coal bricks to stay warm in the winter just around the corner from a high-rise luxury hotel. Although eating Western fast food is a status statement in China, the vast majority of Chinese still prefer traditional Chinese food prepared the same way it has been for centuries. While many Chinese have embraced Western culture, young people still bow to the wishes of their parents, pay their respects to their ancestors and are fiercely proud of their long history and culture.

Above Jack Ma, CEO of Alibaba Group, a giant Internet company, giving a speech in Hangzhou.
Right Young people enjoying themselves at the international outdoor Yoga Midi Music Festival, Huaxi Park, Guiyang Province.

CHAPTER 1
CHINA PAST AND PRESENT

China has the longest continuous history of any country on earth with a standardized writing system that has been in use since around 1000 BCE. China's famous historical and mythological figures are well known in and outside of China and Chinese philosophies are revered the world over. The Great Wall of China and the Terracotta Warriors are Chinese icons recognized by everyone all over the world. China's past has created a fascinating backdrop for China's emergence in the modern world.

HISTORICAL AND MYTHOLOGICAL FIGURES WHO STILL MATTER TODAY

Although some of China's famous historical and mythological figures, such as Confucius and Laozi, are well known around the world, many are unknown to us in the West. Many famous and important people from China, is past—from emperors and philosophers to military generals and poets—are still revered in China today.

CONFUCIUS

Confucius (551–479 BCE) is the most celebrated figure in China's history. He was a philosopher, educator and reformer. His thought and philosophy form the basis of Confucian or *Ru* thought in China and the entire moral codes of China and other East Asian countries like Japan and Korea. Whereas in the West we follow Judeo-Christian ethics, in China people live by a Confucian code of ethics.

Confucian philosophy is rooted in the concept of *ren* or compassion and love for others. This involves deprecating yourself as you show concern for others. Confucius's golden rule was 'What you do not wish for yourself, do not do to others.' He also believed in the importance of reciprocal relationships: ruler to subject, father to son, husband to wife, brother to brother and friend to friend. In each relationship there is responsibility on the side of both parties. For example, a husband treats his wife with kindness and she, in return, is obedient and loyal. One's place and status in society are also important. Confucius's sayings were collected by his disciples and compiled into a book called *The Analects*.

LAOZI

Laozi, literally 'old master', was an ancient Chinese philosopher who is said to have written the short book *Dao De Jing* (Tao Te Ching), often translated as *Classic of the Way and Virtue*. According to Chinese tradition, he was a brilliant thinker who lived in the 6th century BCE during the Zhou Dynasty and was from the state of Chu (present-day Hunan). But there is no hard evidence that he even existed. In religious Taoism he is considered a god. According to early historical records, he was a contemporary of Confucius who consulted him regarding mourning and funeral rites. Confucius praised his wisdom. After Laozi witnessed the decline of the Zhou kingdom, he wandered off to the far northwest border of China. There he met an official at the border crossing who asked him to write down his teachings, whereupon in 5,000 characters he wrote the meaning of *dao* or 'the way' and virtue. He is much revered in China as the founder of Taoist philosophy and religious Taoism.

EMPEROR QIN SHI HUANG

Qin Shi Huang (259–210 BCE) was the first emperor of China and ruled over the short-lived Qin Dynasty (221–206 BCE). He was the ruler of one (Qin) of seven states in China that were vying for power at the time. He was successful in conquering and unifying the other states and creating the first unified kingdom in China. To unify the empire, he instituted reforms and models, such as standardizing the written script, coinage and axle width, which improved the road system. He also began construction of a wall that later evolved into the Great Wall. For all the good he did, he was a ruthless ruler who regularly executed scholars who did not agree with his policies. Thousands of young men were also forced to work constructing the Great Wall as well as his elaborate mausoleum, which includes the famous Terracotta Warriors.

THE MONKEY KING

The Monkey King is the central character in the classic novel *Journey to the West* (also translated as *Monkey*), written in the 16th century by Wu Cheng'en. The story is based on the legendary journey of the Buddhist monk Xuan Zang to India to obtain sacred Buddhist texts. In this fantastical fictionalized account, four guardians accompany him on his journey. One of them is Sun Wukong, a monkey born from a stone nourished by the five elements. He has magical powers that allow him to fly, transform himself into other beings and be immortal. The story is hugely popular all over the Chinese-speaking world and there have been countless adaptations, from comic books to movies, TV series, plays and video games.

CAO CAO AND ZHUGE LIANG

Cao Cao was the emperor of the kingdom of Wei during the Three Kingdoms Period (220–280 CE). He fought to reunify China and was successful in northern China. His forces were

defeated by Zhuge Liang in the famous Battle of Red Cliffs but he was never able to conquer the southern kingdoms.

Zhuge Liang and Cao Cao are still famous today for their roles as the principal characters in the historical novel *Romance of the Three Kingdoms* written by Luo Guanzhong in the 14th century. The novel is part history and part myth. It tells the story of the break-up of the Han Dynasty, the division of China into three kingdoms, Shu, Wu and Wei, and the struggles of Zhuge Liang and Cao Cao to reunite the country. The stories portrayed are well known by the Chinese as there have been countless adaptations, movies, TV series, video games and comic books based on the novel.

LI BAI AND DU FU

Li Bai (701–262 CE) is the the most famous poet in Chinese history. He is as well known in China as Shakespeare is in the Western world. Sometimes referred to as the 'banished immortal', he was considered a poetic genius who spent most of his life wandering, indulging in wine and writing poetry. Every schoolboy and girl in China memorizes a few of his poems. He was heavily influenced by Daoism and Buddhism.

Along with Li Bai, Du Fu (712–770 CE) is a household name in China. He is also a Tang Dynasty poet who was revered for his ability to master all forms of poetry. He was a Confucian who lived in a time of political turmoil. He spent much of his life either working for the imperial court or defending imperial rule when in exile. He is sometimes called the 'poet historian' as many of his poems are about daily life and current events during his time.

ADMIRAL ZHENG HE

Zheng He (1371–1433) was a palace eunuch, diplomat, explorer and mariner during the Ming Dynasty who rose to the ranks of Admiral. Between 1405 and 1433 he commanded large expeditions that explored and traded with countries in Southeast Asia, South Asia, the Middle East and East Africa. He was undoubtedly China's greatest maritime figure. At a time when maritime exploration was in its infancy in the West, and nearly a century before Columbus set sail for the New World, Admiral Zheng commanded fleets of hundreds of ships manned by thousands of sailors. His first voyage left Suzhou in 1405 with 317 ships and 28,000 crewmen. Some of his ships were so large that the combined fleets of Columbus and Vasco da Gama could fit on the deck of a single ship in Zheng's armada. During his various voyages, he presented gifts of gold, silver, silk and porcelain, and in return received such exotic gifts as ivory, ostriches, camels, zebras and even a giraffe. It is speculated that the purpose of his voyages was to expand the Chinese empire by creating tributary states.

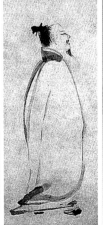

Far left Drawing of the poet Du Fu. **Left** Painting of Li Bai by Liang K'ai called 'Li Po Chanting a Poem'. **Below** Detail of Chinese Running Style calligraphy.

HIGHLIGHTS OF CHINESE HISTORY

During the Warring States Period (481–221 BCE), China was ruled by seven semi-independent kings. Each of their kingdoms had its own language, customs and cultural practices. The Qin kingdom in western China along the Wei River, a tributary of the Yellow River, began conquering its neighboring kingdoms. In 221 BCE, the Qin successfully conquered the other six kingdoms and, for the first time, unified the country under central rule.

The king of Qin declared himself Qin Shi Huang or the first emperor of Qin. The name of this new unified kingdom, Qin, was eventually Latinized as 'China' or China. The emperor of Qin instituted several changes, including a common monetary system. He also built roads and standardized axle widths, established a common language and writing system and a strong central rule with a well-developed bureaucracy. The dynasty was short-lived, however, as the emperor ruthlessly suppressed dissent, imposed heavy taxes, distrusted the scholar class (even burning books and killing intellectuals who he considered a threat to his rule), and was obsessed with finding a means to immortality. Before the emperor died, he conscripted tens of thousands of workers to build a tomb that included thousands of lifelike terracotta warriors.

Above An 18th-century depiction of Emperor Qin Shi Huang's imperial tour across his empire. **Left** Terracotta warriors guarding the tomb of Emperor Qin Shi Huang (r. 221–210 BCE).

THE HAN DYNASTY

Ethnic Chinese today call themselves Han after the Han Dynasty. The Han period is considered one of the most important in China's history, as it was a time when a political system was established that remained intact, with some modifications, until the 20th century. Confucianism became the governing philosophy and helped shape the very character of the Chinese people. This was also a time of great prosperity. During the later part of the Han Dynasty, the capital of Luoyang housed half a million people, the largest city in the world at that time.

One very important development was the examination system whereby scholars could join the ruling elite based on merit. These exams were based on the Confucian Classics, a series of five books that included poetry and history, political speeches and guidelines for ritual practice established by Confucius and his later followers. Those who scored the highest in the exams were given jobs of more importance, such us mayors, governors, even prime minister, and personal aids to the emperor. This system of meritocracy was used in China all the way up to the 20th century.

TANG AND SONG DYNASTIES

The capital of the Tang Dynasty, Chang'an (present-day Xi'an), was the largest city in the world. This was a high point in Chinese civilization, even surpassing the glories of the Han Dynasty. It was a golden age of literature, art, religion and cosmopolitan culture. The Tang Dynasty is best known for its flowering of Chinese poetry. China's most revered poets—Li Bai, Du Fu and Wang Wei—wrote during this illustrious period. Today in China people still study these Tang Dynasty poems and learn to write in these forms. An 18th-century anthology of Tang poetry has become a treasured book familiar to all educated Chinese. Landscape painting also developed and became important during this time.

THE WARRING STATES OF CHINA 250 BCE

Yellow River
Dai • Ji • YAN
Gilf of Jili
ZHAO
Handan •
Ye •
WEI   Wei •
Anyi •
Yang • Wei River   Luoyang • Daliang
Xianyang •   HAN Yangzhai • Chen
Nanzheng •   Han River   Danyang • Chai
QIN   Shouchun •   Wu •
CHU
Shu •   Ying •
Ba •
QI • Linzi
Yellow Sea
Huai River
Yangtse River

Top Tang court ladies, from the tomb of Princess Yongtai, Qianling Mausoleum, near Xi'an, Shaanxi. **Above** Spring outing of the Tang court.

MAJOR PERIODS IN CHINESE HISTORY

Shang Dynasty 1650–1045 BCE	The beginning of Chinese civilization and recorded history; walled cities, writing system, practice of divination, bronze technology, horse-drawn chariots.
Zhou Dynasty 1045–256 BCE	Political and social system ruled by the Zhou royal house based on hierarchy; power and land bestowed on aristocratic families, similar to Europe's feudal system; power broke down among the semi-feudal states during the Spring and Autumn and Warring States periods.
Qin Dynasty 221–206 BCE	The kingdom of Qin conquers the other six kingdoms that fought for power during the Warring States Period and China is unified for the first time; capital near present-day Xi'an.
Han Dynasty 206 BCE–220 CE	Modified and established the foundation for aristocratic rule; Confucianism becomes orthodox and the civil service examination system was introduced where civil servants were selected through merit; capitals established in modern-day Xi'an, then in modern-day Luoyang.
Six Dynasties 220–589 CE	The empire is fragmented; the north is ruled by non-Chinese invaders, the south ruled by successive Chinese dynasties; Buddhism is introduced from India and spreads; several influential forms of religious Daoism emerge.
Sui Dynasty 581–618 CE	China reunified; capital established in modern-day Xi'an.
Tang Dynasty 618–907 CE	Cultural renaissance, a flowering of the arts and literature; continued spread of Buddhism until suppressed in 845 CE; capital established in modern-day Xi'an; Silk Road and Indian Ocean trade flourished.
Song Dynasty 960–1279 CE	Significant economic and social change; growth in commerce and maritime trade; urban expansion and many technological innovations, including woodblock printing; civil service examination system further refined based on neo-Confucianism; capital established in modern-day Kaifeng, then moved close to modern-day Hangzhou.
Yuan Dynasty 1279–1368 CE	Mongol dynasty as part of their conquest of much of Asia and Eastern Europe; Beijing becomes capital of China for the first time.
Ming Dynasty 1368–1644 CE	Beginning of authoritarian political rule and culture; inward-looking state; growth of commercial sector; vibrant literary scene; capital first established in Nanjing, then moved to Beijing.
Qing Dynasty 1644–1912 CE	China ruled by Manchu invaders; further economic expansion and prosperity; dramatic increase in population; authoritarian structure challenged by military and cultural influences from the West.
Republican 1912–1949 CE	Weak central government after collapse of the dynastic system; continued Western influence and promotion of science and democracy; Nationalist government unable to unify the country because of Japanese invasion and civil war with the Communists; the Nationalists fled to Taiwan after their defeat in 1949.
People's Republic of China 1949–present	Communist/socialist government; economic expansion; land reform; gender equality; language reform; now considered a world superpower.

Buddhism gained a loyal following and many monasteries and temples were constructed during this period. It was also during this time that Buddhist doctrine was modified to conform with existing Chinese thought and philosophies.

The Tang Dynasty was so important in Chinese history that to this day many Chinese refer to themselves as 'Tang people', just as they also refer to themselves as Han.

The Song Dynasty continued the flourishing of the arts that began in the Tang Dynasty. New poetic forms were developed and art, religion and philosophy continued to flourish. The invention of woodblock printing led to a significant increase in literacy and many texts became widely available.

The economy expanded considerably during the Song and the country's population doubled, an integrated system of waterways was built, the first paper money was issued and commerce increased through trading of necessities and luxury goods. This resulted in an urban revolution where 10 percent of the population lived in cities. The last innovation was the appearance of large-scale industry, such as the production of iron. Some have argued this was the beginning of capitalism.

HERE COMES THE WEST: THE OPIUM WARS

Until the latter part of the 18th century, China had little contact with the West. Jesuit missionaries arrived in small numbers in the 15th century but had little impact. For centuries China had contact with other Asian nations, particularly Korea, Japan and Vietnam, but contact with the West was sporadic and minimal.

Left British troops land at the western gate of Chinkiang (Zhenjiang) during the First Opium War (1839–42) in their bid to secure ports along the eastern seaboard of China.
Above Painting of fighting between British and Chinese troops at Guangzhou during the Second Opium War (1856–60).

By the 1760s, tea imports to Great Britain were far greater than Britain's exports to China. This trade imbalance had to be made up with British silver. To offset the disparity, Britain began exporting raw cotton from India to China, along with an initially small but lucrative trade in opium, also from India. In time, the opium trade, smuggled into China and distributed by Chinese triads (organized crime gangs) grew until by 1820 the trade imbalance switched in favor of Great Britain. This caused a silver drain in China, making it difficult for peasants to pay their land taxes. Various violent incidents occurred which escalated into the First Opium War (1839–42). The British navy proved far stronger than the Chinese and they took control of ports along the eastern seaboard. In the Treaty of Nanjing in 1842, the Chinese opened five ports to foreign trade and residence. These included Guangzhou, Xiamen, Fuzhou, Ningbo and Shanghai. The Chinese government set up an office of 'barbarian affairs' to deal with the encroaching Westerners.

The Second Opium War (1856–60) was caused by Britain further encroaching on Chinese territory. With the Treaty of Tianjin in 1858, the Chinese agreed to open ten more ports, allowed foreigners, including missionaries, to travel into China's interior, legalized the opium trade and agreed to a British minister residing in Beijing.

For most of China's history, outsiders, whether Asian or European, were considered barbarians with nothing to offer China. It was during the Opium Wars that China realized that its technology, particularly military might, was not up to Western standards. This period in Chinese history marked the beginning of the end of imperial rule in China. As more Westerners arrived in China and trade increased, the Chinese began to realize that a foreign policy of isolationism was not the best way to go. The Manchu government grew increasingly weak and ineffective in ruling a changing China. At the same time, Western powers were forcing China to open up and engage with them.

THE LAST EMPEROR AND THE REVOLUTION OF 1911

On October 10, 1911, now known as 'Double Tenth', a rebellion broke out in Wuchang in Hubei Province. The province declared its independence from the empire. By December all other provinces had followed suit. A republic was declared, with Sun Zhongshan (Sun Yat-sen), a young revolutionary, as provisional president. However, he was not able to consolidate power and did not last long in this position. By this time in China's history, the country was fragmented and ruled by regional warlords, former military men under the Qing Dynasty. The Qing rulers appealed to a military commander in the north, Yuan Shikai, to support their rule. Instead, he sided with the new republic and forced the emperor to abdicate the throne. Yuan Shikai ruled first as president, then declared himself emperor (1912–16). His death left a political vacuum and for the next decade the country was ruled by various warlords.

THE FORBIDDEN CITY: HOME OF CHINA'S EMPERORS

The Forbidden City sits at the center of the ancient city of Beijing. Built between 1406 and 1420, it was the imperial palace of the Ming and Qing emperors, their families and other appointed political figures. It was the ceremonial and political center of China until the Qing Dynasty fell in 1912. It was called the Forbidden City because it was strictly off-limits to anyone outside the imperial household. No one could enter or leave without the permission of the emperor.

The palace complex consists of 980 buildings surrounded by a high wall and wide moat. Four towers stand guard at each corner of the huge complex and large gates are situated on each side. The Meridian Gate faces Tiananmen Square and is the entry point to the palace. The complex has an outer court with large ceremonial halls and an inner court with living quarters, kitchens and informal halls. The Forbidden City was named a World Heritage Site in 1987 by UNESCO for its archeological significance. It is the largest collection of ancient wooden structures in the world.

Above and left The Hall of Supreme Harmony, the largest hall within the Forbidden City, where emperors hosted enthronement and wedding ceremonies.

THE BLOODY TAIPING REBELLION 1849–1864

As China was reeling after the First Opium War, a young man seized the opportunity of a weakened Qing government to launch the most deadly rebellion in Chinese history. Hong Xiuquan, though from a poor family, received a decent education but failed the imperial examinations twice. After a brief encounter with Protestant missionaries, Hong claims to have met a 'bearded, golden-haired man who gave him a sword, and a younger man who instructed him to slay evil spirits, who Hong addressed as "Elder Brother".' Highly charismatic, Hong convinced people that God and Jesus had appeared to him. Studying with local missionaries, Hong began preaching and gaining converts, openly denouncing Confucianism and ancestor worship. By 1849 he had 10,000 converts and his doctrine was to form a new Christian community in opposition to the Qing government. He attracted young and old, rich and poor, and by 1850 his following had grown to 20,000. He became a significant threat, finally coming to the attention of the weakened Qing government. An attempt by Qing soldiers to oust Hong was met with defeat. Spurred on by this, Hong declared himself the Son of Heaven and his followers the Heavenly Kingdom of Great Peace (or Taipings). By the end of 1853 his following had grown to 60,000. Cities were attacked and many fell with little resistance. The Taipings gathered money, food, weapons and followers and seized Nanjing, killing 40,000 Manchu men, women and children, and openly declaring war on the Manchu government. Hong set up a Nanjing-based Heav-

enly Kingdom that survived for 11 years, from 1853 to 1864. The rule of the Taipings was extreme: sexes were segregated; opium, prostitution, dancing and drinking were banned; money was collectively shared; examinations were held on the Bible; and women were allowed into the bureaucracy. Yet, they failed to win over the residents of Nanjing and the surrounding countryside, who were resentful of the Taiping's constant need for food and supplies and their strange ways. Eventually, the Qing crushed the Taipings, in 1864.

CIVIL WAR AND THE RISE OF THE COMMUNISTS

The Communist Party of China (CPC) was organized in Shanghai in 1921. From 1928 to 1937, the Nationalists tried to transform China into a modern state based on Western models. This was unsuccessful as there was political fighting with the Communists. In 1931, Japan invaded China. The Nationalists, under the direction of Chang Kai-shek (Jiang Jieshi), were eager to oust the Communists under the direction of Mao Zedong, but after Japan invaded they were forced into a united front with the Communists against the Japanese. When the Japanese were defeated in 1945, the Communists and Nationalists began a full-scale civil war. The Nationalists had their capital first in Nanjing, then retreated to Chong-qing before being defeated by the Communists in 1949. The remaining Nationalist troops, along with many civilians, fled to Taiwan where they set up a government in exile.

Soldiers from the Chinese Communist People's Liberation Army taking over Fuzhou from the Chinese Nationalist Party (Kuomintang) on August 17, 1949.

Chairman Mao Zedong greeting US President Richard Nixon in Beijing on February 21, 1972, an important step in paving the way for normal relations between China and the United States.

MAO ZEDONG AND THE FOUNDING OF THE PEOPLE'S REPUBLIC OF CHINA

Mao Zedong was born to wealthy parents in Shaoshan, Hunan Province, in 1893. The revolution of 1911 and other movements during the early republican period had a significant impact on him. These incidents contributed to his adoption of Chinese nationalist and anti-imperialist views. He adopted Marxism-Leninism while working at Peking University. He was an early member of the Communist Party of China (CPC) and soon rose to a senior position. He helped to create a revolutionary peasant army and organized rural land reform. Mao was in charge of the CCP when the Japanese were defeated in 1945. He led the Communists to victory against the Nationalists in 1949. On October 1, 1949, Mao stood at the front gate of the Forbidden City overlooking Tiananmen Square and proclaimed the founding of the People's Republic of China, a one-party socialist state.

Under Mao's leadership, radical land reform was instituted, over-throwing feudal landlords, confiscating their huge land holdings and dividing up the land into communes worked by peasants. He was instrumental in industrializing the country, reforming Chinese script, raising the status of women, improving education and health care and providing universal housing. The population of China doubled during his leadership. Mao is not without his critics. Although he is considered to be one of the most important individuals in modern world history, many of his reforms resulted in widespread famine, political chaos and systematic human rights abuses.

SUN YAT-SEN: THE FATHER OF MODERN CHINA

Sun Yat-sen (1886–1925) was an early revolutionary and was instrumental in the overthrow of the Qing Dynasty in 1911. He was the first president and the founding father of the Republic of China (Nationalist China). Revered by both Communists and Nationalists, Sun Yat-sen was a co-founder of the Kuomintang (KMT), organized shortly after the 1911 revolution, and served as its first leader. He is considered the father of modern China and one of its greatest leaders. He is best known for developing a political philosophy known as the Three Principles of the People: Nationalism, Democracy and the People's Livelihood. He died of liver cancer at the age of 58 before

his political ideals could be realized. He is buried in a large mausoleum in the hills outside Nanjing, in Jiangsu Province.

US President Gerald Ford in an informal meeting with Vice Premier Deng Xiaoping in Beijing in 1975.

DENG XIAOPING AND CHINA'S ECONOMIC MIRACLE

Deng Xiaoping (1904 –97) was an early member of the Communist Party of China and a reformist leader. After Mao's death, he rose to power and implemented economic reforms that led China toward a market economy. He was the paramount leader of China from 1978 to 1992. He implemented what is known as 'socialism with Chinese characteristics'. His economic theory and plan became known as a 'socialist market economy'. He brought foreign investment, limited private enterprise and global marketing to China. He is credited with developing China into one of the major world economies and raising the standard of living of hundreds of millions of Chinese.

CHINA'S PRESIDENT

Xi Jinping (1953–) is the current President of China and Head of State, a figurehead under the National People's Congress. More importantly, he has served as General Secretary of the Central Committee since November 2012. This is the highest position within China's Communist Party structure and is widely considered the most powerful position in the country. He also serves as Commander in Chief of the joint battle command center, which ensures that he enjoys the support of China's military. He is originally from Beijing and studied engineering and law at the prestigious Qinghua University.

Xi Jinping, China's current President and Head of State since 2013. He served as Vice President from 2008 to 2013.

Right Three mega skyscrapers in the Pudong district of Shanghai: The Shanghai World Financial Center, Jinmao Tower and Shanghai Tower.
Below The Oriental Pearl Radio and TV Tower by the side of the Huangpu River in Pudong, opposite the Bund, is another distinctive landmark.

THE CHINESE LANGUAGE

To an outsider, the written Chinese language may seem like indecipherable chicken scratchings, but a language that has been in continuous use for thousands of years certainly makes sense to 1.3 billion Chinese. It is true that Chinese is vastly different from Western languages and it does take rigorous study to master. But it is a fascinating language to learn, spoken by more people than any other language.

THE WORLD'S FIRST WRITING

China has the world's oldest writing system still in use. There are older systems, such as Egyptian hieroglyphics and the Sumerian Cuneiform script, but they fell out of use long ago. The Chinese writing system that we can trace back to 1200 BCE is still recognizable to those who know Chinese. Although the system has evolved over time, it is still based on Chinese characters.

The earliest Chinese characters were written on the shoulder bones of oxen and on turtle shells. These early characters were used in divination ceremonies to predict the future. They are commonly referred to as 'oracle bones'. The vast majority of these bones date to the Shang Dynasty (1650–1045 BCE). Most of the characters are pictographs, stylized pictures of an object such as a tiger, a table, an eye or a horse.

By the Zhou Dynasty (1045–256 BCE), Chinese characters were being cast onto bronze vessels. The earliest

Chinese books consisted of bamboo slats with a row of Chinese characters written on them vertically. These slats were then lashed together to form a book. Later, Chinese was written on silk scrolls, then finally on paper.

CLASSICAL CHINESE

Early in Chinese history, the language already consisted of various spoken dialects. When the writing system was developed, a standard written form was promoted from as early as the Qin Dynasty (221–206 BCE) in an attempt to unite the various kingdoms of the

time. This writing system evolved into a written form called 'literary' or 'classical' Chinese. It was based on a spoken dialect but was not associated with any particular one. Over time, the written language and spoken varieties of Chinese grew apart until the situation was similar to the use of Latin in ancient Europe, where Latin was used for written documents but people continued to speak different languages. Classical Chinese was the written standard that all educated people used for written communication and literature of all kinds, but which no one spoke. This classical language was commonly used until the early part of the 20th century.

This literary language became canonized with the introduction of the Confucian Classics. These writings consisted of works that were associated with a classical education. Originally, they consisted of five books that were promoted by scholars as the most important works of literature with the power to improve the common man. We don't know the authors of these books, but they were studied religiously by the scholar-élite ruling class in China.

Oracle bone writing or *jiaguwen*. This is the earliest form of writing in China dating to as early as 1045 BCE. These characters were carved on the shoulder bones of oxen and on turtle shells.

Chinese calligraphy scrolls displayed in the National Palace Museum, Taipei, Taiwan.

The Book of Songs A collection of 305 songs or poems from the 10th to 7th centuries BCE, allegedly compiled by Confucius.

The Book of History A record of events in ancient China, some as early as the 11th century BCE.

The Book of Rites Written in the Han Dynasty, it describes the social customs, administration and ceremonial rites of the Zhou Dynasty (1045–256 BCE).

The Book of Changes A divination manual that dates back as far as 1000 BCE.

Spring and Autumn Annals A history of the State of Lu (722–481 BCE), the kingdom Confucius came from.

During the Han Dynasty (206 BCE–220 CE), four additional books were added to the canon. These were works compiled by disciples of Confucius. Further expounding on Confucian doctrine and ideals, the books were all written before 206 BCE.

The Great Learning Originally a chapter in the *Book of Rites*, said to be written by Confucius, it also contains commentary by one of Confucius's disciples.

Doctrine of the Mean Another chapter from the *Book of Rites*, attributed to Confucius's grandson, it describes how to attain perfect unity in society.

Analects of Confucius A compilation of sayings by Confucius and his disciples, the *Analects* is heavily influenced by the philosophy and moral values of China.

Mencius A collection of conversations that Mencius, a disciple of Confucius's grandson, had with kings of the time.

These important books became known as the Five Classics and the Four Books. They formed the cornerstone of the Chinese education system beginning shortly after the Han Dynasty up to the beginning of the 20th century. What this means is that anyone who was educated in China was well versed in these classics. The classics also became the curriculum of the Civil Service Examination System, which began in a limited way during the Han Dynasty up until the end of the imperial dynastic period. A system of exams based on knowledge of these classics was instituted to select those who would serve as administrative officials. The better one performed in the exams, the higher and more important the administrative assignment one received.

CRAP EGGS WITH BAMBOO FLAVOR A TASTE OF CHINGLISH

With increasing globalization, the Chinese are making enormous efforts to appear international and sophisticated by translating street signs, menus and other signages into English. They also want to help English-speaking visitors to China. A hotel that has English signage will appeal more to foreigners but also to well-heeled Chinese. The demand, unfortunately, has far outpaced those qualified to do these translations, often leading to hilarious results. I was recently staying at a Chinese hotel that caters to Chinese business people and Chinese tour groups. At the typical breakfast buffet, often provided to attract customers, was a small placard next to each menu item in both Chinese and English. I came across this one:

文明交通从脚下起
Civilised Traffic Starts at Home

保护古迹
请勿刻画
RELIC PROTECTED, NO SCRATCH

PAN TRY BREAKFAST BOWEL

This did not sound too appetizing knowing how much the Chinese love to eat entrails. But after lifting the lid on the dish, I discovered it was sausage. The literal translation of the Chinese would be something like 'Fragrant-fry-breakfast-intestine'. A more appropriate translation would simply be 'Pan-fried breakfast sausage'.

Sometimes a single misplaced letter can make all the difference. Crap eggs are actually *crab* eggs or roe.

Here are a few others:
CAREFUL LANDSLIP
SLIP AND FALL DOWN CAREFULLY
DON'T FORGET TO CARRY YOUR THING
DEFORMED MAN TOILET
RACIST PARK
EXECUTION IN PROGRESS

MANDARIN OR CANTONESE?

Although referred to as 'dialects', the languages of China are like the languages of Europe, really distinct languages though related to one another and having many common features.

People in Cantonese-speaking areas such as Guangzhou or Hong Kong speak mainly Cantonese. But in northern China or Taiwan, they say that Chinese is Mandarin. The answer is that both languages are forms of Chinese. In fact, there are seven main language groups in China, each with its distinct pronunciation, vocabulary and grammar. To make matters even more complicated, there are literally hundreds of regional dialects within each of these groups. What makes the language situation in China really complex is that these languages are not mutually intelligible. For example, a Beijing speaker of Mandarin (or more precisely the Beijing dialect of Mandarin) cannot understand the Cantonese spoken in the far south of the country.

THE SEVEN MAIN CHINESE LANGUAGES GROUPS

Mandarin (836 million speakers). Spoken in a broad arc from the northeast to the southwest. Beijing dialect is the prestige dialect.

Wu (77 million speakers). Spoken in Jiangsu and Zhejiang provinces. Shanghainese is the prestige dialect.

Yue or Cantonese (71 million speakers). Spoken in Guangdong and Guangxi provinces as well as in Hong Kong, Macau and parts of Southeast Asia and among many overseas Chinese communities. Guangzhou and Hong Kong Cantonese are the prestige dialects.

Min (60 million speakers). Spoken in Fujian Province, Taiwan and parts of Southeast Asia and in some overseas communities.

Xiang or Hunanese (36 million speakers). Spoken in Hunan Province. Changsha dialect is the prestige one.

Hakka (34 million speakers). Spoken in pockets of numerous provinces in southern China, Taiwan and parts of Southeast Asia.

Gan (31 million speakers). Spoken in Jiangxi Province.

MANDARIN
- Northern
- Eastern
- Southwestern

SOUTHERN
- Wu (Shanghainese)
- Gan
- Hakka
- Xiang (Hunanese)
- Min (Fukienese)
- Yue (Cantonese)

1000 km

THE LIFE OF MA: MOTHER, HEMP, HORSE, CURSE

Chinese is a tonal language. Different pitches or intonations are attached to a syllable to give it a distinct meaning. Different words may have the same sound (i.e. homophones) but the different pitches give them different meanings. Take, for example, the syllable *mā*.

Mā (妈) with a high level tone means 'mother'
Má (麻) with a rising intonation means 'hemp'
Mǎ (马) with a falling then rising intonation means 'horse'
Mà (骂) with a sharply falling intonation means 'curse'

Because Chinese has relatively few sound combinations (only 413), the addition of four tones to each sound combination allows for a much richer language. This is not to say that there are only 1,652 words in Chinese as there are many homophones as well. In fact, when you

look up a word in the dictionary, let's say the word *fàn*, you will get several different words, such as 'cooked rice', 'to violate', 'to float', 'a surname', and so on. The words are distinguished by how they are written. Each word is written with a different character.

It is extremely important when speaking Chinese to pronounce words with the correct tonal contour or you might be saying something that you didn't intend.

THE COMMON LANGUAGE

Mandarin Chinese is considered 'standard Chinese' or the 'common language' (*putonghua*) because it is the language of the central government, commerce, education, the media and so on. All children learn Mandarin at school, thus anyone with some education can speak and understand Mandarin. Mandarin Chinese is also the language taught and learned by foreigners. Learning Mandarin Chinese enables the visitor to China to communicate with educated people all over China.

CHINESE CHARACTERS

It is commonly believed that Chinese characters are composed of little pictures that represent ideas. While this may have been true in the early stages of the Chinese writing system, today less than 2 percent of Chinese characters are pictographic in nature. It is true, however, that there is no alphabet in Chinese and characters have to be memorized. This is the greatest challenge in learning Chinese, even for native speakers. Chinese children spend countless hours memorizing characters and practicing writing them. Although there are nearly 50,000 Chinese characters in the largest dictionaries, about 2,000 are commonly used by educated people.

Most Chinese characters have a radical, which gives an indication of the meaning, and a phonetic component that gives an idea of how to pronounce

it. Sometimes this phonetic component is an exact representation and sometimes an approximation. Here are some examples:

河 This is the character for 'river' and is pronounced *hé*.
The component on the left side of the character, the three dots (氵), are the radical and mean 'water'. This indicates that this character (or word) has something to do with water. The component on the right side of the character (可) is the phonetic and is pronounced *kě*. As you can see, the vowel sound in this component is retained in the pronunciation of the word *hé*.

湖 This is the character for 'lake' and is pronounced *hú*.
As you can see, the component on the left is the water radical (氵), so we know this character has something to do with water. The phonetic component on the right is pronounced *hú* (胡), which is an exact match for the pronunciation of the word.

THE DIFFERENCE BETWEEN A WORD AND A CHARACTER

All characters in Chinese are pronounced as a single syllable. Some words consist of a single character but most have two characters and occasionally three or more. Learning the characters, then, is only part of the job of learning Chinese. One must also learn word combinations in order to become literate. In a Chinese text, all characters are written equidistant apart. Traditionally, Chinese was written top to bottom and right to left. Nowadays, it is written like English, from top to bottom and left to write.

Single character words:
我 wǒ I, me
书 shū book
姜 jiāng ginger

Multisyllabic words:
老师 lǎo shī teacher
书桌 shū zhuō desk
筷子 kuài zi chopsticks

Right Traditional Chinese writing tools: ink stone, brush stand and brushes. **Far right** The Chinese character *fo* for 'Buddha'.

CHINA'S MANY RELIGIOUS AND PHILOSOPHICAL TRADITIONS

There are two religious and philosophical traditions native to China: Confucianism and Taoism. Both have their beginnings in the 5th to 6th centuries BCE. Buddhism has also shaped Chinese culture. Elements of these are incorporated into folk religion and ancestor worship, which include respect for the forces of nature, ancestors, gods of human groups and figures from mythology.

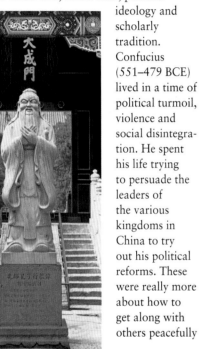

The character for filial piety (*xiao*).

Confucianism is not only considered a religion and philosophy but also a worldview, social ethic, political ideology and scholarly tradition. Confucius (551–479 BCE) lived in a time of political turmoil, violence and social disintegration. He spent his life trying to persuade the leaders of the various kingdoms in China to try out his political reforms. These were really more about how to get along with others peacefully than about politics. To Confucius, politics meant moral persuasion. The core of Confucianism is thus humanistic, with particular emphasis on the importance of the family and social harmony. In particular, Confucian doctrine is based on the Five Relationships—reciprocal relationships that if adhered to bring peace and prosperity. Inferiors must be subject to superiors, but those superiors have a responsibility to care for their inferiors. The relationships emphasize respect by the younger for the older and by women for men. But there is a responsibility on both sides that are mutually beneficial.

BASIC PRINCIPLES OF CONFUCIANISM

Benevolence (*ren*) 仁

Also described as human-heartedness, this carries the idea of being kind and respectful to others. The supreme moral achievement in life is excellence of character, to become a gentleman.

The Gentleman (*junzi*) 君子

The ultimate individual ('superior person') attains nobility through character rather than inheritance.

Filial Piety (*xiao*)

This refers to unquestioned loyalty and respect for elders, especially parents and grandparents.

THE VALUE OF EDUCATION

To Confucius, the purpose of government was not only to provide food and protection but also to educate. Education became a serious focus of Confucian thought. By 50 BCE, enrollment in the state university was 3,000, but by 1 CE all bureaucratic positions in the government were staffed by those with a Confucian education. In the year 58 CE, all government schools were required to make sacrifices to Confucius. Toward the end of the Han Dynasty, up to 30,000 students attended the Imperial University and a Confucian temple eventually stood in all of China's 2,000 counties.

The curriculum for a Confucian education comprised the Five Classics and Four Books (see pages 18–19). These nine books espoused Confucian thought and practices. The Five Classics are said to have been compiled by Confucius himself, whereas the Four Books were compiled by his disciples.

This Confucian education system began in the Han Dynasty (206 BCE–220 CE) and was in place until the early part of the 20th century. What this means is that anyone who was educated in China was thoroughly familiar with Confucian ideals and practices.

THE FIVE CONFUCIAN RELATIONSHIPS

Ruler to subject If a ruler is kind and cares about his subjects, the people, in turn, will be loyal.

Father to son If a father cares for his son and treats him well, his son will be obedient and want to care for his father.

Elder brother to younger brother If an elder brother treats his younger brother with kindness, the younger brother will respect the elder.

Husband to wife If a husband takes care of his wife, she will, in turn, be loyal to him.

Friend to friend Friends treat each other with mutual respect and kindness.

Confucius believed that if we treat each other with respect and dignity, then everyone will benefit. He advocated self-cultivation. If you want to change society, you must begin by changing yourself. Your actions will then influence those around you and extend from your immediate community to the city, to the state and, eventually, to the whole country.

TAOISM

Taoist thought pervades Chinese society. At the core of Taoism, which links Confucian tradition with folk traditions, is a book regarded by many as scripture, the *Dao De Jing* (Tao Te Ching) (*Classic of the Way and Virtue*). Tradition has it that it was written by Laozi ('the old one'), but in fact scholars are unsure who the author is. It was originally meant as a handbook for rulers. Ideal Taoism describes a sage whose actions are so unnoticed that his very existence is unsure. The term *dao*, meaning 'way', has been used by all other religious and philosophical traditions in China, including Confucianism and Buddhism.

Taoism is all about the natural order of things. In fact, civilization is a corruption of the natural order, thus reform for the Taoist is to look to the past and the ideals established then. It is about maintaining balance and order according to natural laws. Taoism emphasizes spontaneity and non-interference by letting things take their natural course.

Taoism is sometimes regarded as passive and lacking in strength and vigor. But the Taoist would respond by using the analogy of water. Though water seems weak (not hard), it carves great canyons in the earth by following a natural course.

Taiwan has a thriving Taoist community with Taoist temples dotting the island. Religious Taoism was suppressed by the Communists in mainland China when they came to power, but in recent years there has been a surge in interest in and tolerance for Chinese religions in the country, among them Taoism.

A priest conducting a Taoist rite at a temple. Taoism is one of five religions officially recognized by China.

PRINCIPLES OF TAOISM: HARMONY YIN AND YANG

Yin refers to darkness and *yang* to light. They represent harmony in the universe, that everything has an opposite force. They are not considered positive or negative but complimentary, independent forces. A fruitful and happy life lies in having a proper balance of all things, such as food, exercise and sleep.

Virtue (*de*) 德

Taoists seek virtue in their life. It is a passive power that never lays claim to achievements. It is an inner strength and confidence.

Non-action (*wu wei*) 无为

The *Dao De Jing* says, 'The man of superior virtue never acts, and yet there is nothing he leaves undone.' It does not imply there is no action, but that the actions are so in tune with the natural order of things that the author leaves no trace of himself.

ANCIENT PRACTICES OF ANCESTOR WORSHIP AND FOLK RELIGION

Confucius believed that the bonds we form with our loved ones in this life are still there when they pass on. Up until the early 20th century, a child would engage in a three-year mourning period when a parent died, consisting of wearing coarse clothing, eating a restricted diet of rice porridge twice a day, living in a mourning hut next to the house and other rites. The three-year period was symbolic of the first three years of life, when a child's parents carried, fed and cared for him.

These mourning rites also resulted in ancestor worship. Family members had a responsibility to care for their deceased loved ones after their death. Ancestors are thought to be deities with power to affect the lives of those still living.

Ancestor worship still persists in rural areas and among Chinese living overseas. The practice includes having a place in the home

where offerings are made to ancestors and where photographs of ancestors or tablets with their names carved on them are kept. Offerings of food are placed periodically and incense is burned. Family members pray in front of these ancestral shrines. In some cases, they also burn fake banknotes, paper cars and houses, even paper iPhones and iPads, to ensure their ancestors are comfortable in the afterlife.

Spirit mediums are sometimes called on to communicate with ghosts (the spirit form of a deceased relative and ancestor), who can help them if properly respected and rewarded with food and other offerings.

Rituals and spirit mediums are part of ancestor worship and folk religion.

CHINESE BUDDHISM AND OTHER BELIEFS

Buddhism is an Indian religion that was founded sometime around the 6th to 4th centuries BCE by a young wanderer, Siddhartha Gautama, who later become known as Buddha or the 'Enlightened one'. It is China's oldest foreign religion. It spread gradually to China during the Han Dynasty (206 BCE–220 CE) where it merged with the prevailing Taoist thought as well as folk religion. When the first Buddhist scriptures were translated into Chinese, Taoist terms based on folk religion were often used so that the Chinese could understand and interpret the principles.

By the 5th and 6th centuries, Buddhism had become a powerful intellectual force and was well established among the peasant class. The golden age of Buddhism however, was during the Tang Dynasty (618–907 CE), when it enjoyed state sponsorship (temples and monasteries were supported by the government), and widespread acceptance among the élite as well as peasant classes. Buddhist ideas and practices shaped Chinese culture in a wide variety of areas, including art, politics, literature, philosophy, medicine and material culture.

Buddhism, however, never fully displaced Confucianism and Taoism, but was accepted alongside these native religions. In fact, many in China felt perfectly comfortable adhering to the principles of all three religions at the same time. In order for this to happen, Buddhist philosophy and practices were altered so that they were compatible with existing beliefs in China.

BASIC PRINCIPLES

Samsara This is the belief that life is an endless cycle of birth, death and rebirth.

Reincarnation This is rebirth of the soul into a new body. That new body depends on how someone lives their life. If they live a bad, evil life, they may be reincarnated as a dog or a rat in their next life. If they live a good, virtuous life, they may come back as a more enlightened person.

Karma This refers to acts or deeds. Good conduct and deeds bring happiness and lead to similar good acts and further happiness. Bad conduct brings misery and evil and leads to more bad conduct. Good karma results in a better reincarnation.

Nirvana Once one has overcome these obstacles, they reach a state of enlightenment or nirvana. The endless cycle of rebirth is overcome and one is released from suffering and becomes a Buddha.

Although Buddhism was suppressed in mainland China, most recently during the 1960s and 1970s, it has slowly regained importance to many people. The government is also restoring monasteries and temples, although this is more for the sake of tourism than for any adoration of the religion.

Buddhist monks dressed in saffron robes chant inside the Grand Hall of the Jade Buddha Temple, founded in 1882 in the west of Shanghai.

THE FOUR NOBLE TRUTHS

The Four Noble Truths are at the core of Buddhist thought.

1. Life is suffering
To live means to suffer because human nature is not perfect. Suffering comes from pain, sickness, injury, old age and death.

2. The origin of suffering is attachment or desire
When we become attached to things and ideas, we suffer. The causes of suffering are desire, passion and seeking wealth, prestige, fame or popularity.

3. Suffering can be eliminated
Suffering can be eliminated by getting rid of desires or attachments. Our suffering will then go away because we will realize that all things and ideas are transient and thus unimportant.

4. There is a path to the end of suffering
The path to the end of suffering is a gradual one of self-improvement. This path has eight principles called the Eightfold Path. This path seeks a balance between excessive self-indulgence (hedonism) and strict sacrifice (asceticism). The goal is to get rid of ego and to extinguish illusions, passions and cravings. Following the Eightfold Path (below) leads to Enlightenment or nirvana.

Right views
Right intentions
Right speech
Right actions
Right livelihood
Right efforts
Right mindfulness
Right concentration (meditation)

Chinese Muslims leave the Id Kah Mosque in Xinjiang Province after prayers marking the end of Ramadan.

CHINESE MUSLIMS

Approximately 1–2 percent of the people living in the People's Republic of China are Muslims, among them Chinese Muslims as well as those from many ethnic minority groups, such as the Uyghurs, Kazaks and other Central Asian groups. Although Chinese Muslims are ethnic Hans and speak Chinese, they are considered Hui or Muslim because of their religious beliefs and cultural practices.

Muslims arrived in China as early as 650 CE during the Tang Dynasty, just 18 years after Prophet Muhammad's death. Their primary interest was trade. The first mosque was built in the southern city of Guangzhou. Muslims came to dominate the import–export business in China. They intermarried with Han Chinese, learned to speak and read Chinese, and by the Ming Dynasty could not be distinguished from Han Chinese even though they maintained their religious beliefs and customs.

There are more than 32,000 mosques in China, most of them in Xinjiang Province. The biggest and most important mosque in China is located in the city of Xi'an and is called the Great Mosque of Xi'an. It has a distinctive Chinese feel to it, with elements of Chinese and Buddhist architecture mixed with Muslim features.

GOD IS RED: ATHEISM AND THE CULT OF MAO

With the establishment of the Communist People's Republic of China in 1949, religions were outlawed. Superstition, traditional beliefs and customs and religious practices were viewed as backward and not contributing to forward progress, not to mention their incompatibility with Communist ideology. As such, all religious practices, including Taoism, Confucianism, Buddhism, Christianity and ancestral worship, were suppressed. Mao Zedong established himself as the Great Helmsman and unquestioned leader and authority in China. His many sayings were compiled into a book, which became known as the 'little red book'. These sayings were committed to memory by many and quoted with religious fervor. The little red books were carried around by nearly everyone and considered as sacred as scripture. Those speaking out against Mao or his sayings were punished. Mao was considered by many to have reached godlike status among the Chinese. This Cult of Mao subsided after his death in 1976 and has faded since then.

CHRISTIANITY IN CHINA

Nestorian Christianity first came to China in the 8th century during the Tang Dynasty but did not meet with much success. By the Mongol period in the 13th century, some Mongol tribes were primarily Nestorian Christian, an early branch of Christianity from Persia. Franciscan friars from Europe also began proselytizing in China during this period. Through the years, various Christian missionaries traveled to China preaching their faith, the most famous being Matteo Ricci who arrived in 1582 and introduced Western science, mathematics and astronomy. Other Christian missionaries continued to go to China in search of converts through the 17th and 18th centuries. Often these missionaries were met with strong resistance from the ruling emperors. Qing Dynasty emperors in the early 19th century outlawed Christianity and attempted to expel or kill all foreign and domestic Christians. Nevertheless, Christian proselytizing continued up into the 20th century.

Today, the Catholic and Protestant churches are officially recognized by the Chinese government and Christian chapels are located in large cities, some dating back to the late 19th and early 20th centuries. There is increasing interest in Christianity, with many informal 'house churches' throughout the countryside. Although not officially recognized by the government, they have become quite popular. Believers meet in private homes and traveling ministers often preach at these gatherings.

An old Christian church beside a canal in the city of Huangzhou.

FAMOUS HISTORICAL AND CULTURAL SITES IN CHINA

China's long history and its vast and varied geography have given rise to numerous tourist attractions, including 48 UNESCO World Heritage sites that are both cultural and natural.

THE FORBIDDEN CITY

The 90 palaces and courtyards of the Forbidden City, situated in the very heart of Beijing, were home to 14 emperors of the Ming (1368–1644) and Qing (1644–1912) dynasties. Covering an area of 178 acres (72 ha) and entered through Tiananmen, the Gate of Heavenly Peace, this largest ancient palatial structure in the world and the former ceremonial and political center of China is well worth a visit to see its traditional palace architecture and the many treasures housed in the Palace Museum.

THE GREAT WALL

The Great Wall of China stretches approximately 5,500 miles (8,850 km) across northern China from east to west. It begins at the sea in eastern China and winds up and down mountains and across deserts before it comes to an end in northwestern China. Construction began on the Great Wall during the Warring States Period (476–221 BCE) and was added to and rebuilt over the next 2,000 years. Much of what you see today was built during the Ming Dynasty and restored in the modern era. The wall was originally built by independent kingdoms to prevent invasion by nomadic tribes on the steppes of Asia. During the Qin Dynasty (221 BCE–206 CE), the various walls were connected to make a more complete structure to protect the country. It was built primarily by conscripted laborers using stone, brick, wood and tamped earth. The Ming Dynasty sections of the wall are 18–26 feet (6–8 m) tall and 15–30 feet (4–9 m) wide at the base, sloping to about 12 feet (4 m) wide at the top. Of the estimated 25,000 watchtowers built along the wall, some of which were large enough to house dozens of soldiers, many still remain. The Great Wall is a popular tourist attraction for both foreigners and Chinese. Many parts of the Wall are easily accessed from Beijing.

THE TERRACOTTA WARRIORS OF XI'AN

In 1974, on the outskirts of Xi'an, a farmer was digging a well and discovered a life-sized clay soldier. He had inadvertently discovered a huge tomb complex for the first emperor of the Qin Dynasty (221–206 BCE). The complex contained thousands of these life-sized warriors, many holding bronze weapons. The pit also contained life-sized chariots and terracotta horses. Most of the figures were broken into pieces but have since been painstakingly pieced back together. Although the figures appeared gray, there were remnants of vivid paint clinging to some of them. The actual tomb of the Qin emperor is just over a mile (2 km) away. These soldiers, lined up in formation in underground corridors, were built to protect the emperor's tomb from invaders. A large structure has been built directly over the excavation site and is now one of the most important, interesting and popular museums in China.

YELLOW MOUNTAIN

SUN YAT-SEN MAUSOLEUM

BEIJING'S TEMPLE OF HEAVEN

The Temple of Heaven in Beijing is a complex of religious buildings used by the emperors of the Ming and Qing dynasties for annual ceremonies and prayers to heaven to ensure a good harvest. It was constructed in the early 1400s, at the same time the Forbidden City was built. The central building in the complex, a circular three-tiered structure, is the Hall of Prayer for Good Harvests. It is built entirely of wood with no nails. The other important structure is a large circular altar called the Circular Mound Altar. It consists of a large three-tiered circular platform with a round stone in the center. The emperor would stand on this stone to offer prayers for good weather and a good harvest.

HUANG SHAN

Huang Shan or Yellow Mountain is a mountain range, 6,115 feet (1,864 m) high, located in southern Anhui Province. The area is known for its stunning granite peaks, spectacular sunsets and sunrises, misty clouds, evocative pine trees, hot springs and high-quality green teas. It is a UNESCO World Heritage Site and a popular tourist destination. Like Guilin in south-central China, Yellow Mountain has been the subject of countless landscape paintings and poems. A number of guesthouses and small restaurants are dotted among the peaks. Travelers can either take trams to the top of these or go the old-fashioned way, walking up some of the 60,000 stairs carved into the rock in the Yellow Mountain area.

THE SUN YAT-SEN MAUSOLEUM

The mausoleum of the father of modern China, Sun Yat-sen (1866–1925), is located on the outskirts of the city of Nanjing in Jiangsu Province, in an area called Purple Mountain. The mausoleum complex covers 20 acres (8 ha) and was completed in 1929. The complex consists of arched gateways, characters carved on stone tablets and an impressive series of stairways and platforms that lead to the actual tomb, which is a combination of Chinese and Western architecture. Inside the tomb building is a large marble statue of Sun Yat-sen dressed in traditional long robes. There are several other ceremonial buildings in the area, all located in a beautiful forested area to the east of Nanjing. The tomb of the first emperor of the Ming Dynasty is located nearby. This makes a pleasant excursion outside the hectic city.

Fisherman using cormorants to catch fish in the Li River.

THE KARST MOUNTAINS OF GUILIN

The city of Guilin in south-central China lies on the banks of the Li River. It is one of the most popular tourist attractions in all of China and has been the subject of countless Chinese landscape paintings for thousands of years. People flock here to see the natural and strange beauty of the karst mountain formations. These steep, jagged limestone peaks loom over the city and the surrounding countryside. The area also has an abundance of caves and sinkholes. It is popular to take a boat down the Li River to view the karst hills and the peaceful countryside and small villages in the area. Most river cruises begin in Guilin and end in the backpackers' haven of Yangshuo. Here you will find all kinds of small shops and Western cafés and bars.

SUZHOU, CHINA'S VENICE

Suzhou is a major city located in Jiangsu Province, between Taihu Lake and the Yangtze River, about 60 miles (100 km) west of Shanghai. This ancient city was originally founded in 514 BCE. It is often referred to as the 'Venice of the East' because 42 percent of the city is covered by water. The city is divided by China's Grand Canal from north to south, an artificial canal built in the 6th century to link Hangzhou with Beijing. Many small canals criss-cross the city. But Suzhou is most widely known as a centerpiece of the Chinese Classical Garden. Originally, there were hundreds of gardens but now only 69 remain, some of them over a thousand years old. The gardens of Suzhou have been named a UNESCO World Heritage Site. The gardens contain a mixture of hills, ponds, bridges, terraces, corridors and pagodas. Marco Polo described Suzhou as one of the most beautiful cities in China. Suzhou is also known for its whitewashed houses that line the canals.

BEIJING'S SUMMER PALACE

Located 9 miles (15 km) northwest of central Beijing, the Summer Palace, another World Heritage Site, is a vast grouping of lakes, gardens and palaces that began as a royal garden for the emperor and his family during the Qing Dynasty (1644–1912). Royalty often took refuge here during the hot summer months. The largest and best preserved royal park in China, it is divided into four areas: Court Area, Front Hill Area, Rear Hill Area and Lake Area. The main attraction is Kunming Lake and the Front Hill Area where beautiful pagodas and towers are built on the side of a hill overlooking the lake.

Left The white marble Yudai (Jade Belt) Bridge in Beijing's Summer Palace.
Below Traveling by canal in Suzhou, Jiangsu Province.

THE BUDDHIST GROTTOES OF DUNHUANG

The Mogao Caves or Grottoes, also known as the 'Caves of the Thousand Buddhas', are located in northern Gansu Province in western China, along the ancient Silk Road route. The caves form the largest, best preserved and longest used depository of Buddhist art in the world. They were dug and stocked with Buddhist art and scriptures from 366 CE until the 14th century. Of the caves, 492 have been preserved along with 2,000 painted murals and sculptures. In 1900, a Taoist priest discovered a walled-off cave that contained a treasure trove of manuscripts, including 1,110 bundles of scrolls and 15,000 paper books dating from the 4th to the 11th centuries. These documents were written in a number of languages, including Chinese, Tibetan, Uyghur, Sanskrit, Sogdian and the obscure Khotanese, all languages important along the ancient Silk Route that connected China with Central Asia.

A pathway on sacred Mount Emei in western Sichuan Province.

The Big Wild Goose Pagoda in the Ci'en Buddhist Temple complex in Xi'an.

BIG WILD GOOSE PAGODA

The Big Wild Goose Pagoda, the most famous landmark in Xi'an City in Shaanxi Province, was built in 652 during the Tang Dynasty. It sits within the Ci'en Buddhist Temple complex, which consists of numerous buildings and courtyards. One of the largest Buddhist temples in the area, the Big Wild Goose Pagoda was originally built to house Buddhist relics taken from India by the early Chinese Buddhist pioneer Xuan Zang, who became the first abbot of the temple. His travels to India inspired one of China's most famous novels, *Journey to the West*. The pagoda has seven stories (originally five) and stands 211 feet (64 m) high. Visitors can climb the narrow stairway to the top.

MOUNT EMEI

Mount Emei is one of China's four sacred Buddhist mountains and is regarded as a place of enlightenment. It has been an important Buddhist site for hundreds of years. It rises to 10,167 feet (3,099 m) in western Sichuan Province. There are footpaths up the mountain and numerous teahouses and guesthouses along the way. Many of the Buddhist monasteries also have basic lodging. There are also cable cars to the top. Over a hundred Buddhist temples and monasteries dot the mountain. It is very popular to be on the summit for the spectacular sunrise and to view the sea of misty clouds below. It is about a two-hour train ride from Chengdu. Though you can reach the summit in a day, you really need three days to fully explore the mountain. Popular sites to visit are the Golden Summit, Baoguo Temple, Wan-nian Monastery and Jiu Lao Cave.

THE YANGTZE RIVER AND THE THREE GORGES

The Yangtze is the world's third longest river and the longest in China. The Three Gorges, along the middle reaches of the Yangtze, are one of China's top scenic destinations. The gorges range from 330 to 900 feet (100 to 300 m) wide with towering walls on either side. The gorges have been part of Chinese history, literature and folklore for thousands of years. Cruise boats ply the waters between Chongqing in the west to Wuhan or Yichang downriver. Travelers can take luxury cruise ships or local ferry boats. Although there are scenic temples and small towns to visit along the way, the biggest attraction is the gorges themselves.

CHAPTER 2

CHINESE CULTURE AND FOOD

China has a deep and long cultural tradition dating back to prehistoric times. China's traditional arts reflect this long history with refined arts and practices. Traditional Chinese medicine draws on philosophical knowledge grounded in cultural practices, while Chinese cuisine reflects the variety of a large, complex and diverse nation.

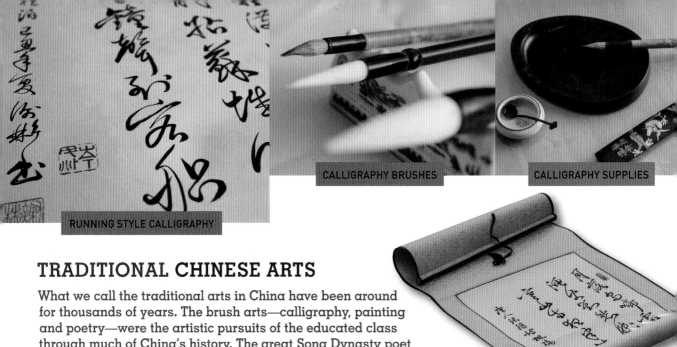

RUNNING STYLE CALLIGRAPHY

CALLIGRAPHY BRUSHES

CALLIGRAPHY SUPPLIES

CALLIGRAPHY SCROLL

TRADITIONAL CHINESE ARTS

What we call the traditional arts in China have been around for thousands of years. The brush arts—calligraphy, painting and poetry—were the artistic pursuits of the educated class through much of China's history. The great Song Dynasty poet Su Shi (1037–1101) was also a renowned calligrapher and painter, and the great Tang Dynasty poet Wang Wei (699–759) was equally well known for his landscape paintings.

POETRY

Whereas the West is known for Greek philosophy, Roman law, Renaissance art and Italian opera, poetry is the most striking cultural element of Chinese civilization. It was one of the earliest forms of written expression in China, with the *Book of Songs* dating back to the 7th century BCE. Poetry became the highest form of creative expression throughout Chinese civilization, and for most of China's history poetry was an integral part of daily life for the educated class. It was promoted by the government and pursued as a vehicle for personal pleasure and communication. In the Tang Dynasty (618–907) alone, more poetry was composed than in the rest of the world combined up to the 18th century. One anthology, the *Complete Tang Poems*, which is considered incomplete, contains 48,900 poems by 2,200 poets. People in the Chinese-speaking world today continue to read and compose classical poems in the styles developed during the Tang and Song dynasties.

There are numerous anthologies of Chinese poetry translated into English but two that provide a good introduction to classical Chinese poetry are *Sunflower Splendor: Three Thousand Years of Chinese Poetry* by Wu-Chi Liu and Irving Yucheng Lo (1975) and *Classical Chinese Poetry: An Anthology* by David Hinton (2010).

The most famous Chinese poems are short, either four or eight lines long. Common themes include longing for a lover, nature and recalling the past. Many Chinese school children memorize this famous poem by the Tang Dynasty poet Li Bai.

Moonlight shines on my bed
Like frost on the ground
I look up and gaze at the moon
Then lower my head and think of home.

chuáng qián míng yuè guāng
yí shì dì shàng shuāng
jû tóu wàng míng yùe
dī tóu sī gù xiāng

CALLIGRAPHY

Calligraphy, the writing of Chinese characters with a brush and ink, is considered one of the highest forms of Chinese art. In ancient China, calligraphy was practiced by the educated élite, who comprised a small percentage of the population. Calligraphy may consist of a single character, common sayings, poetry, essays and other writings. It

is still valued and practiced in China today. Bookstores usually have a department that sells calligraphy supplies, including brushes of various sizes, brush stands made of wood or ceramic, ink stones, ink sticks and liquid ink as well as various kinds and sizes of paper and silk scrolls. There are also dedicated calligraphy shops.

There are five basic styles of calligraphy:

Ancient Style This is the earliest calligraphic style, dating back to the Shang (1650–1045 BCE) and Zhou (1045–256 BCE) dynasties. It includes large and small seal scripts as well as the ancient script that was carved onto animal bones and inscribed onto bronze vessels in ancient times.

Li or Official Style This style was invented during the Qin Dynasty (221–206 BCE) and was adopted for almost all government and official purposes. It became more standardized during the Han Dynasty (206 BCE–220 CE) when it was used for all kinds of stone monuments and official records.

Regular Style This style was developed during the later part of the Han Dynasty. By the time of the Tang Dynasty (618–907 CE), it was firmly established as one of the standard styles. It is more

regular in that there is little room for artistic flair. In fact, many Chinese print fonts are based on the regular style.

Running Style This style was also developed in the later Han Dynasty and was used alongside the Regular Style. It is more artistic than previous styles in that it resembles cursive handwriting, with freer, more vivid and flowing movements. It is the most common style for regular writing with a brush.

Grass Style This style was also developed simultaneously with the Regular and Running styles. It is the most highly artistic, a kind of carefree, highly stylistic cursive form. But for those untrained in calligraphy, it can be difficult to decipher the characters.

Learning calligraphy can be a daunting task as it requires a great deal of practice. Most universities in China offer a Chinese calligraphy class, especially those with foreign student populations. In these classes students learn about the basic supplies needed before practicing writing in the Regular Style. They may also learn the Li or Running styles. The Ancient and Grass styles are usually reserved for advanced students. Some universities in the United States with larger, more established Chinese programs as well as some community adult education programs also offer Chinese calligraphy courses.

After learning the basics of how to hold the brush and do basic stroke patterns, students can also practice calligraphy using self-instruction booklets sold at most Chinese bookstores, which provide a way for the student to trace the characters, either using tracing paper over the characters or following the arrowed outlines of characters. Booklets like these are very suitable for children.

Scrolls with Chinese calligraphy are not only a popular art form in China but are also popular souvenirs. Scrolled calligraphy is sold in many bookstores, souvenir shops and dedicated calligraphy shops. Souvenir shops catering to tourists usually sell cheap replicas of Chinese calligraphy done by master calligraphers. True original works of art can cost up to several thousand dollars.

CHINESE CERAMICS

When one thinks of Chinese ceramics, the iconic blue and white Ming vase usually comes to mind, but many kinds of Chinese ceramics were produced during different historical eras, as can be seen in museums in China. These range from early hand-built, low-fired pottery intended for everyday use to sophisticated fine porcelain wares made for the imperial court. Two separate production areas, in the north and south, each with different raw materials, collectively produced three-color lead-glazed ceramics, celadon, blackwares (used for teapots and cups), underglaze blue and white wares, delicate white porcelain, and much more.

Porcelain was being made in China as early as the Han Dynasty (206 BCE–220 CE), but it was during the Ming Dynasty (1368–1644) that most innovation occurred. It was also during the Ming that China began exporting ceramics, produced even then on an industrial scale, to other parts of the world, giving rise to the term 'china' to refer to dinnerware.

When shopping for ceramics, keep in mind that those sold in antiques markets around China are not genuine. They are replicas. That doesn't mean you can't find some nice pieces, just don't believe that you are getting a genuine antique worth thousands of dollars even if that is what they are charging. Once at an antiques market in Nanjing, I was approached by two peasants who said they had some original ceramics unearthed in the countryside. I was skeptical but decided to take a look. I selected a small covered dish that had an inscription on the bottom indicating it was made during the Qianlong Emperor's reign of the Qing Dynasty, which would make it more than a 200 years old. It was more expensive than what was selling in the market but was still fairly cheap. Of course it was not authentic but it was a pretty good replica. This is a common strategy near antiques markets. In reality, it is illegal to take anything out of China that is more than 100 years old, and anything that is truly antique will have a special seal and documentation to prove its authenticity.

Top left A gently sloping tunnel-like brick and earth 'dragon' kiln, developed in China 3,000 years ago for firing pottery and ceramic ware. **Top right** An antique blue and white Chinese vase. **Left** Traditional Chinese decorative porcelain vases and jars.

If you just want some Chinese calligraphy to display on your wall at home, a bookstore is a good place to shop. It will usually carry a wide range of styles and texts, sometimes mixed with a landscape. Remember that calligraphy is an art form and what is written is less important than the style and aesthetic of the work. Once you have decided which style of calligraphy you want, inspect the scroll. Look for a heavy, good quality silk and characters that look original, not photocopied. Black ink on white silk is typically of higher quality than colored paintings. The other option is to have a calligrapher do a scroll for you with your choice of wording, such as a favorite poem or an excerpt from the *Confucian Analects* of the Tao Te Ching.

Although I personally own calligraphy scrolls in many different styles, I tend to favor the Running Style because the characters are recognizable yet have a beautiful flowing character to them, much like well-written cursive. My second favorite style is the Li Style. Sometimes the style of the calligraphy for me is dictated by the text. For example, I have a line from the *Confucian Analects* which I had written in the Li Style, which would have been roughly contemporary to Confucius's time.

LI OR OFFICIAL STYLE CALLIGRAPHY

LANDSCAPE PAINTING

Among a number of different types of Chinese painting themes and styles, landscape painting remains one of the most highly regarded and is certainly the most commonly seen in the West. Landscape painting evolved into an independent genre of Chinese painting in the last years of the 9th century as the Tang Dynasty disintegrated into chaos and cultivated Chinese intellectuals (painters and poets alike) attempted to escape society and withdraw into the natural world to commune with nature through their paintings and poems. The genre reached its epoch in the Northern Song Period (907–1127 CE), which became known as the 'Great Age of Chinese Landscape'. As landscape painting evolved during the Song, it became more than just a description of nature and began to be an expression of the inner landscape of the artist's heart and mind, how the artist perceived the world around him, commonly referred to as the 'mind landscape'.

While Chinese landscape painting has been transformed over the centuries, images of nature have remained a potent source of inspiration. Early landscapes often depicted the Five Sacred Mountains and Four Great Rivers, places of imperial and religious significance, and they were often judged in terms of how well the subject matter served the gods,

buddhas, sages and emperors. Depictions of wild nature, with waterfalls, towering peaks, rivers and trees and the occasional building or person were common, as well as more restrained depictions of well-ordered imperial gardens. Figures in landscape paintings were, and still are, often very small, and usually in one corner of the painting. This reflects Chinese attitudes about man's relationship with nature, that of being part of nature but being overshadowed by the permanence of it. It was also common to annotate a landscape painting with a poem written in one of the standard calligraphy styles, often the Running Style.

Landscape paintings, as with other types of painting, were often done with a single brush and black ink. Although natural color pigments were used, black was the predominant choice among Chinese artists, rendered boldly or subtly.

Chinese landscape paintings can be viewed in museums in China, such as the Palace Museum in the Forbidden City, the National Museum in Beijing and the Shanghai Museum. The National Palace Museum in Taipei, Taiwan, has an excellent rotating collection of Chinese landscape paintings. In the US, the Metropolitan Museum of Art in New York City, the Museum of Fine Arts in Boston and the Art Institute in Chicago all have large collections of Chinese art, as does the British Museum in London.

A LONG TRADITION OF **CHINESE SILK**

Silk, one of the oldest fibers known to man, is produced from silkworm cocoons, the best of which come from the larvae of the mulberry silkworm. A single silkworm can produce over 3,000 feet (900 m) of silk thread in its short 28-day lifespan. Silk was first produced in China as early as 3500 BCE. Archeologists have found intricately dyed and woven silk textiles dating back to the Zhou Dynasty (1045–256 BCE).

Although the lengthy, labor-intensive process of producing silk was kept a strictly guarded secret in China for 3,000 years, where silk was regarded as a luxury item and its use was strictly controlled, silk gradually spread, both geographically and socially, as Chinese traders ventured forth, taking with them their products and their culture. In the 2nd century, demand for the exotic fabric created the lucrative trade route now known as the Silk Road, which stretched 4,000 miles (6,400 km) from eastern China to India, Europe, the Middle East and northern Africa.

Silk has played a significant role in almost every aspect of Chinese society, politics, economics and culture, but nowhere more obviously than in clothing. Because silk is a wonderfully light, soft, lustrous and yet strong material, which also has a sensuous sheen but is not slippery (unlike many synthetic fibers), it has always been used primarily for clothing. It is cool in hot weather and warm in cool weather. Although it was initially reserved exclusively for the use of the emperor and his close relatives and highest dignitaries for making ankle-length robes, and as gifts for others, silk is now available to people all around the world, especially for fashioning into clothing for special occasions.

Silk was also used as a medium for painting and calligraphy and for weaving into fine rugs.

China remains the largest producer of silk in the world, producing more than two-thirds of all output. The raising of silkworms is still very much a cottage industry in rural households but silk production is largely automated, carried out in factories on high-end machinery.

Silk is still commonly worn in China for formal and celebratory occasions. Fabric shops have a wide selection of silk available in just about every type to suit all pockets—chiffon, crepe, jacquard, raw silk, shantung—and any color to suit all tastes, for tailoring into formal gowns, dresses, blouses, jackets, trousers and shirts. As in the US, silk is sold by the meter.

The slim-fitting traditional Chinese dress called the *qipao* or cheongsam, as the Cantonese call it, is a popular item for purchase while in China. These can be bought off the rack in a department store or can be custom-made by a tailor. Many fabric stores have in-house tailors who can make clothing to measure. The quality of custom-made clothing in China varies widely. Typically, higher quality products sell for more.

Another common item that tourists look for are silk robes. These usually can be found in shops catering to tourists as they are not that popular among the Chinese. One can also buy silk handicrafts such as embroidered silk wall hangings, children's clothing and accessories like neckties.

Top Bolts of colorful Chinese silk for sale in a fabric shop. **Left** The iconic slim-fitting traditional *qipao* or cheongsam in 'lucky' red Chinese silk. **Center and above** Silk robes and neckties are popular items among visitors to China.

TRADITIONAL CHINESE MEDICINE (TCM)

The traditional Chinese approach to treating illness is much more holistic than in the West. A traditional Chinese doctor will not only look at the symptoms of an illness but seek to understand the cause and how it relates to other functions of the body. The emphasis is on balance in the body, manifested through the principles of yin and yang. Too much of one thing, such as heat, causes an imbalance leading to a variety of illnesses. The five elements (air, earth, fire, metal and wood) are also integral to traditional Chinese medicine as they are part of the life force (*qi*) that flows through the body. The qi of the elements waxes and wanes in the body in daily and seasonal cycles.

If you have a headache, the problem may not be in your head. Traditional Chinese medicine tries to solve the underlying problem instead of treating your headache. After taking traditional medicine, you may not feel the effect immediately and you may still have a headache, but over a certain time the underlying problem will be treated and the headache will go away. While Western medicine may make your headache go away quickly, it is a temporary fix.

In general, for acute diseases the Chinese prefer Western medicine, but for chronic diseases they usually think traditional Chinese medical methods are more effective.

CUPPING THERAPY

Cupping therapy is another way to stimulate points along the acupuncture meridians. It is believed that cupping draws out toxins and waste from the body. It also can stimulate the body's immune system, promote the flow of blood and *qi* and increase metabolism.

A man receiving cupping treatment, an ancient form of Chinese alternative medicine for drawing out toxins and waste from the body.

It is done by suctioning small glass, metal or wood jars on the affected area. The suction is created by placing a small flame in a jar, then quickly placing it on the body. This stimulates the area by causing coagulation of the blood. Once all the jars are in place, you feel a strong pulling sensation as the skin is drawn about an inch inside the cups, but this eases within a few minutes. Cupping therapy is commonly used for back-

aches, soft tissue injuries, sprains, acne, colds and asthma. It leaves large, round red marks on your body that gradually disappear over 4–5 days. Sometimes cupping therapy is done publicly in parks or at night markets.

I discovered cupping therapy several years ago when my neck and shoulders were very tight after a long flight to China. After the first time, I was hooked. Up until then, I had only had traditional Chinese massages. After the therapist began massaging me, he suggested cupping therapy as another way to loosen my neck muscles. He placed about 18 glass cups on my back. At first the pulling sensation was fairly intense, not painful, but almost. After about 5–10 minutes, it reduced to a long pulling sensation, then I began to relax. After about 30 minutes, he returned and began taking the cups off my back. Once they were all off, I felt really loose and relaxed, much more so than with massage alone. Every time I go to China now, I get cupping therapy to loosen me up and help me relax. My wife and kids are always amused to see the big red marks all over my back when I return.

TRADITIONAL CHINESE MASSAGE

Traditionally, massage therapists in Chinese were blind but most clinics today employ both blind and sighted therapists. A Chinese massage is usually done with the client fully clothed. The therapist will put a sheet or light towel over your clothes so that their hands are not in direct contact with your body.

Massage is a common way to deal with stress or problems with your back, neck or other areas of your body.

In many hair salons, a scalp, neck and shoulder massage is part of the cost of a haircut, and can be quite relaxing. In other salons, you can get a hair wash and massage without having a cut.

I'm a big fan of traditional Chinese massage. I began going to a local traditional massage therapy clinic for neck and shoulder tension when I was living in Nanjing. It was a great way to relax and get loosened up. Not only is it convenient and therapeutic, it is also very cheap. You can typically get a full body massage, which includes your head, neck, shoulders, back, legs, arms and upper chest for less than US $15. There is nothing sleazy or erotic about a traditional Chinese massage. Legitimate clinics are clearly marked outside and typically have a 'menu' of the services available.

Most traditional Chinese massage clinics also provide the option of a foot massage. Foot massages can also be found on the street near night markets. There are various kinds of foot massage, which are particularly relaxing if you have been on your feet a lot. Most begin by soaking your feet in an herbal solution to soften and relax them. After about 15–20 minutes, you lie back in a reclining padded chair for the massage. The service often includes a pedicure to remove rough, callused skin. This is typically done with scary looking knives, but there is nothing dangerous about it.

The best way to find a traditional massage clinic is to ask around. Some larger hotels may also have clinics or can refer you to one.

QIGONG AND TAICHI

Qigong is the blending of breathing techniques, postures or gentle movements and meditation to cleanse, strengthen and circulate the *qi* or life energy in your body, which circulates through channels called meridians. Qigong attempts to keep this system strong and healthy. It is not only practiced for health but also as a form of martial arts and for spiritual practice to bring the practitioner more in harmony with nature. Qigong has been an integral part of Chinese life throughout history and is mentioned in texts dating back 2,000 years. It is usually associated with Taoist principles and combines principles of Chinese medicine, martial arts and meditation. Practitioners of qigong claim great health benefits, including the ability to prevent and cure disease.

Taichi (*taiqi*) is a form of martial arts that emphasizes slow, fluid movements. It is usually considered a form of exercise and can be seen all over China when groups gather in parks, college campuses and open spaces in the morning to practice the various taichi forms. Practitioners wear loose, flowing, traditional clothing. Most universities with foreign student programs offer taichi classes but you can also show up at just about any park or public space early in the morning and find people doing taichi. It may be possible to join one of these groups and learn by observation and mimicry. Many Chinese will be happy to coach you, although most Chinese who practice taichi outdoors tend to be older. You can also buy DVDs of taichi lessons at most bookstores, or simply go online and find video instruction of taichi. Taichi is not terribly difficult to learn but it is difficult to master. I have taken taichi courses on at least three different occasions but it is easy to forget the moves if you don't practice regularly. Most beginner-level courses teach 24 basic forms. Once you have mastered these, you can move on to more complicated forms. Taichi is also a great way to learn to relax, breathe and have more control over your body.

Above Young women practice taichi in a park. **Right** Participants at a taichi wushu festival, Dalian, 2009.

CHINESE HERBAL MEDICINE

Chinese herbs are generally classified into food and medicinal herbs. Food herbs are eaten with food or added to dishes to strengthen, nourish and maintain health. For example, Chinese wolfberries or goji berries are often steeped in tea or added to soups to give general nourishment or when nursing oneself back to health after an illness.

When the Chinese get sick, they often take traditional Chinese medicine as prescribed by a traditional Chinese doctor. Medicinal herbs are much the same as food herbs but are taken differently, usually in greater quantities and often in the form of a tea. There are more than a thousand common herbs used for colds, flu, bronchitis and a variety of other ailments.

Most formulas consists of 10–15 different herbs selected to work together to treat a particular illness. In general, one bag of the prescribed herbs is boiled twice a day and drunk as a tea, once in the morning and again at night after the water has been topped up. The next day, a new bag of herbs is used. Doctors will tell you when to drink the herbs, either before or after meals, what you can and cannot eat when taking them, and how

to prepare them. They may explain a little about the formula, such as which herbs are used for what purposes, but sometimes these formulas are a secret and the doctor will not tell you exactly what is in them.

The Chinese herbs below are very commonly used in China and abroad:

Ban Lan Gen or Isatis Root This is probably the most common Chinese medicinal herb in China and has been used for 2,000 years. It is sometimes translated as indigo woad root, Chinese indigo or isatis root. It is the root of the isatis plant and is also a source of indigo dye. It is commonly used for treating common colds, sore throats and other nose and sinus infections. It is said to fight viruses and bacterial infections and reduce fever and swelling. It was used by many Chinese during the SARS epidemic that swept the country in 2002–3.

Huang Qi or Astragalus Root This common Chinese medicinal herb is also a root frequently used to treat colds, flu and other respiratory infections. It is also effective in treating chronic hepatitis and is said to stimulate the spleen, liver, lungs, circulatory and urinary systems, and to treat arthritis, asthma, low blood

pressure and low blood sugar. It is usually taken in combination with other herbs depending on the patient's condition.

Gan Cao or Licorice Root This sweet root is often used in conjunction with other herbs to offset the bitterness found in many herbal recipes. It is often used for digestive problems as it promotes the secretion of insulin, protects the liver from toxins and is anti-ulcer. It is also used to reduce inflammation and allergic reactions and poisoning. It is used to treat some kinds of cancer and HIV and to fight viruses and bacteria.

Ginseng This root enhances energy, combats fatigue and is used to boost the immune system. It may also lower blood sugar levels and increase concentration, improve mood and boost endurance, as well as treat a number of ailments such as high blood pressure, cancer and heart disease.

Dang Gui or Sacred Lotus This root is used to treat menstrual disorders, move the bowels by moistening the intestines, and to decrease swelling, alleviate pain, and heal wounds. It also improves the blood to help with heart and liver blood deficiency and can help alleviate dry hair, brittle nails, palpitations, anemia, blurry vision and tinnitus.

On my first visit to China in 1985, I had a badly sprained ankle. I hobbled around on it for days until one of the cleaning ladies in my dorm dragged me off to the campus medical clinic. The doctor took one look at my badly swollen ankle, took out some Chinese medical lotion and began vigorously kneading it into my ankle. This was extremely painful but he insisted it was necessary. After several minutes of massage, he pulled out what looked like a round piece of paper with a thick, black, sticky tar-like substance on it. He held it up to a light bulb to soften it, then stuck it on my ankle and told me to leave it there until it fell off in a week or so. He also gave me a prescription, which was some kind of powder that I was to mix with hot water to make a

tea to drink every day. It was extremely bitter and difficult to swallow. I followed his instructions and to my great surprise and relief my ankle healed very quickly. In fact, within two weeks I was playing soccer. To this day, I am not sure what he treated me with but I am a firm believer in the benefits of certain kinds of traditional Chinese medicine.

Chinese Tea

For most Chinese, tea is considered an herb and has healing properties. The line between medicine and tea can be blurry as many Chinese herbs are steeped in hot water like tea, then drunk. The Chinese have been drinking tea for hundreds of years. The mere fact that water must be boiled to make tea has provided safe drinking water for millions of people over the years. Chinese green tea is known to be high in antioxidants, which has many health benefits. Various kinds of Chinese tea are said to have the following benefits:

• regulating cholesterol and high blood pressure
• reducing fatigue and stimulating the central nervous system
• preventing tooth decay
• controlling insulin secretion
• improving skin because of its high vitamin C content
• regulating body temperature
• aiding digestion
• improving blood flow

ACUPUNCTURE

Acupuncture is commonly practiced in China to treat a wide variety of illnesses and ailments, including repetitive stress injuries like carpal tunnel syndrome, pain relief autoimmune disorders like Crohn's disease, skin problems, gastrointestinal conditions like heartburn and diarrhea, OB/GYN issues such as PMS and menopausal symptoms, neurological conditions such as chronic headaches, respiratory problems like asthma, and insomnia. The Chinese believe that all living things have a vital force or energy (*qi*) that circulates through energy channels called meridians that promote healing. When there is a blockage of *qi*, pain or illness results. Acupuncture works to restore normal functions to the body by stimulating the energy channels along these meridians with very fine needles. I have known both Chinese and Westerners who have benefitted from acupuncture. Seldom do the needles cause any pain. There is merely a mild tugging or tingling sensation. Although I have not personally tried acupuncture, there is ample evidence that it works on a variety of ailments and can also be used in place of anesthesia during surgery.

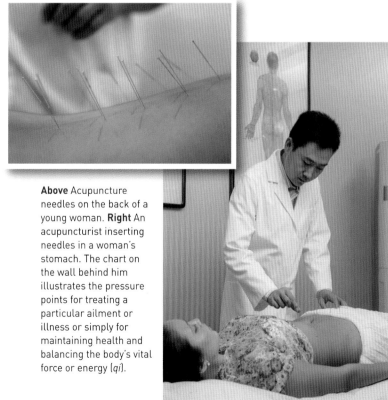

Above Acupuncture needles on the back of a young woman. **Right** An acupuncturist inserting needles in a woman's stomach. The chart on the wall behind him illustrates the pressure points for treating a particular ailment or illness or simply for maintaining health and balancing the body's vital force or energy (*qi*).

CHINA'S MARTIAL ARTS TRADITIONS

Contrary to popular belief, the term the Chinese use for martial arts is wushu, not kung-fu, and not all Chinese are kung-fu masters. The word kung-fu comes from gong-fu, which means a skill or art. Whereas in the past martial arts were developed for self-defense, nowadays they are considered a form of physical exercise and culture.

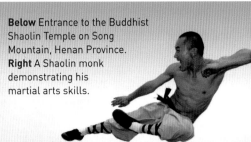

Below Entrance to the Buddhist Shaolin Temple on Song Mountain, Henan Province. **Right** A Shaolin monk demonstrating his martial arts skills.

WUSHU OR KUNG-FU

The birth of martial arts in China can be traced back to at least the 5th century BCE when hand-to-hand combat theory is mentioned in historical texts. By the Han Dynasty (206 BCE–220 CE), there were training manuals written for weaponless fighting.

Chinese wushu as we know it today probably got its start at the legendary Buddhist Shaolin Temple on Song Mountain in Henan Province, central China. Shaolin- style wushu is considered the first institutionalized Chinese martial arts and dates back to the 7th century CE. Other legends suggest that the Buddhist monks of the Shaolin Monastery devised a type of exercise mimicking the movements of animals. This was to provide some relief from long hours of meditation. These exercises evolved into different forms of martial arts used to defend themselves from bandits and corrupt government officials. Many different styles of martial arts have evolved since that time. Although most are weaponless, some styles use a sword, staff or other weapon.

In addition to Shaolin-style wushu, other important styles of wushu include the Wudang style from the Mt Wudang area of Hubei Province, and the Southern Fist style, which has a 400-year-old history in the Guangdong and Fujian provinces of southern China.

Martial arts are popular sports today in China, with schools and training facilities all over the country. Competitions are also popular. It is not uncommon to see people practicing martial arts in parks.

TAICHI

Taichi (*taiqi*) is an internal form of martial arts that emphasizes relatively slow, fluid movements with a focus on inaction. It is practiced for both its self-defense training, incorporating solo hand and weapons routines, and for its health and health maintenance benefits, including longevity. Routines include breathing, movement and awareness exercises and meditation.

ELDERLY MAN DOING TAICHI

THE MIGHTY MONKS OF SHAOLIN TEMPLE

The Shaolin Temple is a Chan (Zen) Buddhist temple and monastery located on Song Mountain in Henan Province outside the city of Zhengzhou. It is the most famous martial arts location in China, and perhaps the world. It was originally built during the 5th century BCE and has been rebuilt many times since then. It was named a UNESCO World Heritage Site in 2010. The first abbot of the monastery was an Indian Dhyana named Batuo who had come to China to spread Buddhist teachings. The monastery has long been associated with martial arts.

The Shaolin Temple is also a major tourist site for both Chinese and foreign tourists. The Shaolin monks put on an impressive performance demonstrating their martial arts skills, which can be divided into external and internal. External skills are what we traditionally associate with martial arts and include punches, kicks and the like. Internal skills include breathing techniques, meditation and qigong. In these performances, the monks will break iron bars over their heads, suction metal bowls to their stomachs that cannot be removed and press sharp spear points to their throats, all without injury. This is done through years of practice and focusing the *qi* within their bodies as protection.

A few years ago, I was with a group of students at a Shaolin monk demon-

THE JIN YONG KUNG-FU NOVELS

Jin Yong is the pen name of Hong Kong author and co-founder of the newspaper *Ming Bao*, Louis Cha. Between 1955 and 1970, Jin Yong wrote 14 *wuxia* (martial arts and chivalry) novels). This genre of fiction has a huge following in the Chinese-speaking world. His books and characters are well known to readers in Hong Kong, Taiwan and mainland China. Most of his stories have been adapted into movies, television shows, radio shows, comic books and video games. One of his most famous novels is his first, *The Book and the Sword* (1955), which has been translated into English. It is set during the Qing Dynasty and tells the story of the secret Red Flower Society and its attempts to overthrow the Qing Dynasty. It is full of intrigue, elaborate kung-fu fight scenes, adventure and romance. His novels are historical, sometimes using real historical figures to emphasize Chinese patriotism. The novels generally espouse traditional Chinese Confucian values and include topics such as traditional Chinese medicine, acupuncture, music, calligraphy and Chinese philosophy (Confucianism, Taoism and Buddhism). His fictional characters often interact with historical figures, sometimes making if difficult for the average person to distinguish them. Many of his plots deal with periods when the country was ruled by invaders or was under threat of invasion from northern tribes such as the Mongols.

stration. At one point in the show, a young monk took off his shirt, spent a few minutes focusing his *qi*, then suctioned a ceramic-coated metal bowl to his stomach. Members of the audience were then invited to come up and try to pull the bowl off his stomach. After several people tried and failed, my students encouraged me to give it a try. I went up, grabbed the shallow pedestal base of the bowl and began to pull. A couple of students held onto me and we pulled until the base of the bowl suddenly tore from the body of the bowl in a crackling of ceramic. In the process it cut deep into my thumb, creating quite a bloody mess. The monks seemed a bit surprised but simply changed the bowl and went on with the show as I wandered out of the auditorium. A Chinese doctor in the audience followed me out. He sprinkled a traditional Chinese medicinal herb, a coagulant called *bai yao*, translated as 'white medicine', on my thumb, which almost immediately stopped bleeding, then bandaged me up. The story goes that the only person successful in getting the bowl off the monk's belly was an attractive young girl who walked up and kissed the monk on the cheek, whereupon, his concentration broken, the bowl slipped off his belly.

At the Shaolin Temple near Zhengzhou in Henan Province, the monks put on daily performances for tourists demonstrating their 'internal' skills as well as their 'external' martial arts skills.

WONG FEI-HUNG (1847–1924)

Wong Fei-hung (Huang Fei Hong), a martial artist and traditional Chinese physician and acupuncturist, was born in Foshan in Guangdong Province in China's far south. His father, Wong Kei-ying, one of the Ten Tigers of Canton, the ten most famous martial artists of the time in that area, was his teacher. Wong was famous for his skill in the Hung Gar style of martial arts, which features deep low stances, horse stances and strong hand techniques. He was also skilled in fighting with weapons and one legend says that he once defeated 30 gangsters with a staff on the Canton docks. He further developed Hung Gar by incorporating his Ten Special Fist technique. It is said that Wong was also involved in revolutionary activities against the Qing Dynasty rulers. The Southern Shaolin Temple in Fujian Province was a legendary training place for those against the foreign Qing rulers. After his death in 1924, his wife and sons moved to Hong Kong and continued teaching his style of martial arts. Wong is the most famous martial artist in the modern era and there have been more than 100 films made about his life. The most famous is the *Once Upon a Time in China* series (1991) directed by Tsui Hark and starring Jet Li. There is a museum dedicated to the life of Wong Fei-hung at the Ancestors Buddhist Temple in the city of Foshan, just outside Guangzhou.

BRUCE LEE (1940–1973)

Bruce Lee brought Chinese martial arts to the Western world through his many Hong Kong and Hollywood films. He is considered the most famous martial artist of all time and a pop culture icon of the 20th century. He was born in San Francisco's Chinatown but was raised primarily in Hong Kong until the age of 18 when he returned to the US. He was originally trained in the Wing Chun style of martial arts by the famous grandmaster Yip Man, but later developed his own style that he called Jeet Kune Do ('The way of the intercepting fist'). He had kung-fu studios in Seattle, then Oakland and later San Francisco. He was 'discovered' by Hollywood when he participated in the Long Beach International Karate Championship where he performed several demonstrations of his kung-fu style. He starred in several Hollywood movies, such as *Fist of Fury* and *Enter the Dragon*, which revolutionized the martial arts film genre in the US and Hong Kong. He died from a cerebral edema when he was only 32 years old.

JACKIE CHAN (1954–)

Jackie Chan is a Hong Kong-born martial artist, actor, film director and producer, comedian, action choreorapher, stuntman and singer. He is best known for his acrobatic fighting style and his use of improvised weapons and innovative stunts in his numerous movies, many in the comedic kung-fu genre, made in both Hong Kong and Hollywood. He is also known for being one of the very few actors who performs all of his own stunts. Jackie Chan is also known by his stage name, Sing Lung (Cheng Long), literally 'become the dragon'. He has starred in and directed over a hundred Hong Kong and Hollywood films in a 40-year career, but it was *The Young Master*, *Dragon Lord* and *Drunken Master* that propelled him to mainstream success and established him as Hong Kong's top cinematic star. His most famous American films, *Rumble in the Bronx*, the *Rush Hour* series with Chris Tucker and *Shanghai Noon* and *Shanghai Nights* with Owen Wilson, made him a Hollywood star.

YIP MAN (1893–1972)

Yip Man was a famous martial artist born in Foshan, just outside Guangzhou in southern China. He helped spread the martial arts style called Wing Chun, a form of self-defense that utilizes both striking and grappling while in close range combat, in southern China and Hong Kong. He began learning martial arts at a young age in Foshan, then moved to Hong Kong at 16. He returned to Foshan when he was 24 to become a policeman. He continued to practice his martial arts under several masters, but in 1949 returned to Hong Kong for good where he taught Wing Chun kung-fu to many students, including Bruce Lee. In 1967, Yip Man and some of his students, including his sons Yip Ching and Yip Chun, established the Ving Chun Athletic Association martial arts school in Hong Kong. Several movies have been made about his life, including the 2008 Hong Kong film *Yip Man* starring Donnie Yen, and Wong Kar-wai's 2013 film *The Grandmaster* starring Tony Leung. There is now a museum about the life of Yip Man at the Foshan Ancestral Temple in Foshan.

Above and left A portrait of Wing Chun kung-fu master Yip Man and a kung-fu wooden dummy at the Foshan Ancestral Temple.

In the mid-1990s, I helped a Wing Chun master who owned a martial arts school to translate some Chinese terms into English and with the Cantonese pronunciation of some kung-fu terms. He had trained in Hong Kong under the Wing Chun Grandmaster Yip Ching and is one of five living grandmasters trained by Yip Man. A year later, he asked if I would interpret at a three-day kung-fu camp where the Grandmaster Yip Ching would be teaching. I later met Yip Ching in Hong Kong, where he showed me around his studio and school. In 2013, I had the chance to visit the Foshan Ancestral Temple, where I discovered a new hall dedicated to Yip Man and another to the spread worldwide of Wing Chun. I was surprised to find a small display and photo about Yip Ching's trip to Utah and the kung-fu retreat where he taught, and even more surprised to see myself in the group photo. Needless to say, my Chinese traveling companions were quite impressed.

Jet Li (1963–)

Li Lianjie, better known as Jet Li, is a martial artist, wushu champion, film actor and film producer. He was born in Beijing, the youngest of five children, to a poor family, but is now a naturalized Singaporean citizen. He took up martial arts at a sports school when he was 8 years old. By the time he was 11, in 1974, he had become the All-round National Wushu Champion, a title he held for five consecutive years. He traveled with the Beijing Wushu Team to more than 45 countries, including the US, where he performed for President Richard Nixon. Although he was a master of several styles of wushu, he retired from the sport when he was just 17 to pursue a career in acting. He has become a popular and wealthy actor starring in both Chinese films and Hollywood English language films. Some of his more popular martial arts films include the Chinese films *Once Upon a Time in China* where he portrayed the kung-fu master Wong Fei Hung. He also starred in the Zhang Yimou film *Hero* that was nominated for an Academy Award. His Hollywood films include *Lethal Weapon 4* with Mel Gibson and *Romeo Must Die*, in which he had the lead role.

CHINESE LITERATURE AND LEGENDS

China has a rich literary history built on its thousands of years of civilization. Different literary styles developed in subsequent dynasties, from the earliest poems to folk ballads, myths and legends, dramas, novels and contemporary literature.

THE COWHERD AND THE WEAVER GIRL

This folk tale, the most famous in China, was first told 2,600 years ago in a poem from the *Classic of Poetry*. It has since been the subject of numerous poems and stories and is a popular opera. The tale is about a human cowherd who falls in love with a weaver girl who is a fairy. Their love is forbidden and they are banished to opposite sides of the heavens, separated by the Silver River (the Milky Way). The cowherd is symbolized by the star Altair and the weaver girl by the star Vega. Once a year, on the seventh day of the seventh lunar month, a flock of magpies forms a bridge to reunite the lovers for one day. This legend is celebrated every year in the Qixi Festival and is similar to Valentine's Day in the West.

THE DREAM OF THE RED CHAMBER

Also known as *The Story of the Stone*, *Dream of the Red Chamber* is generally considered the greatest work of traditional Chinese fiction. Written in the mid-18th century by Cao Xueqin and first published in 1791, it is an epic story covering a number of themes in 120 chapters, including love, Buddhist-Taoist disenchantment and enlightenment and social observation, all within the context of a large aristocratic family in the Qing Dynasty. It is widely praised for how its hundreds of characters are portrayed through both physical and psychological observation. The story is known to all Chinese and has been adapted into children's versions, comic books, plays and other literary and popular forms.

THE BALLAD OF MULAN

The famous Han Dynasty folk tale of the girl turned warrior to take her father's place in the army comes from an anonymous poem written in the 5th or 6th century in 31 couplets of 5–9 character lines. A popular story known all over China, it has been dramatized and incorporated into a historical novel. It has also inspired many screen and stage adaptations. Below is an excerpt from the poem.

Last night I saw the draft posters,
The Khan is calling many troops,
The army list is in twelve scrolls,
On every scroll there's Father's name.
Father has no grown-up son,
Mu-lan has no elder brother.
I want to buy a saddle and horse,
And serve in the army in Father's place.
In the East Market she buys a spirited horse,
In the West Market she buys a saddle,
In the South Market she buys a bridle,
In the North Market she buys a long whip.
At dawn she takes leave of Father and Mother,
In the evening camps on the Yellow River's bank.
She doesn't hear the sound of Father and Mother calling,
She only hears the Yellow River's flowing water cry
tsien tsien.

(Translated by Hans H. Frankel, *The Flowering Plum and the Palace Lady: Interpretations of Chinese Poetry*, 1976.)

THE BUTTERFLY LOVERS

This is China's version of Romeo and Juliet about forbidden and unrequited love. It is the tragic love story of Liang Shanbo and Zhu Yingtai, set in the Eastern Jin Dynasty (265–420 CE). The story is often abbreviated with their names and simply called *Liang Zhu*. Zhu Yingtai is an attractive and intelligent young woman from a large family. She convinces her father to let her dress like a boy in order to attend school. On her way to Hangzhou, she meets Liang Shanbo, a young scholar also on his way to attend the school. They get along well and become the best of friends. After three years studying together, Zhu falls in love with Liang. She eventually reveals that she is a woman and they vow to be together forever. But Zhu's father has arranged for her to marry a local man. When Liang learns of this, his health declines and he dies. During the wedding procession, Zhu wanders off to Liang's grave and, kneeling there, begs the grave to open up and take her. With a clap of thunder, the grave opens and Zhu throws herself in. Their two spirits turn into a pair of beautiful butterflies and they fly off together.

THE ROMANCE OF THE THREE KINGDOMS

Romance of the Three Kingdoms is a historical novel widely considered one of the most influential novels produced in traditional China. Attributed to Luo Guanzhong, it is a fictionalized story based on historical figures and is set in the time of the Three Kingdoms Period, Shu, Wu and Wei (220–280 CE). The characters in the novel have become symbols of Chinese culture: Zhu Geliang as the idealization of wisdom, Hua Tuo as the perfection of professional skills and Cao Cao as the personification of political power. It is a story full of intrigue, military prowess and adventure. It has been become an important part of folk culture and has been adapted countless times for theater, movies, television and books, including simplified versions for children, and comics.

OUTLAWS OF THE MARSH

The late 16th-century novel *Outlaws of the Marsh*, also known as *Water Margin*, is set during the Song Dynasty (960–1279) and is loosely based on a Song Dynasty bandit named Song Jiang. It tells the story of 108 outlaws who gather at Mt Liang to form an army to fight corrupt government troops. Its theme of commoners standing up to oppression is similar to the oral tradition of Robin Hood. The bandits are eventually granted amnesty and hired by the emperor to fight foreign invaders and rebel forces. *Outlaws of the Marsh* is one of the four great classical novels of China, along with *Dream of the Red Chamber*, *Romance of the Three Kingdoms* and *Journey to the West*. The characters in the novel, Song Jiang, Wu Song, Lin Chong, Lu Zhishen and others, have become household names and are some of the best-known characters in Chinese fiction.

THE ART OF WAR

The Art of War is an ancient military treatise attributed to Sun Tzu, who was a high-ranking military general at the end of the 6th century BCE. Each of the 13 chapters is devoted to one aspect of warfare, such as 'Laying Plans', 'Maneuvering' and 'Terrain'. It is China's most famous and influential of the seven military classics and is considered the definitive work on military tactics and strategy of the time. It was first translated into French in 1772, and the first English translation came out in 1910. It has been translated into multiple languages and continues to be widely discussed in military circles. It is also considered a philosophical text.

Below Statue of Sun Tsu at the Liu Bei Peach Temple, Chengdu, Sichuan Province.
Bottom A copy of Sun Tsu's famous military treatise, *The Art of War*.

TO THE CHINESE, FOOD IS HEAVEN

The Chinese have a saying, 'Min yi shi wei tian', which means that to the people food is heaven or that food is the most important thing in society. The Chinese place great importance on eating. In fact, Chinese culture seems to revolve around thinking about food, talking about food and buying and eating food. A sure way to start a conversation is to ask people about their favorite dishes or the specialty dishes of the city you are visiting. I have had countless surly taxi drivers become friendly and animated after I've asked them about the local cuisine.

There is a common joke that the Chinese will eat anything with four legs except a table and anything that flies except an airplane. It has also been said that China is a nation of one billion foodies. This obsession with eating probably stems from the fact that over the centuries life in China has been difficult for most people. The supply of food was always low but the demand was always very high, resulting in a culture that is obsessed with food and eating.

To the Chinese, eating is an important social activity. It plays a central role in all Chinese holidays and is at the center of business negotiations and nearly every other social engagement like weddings, parties and reunions. No business deal is complete without starting and ending with a banquet. Potential business partners get to know each other over a meal, maybe two or three, to establish trust before any business talk begins, always around the table. It is also very common for Chinese friends to meet at a favorite restaurant for a meal. This is the default way to socialize and spend time together.

The Chinese view food in the same way they view medicine, as a means to support, nourish and maintain good health. In fact, in Chinese one does not 'take' medicine but 'eats' it. Based on Taoist philosophy, the Chinese view food as having either cooling properties or warming properties linked to the *yin* and *yang* in the body. When the body is out of balance, causing someone to be ill, they need to eat either hot or cold foods to restore the balance. Cooling foods clear heat and toxins in the body and have a calming effect on the blood.

They nourish the *yin* by helping with such things as anxiety, thirst, headaches and constipation. Cooling foods include apple, banana, lemon, orange, watermelon, asparagus, celery, cucumber, eggplant, lettuce, tofu, whole wheat, barley, clam, chicken egg, crab and tea. Warming foods affect the *yang* in the body by increasing energy in the organs, improving circulation and dispelling the cold. Common symptoms include cold hands and feet, diarrhea, stomach pain, lack of energy and sore joints. Warming foods include cherries, dates, coconut, guava, lychee, chives, leeks, mustard, onion, squash, chestnut, walnut, glutinous rice, butter, chicken, eel, ham, lamb, brown sugar, cinnamon, cloves, coffee, garlic and ginger. There are also a number of foods that are considered neutral, neither warming nor cooling. If you are not feeling well, a Chinese friend or colleague may encourage you to eat something with healing properties to address the problem.

Chinese food in China varies widely geographically but there are four main regional cuisines. The Chinese will eat just about any kind of meat, an astonishing array of fruits and vegetables as well as many kinds of grain, the main ones being rice and wheat. Common seasonings include chili pepper, garlic, ginger, vinegar and soy sauce.

Eating in China is a great adventure and is the thing I most look forward to when I travel there. Although I love a good banquet with a wide variety of exotic and interesting dishes, my favorite kind of food in China is what we call *bian fan* or ordinary food, the kind of food that people eat all the time, nothing fancy, just good common dishes. My favorite places to get this are the countless small, informal restaurants on any city side street. They are typically inexpensive, the food is freshly prepared and is delicious. Gathering in a small, casual restaurant with a few friends is a great way to spend an evening. And since Chinese food is served family style, with everyone sharing the dishes arranged in the center of the table, it is a great social activity.

Banquets offer a chance to taste a wide variety of often exotic Chinese dishes.

A Chinese New Year banquet for CEOs from various industries at the Foshan Hotel, Foshan City.

THE CHINESE BANQUET AND DRINKING

Banquets are practically a national sport in China. They are held to celebrate events (holidays, promotions, retirements, birthdays, baby's one-month parties), to entertain guests and to get to know business partners, the overriding purpose being to create and maintain social harmony. Banquets and hosting are so important in Chinese culture that most organizations have a special budget for them. Banquets may be small, consisting of just one table, or very large, with hundreds of tables. I had heard that the Great Hall of the People could seat 5,000 people. When I was invited there with a group of educators for a formal banquet, I saw with my own eyes the vastness of this huge dining hall, with swarms of waiters everywhere. The food was not only excellent but visually stunning.

The main table at a banquet is always reserved for VIP's, dignitaries, bosses, etc. When you arrive, the table will usually already be set with 4–6 cold appetizer dishes. Once your host starts to eat, you may also begin. After the cold dishes are eaten, the hot dishes will begin to arrive, one or two at a time, which are placed on a lazy Susan in the center of the table.

There are a few things to remember at a banquet. First, pace yourself. At most banquets, 10–15 dishes will be served, sometimes more. Guests are expected to try each dish. Even if you really like a dish, don't take too much as there are many more to come. It is also very bad form to eat too much early in a banquet and not eat any of the later dishes. Sometimes the better, more expensive dishes are served later. At large formal banquets, a soup dish may be served after every 4–5 dishes.

Second, try everything. The food at formal banquets is not ordinary fare found at casual restaurants. It may be rich, expensive, exotic and often unidentifiable, such as duck web, duck blood, soup snake meat and sea slug. If you don't like a dish, simply leave it in your bowl or place it on the small plates reserved for shells and bones. If there is an item that you are prohibited from eating, such as pork for Muslims, it is perfectly fine not to eat it.

You are probably used to eating rice with Chinese food, but the emphasis at a banquet is on a variety of delicious dishes, not to fill up on cheap rice. Near the end, rice, noodles, dumplings or other starchy food will be brought out to 'top you off' if you are still hungry, although you will probably be full to the brim. Nearly all banquets end with a plate of fresh fruit.

Third, keep banquet conversation light. This is not the time to discuss politics, religion or other potentially sensitive subjects. Also avoid serious business discussions or negotiations. The purpose of the banquet is to relax and to build and maintain relationships.

Drinking and Toasting at Banquets

Drinking alcohol and toasting is an integral part of most banquets. There may be up to three different glasses: a medium size for beer, soda or juice, a smaller wine glass and an additional glass like stemware or a shot glass for hard liquor. The host will usually begin the banquet with a short speech to welcome everyone and a toast. Don't drink any alcohol until the host starts. If you don't drink alcohol, ask for a soda or juice and join in the toasts. Many Chinese feel that in order to trust someone, they need to drink together so you may be pushed to drink even if you don't want to. This is often *baijiu*, a very strong white liquor produced from white rice or sorghum (40–60 percent alcohol, so be careful). Getting drunk on it is not uncommon. The host usually goes from table to table offering a toast. As a guest, you may also be expected to return the toast, so come prepared to say something. After a toast, it is common to bump glasses with those at your table. Hold your glass lower than the host or others of higher position. You are not expected to pay the bill or to share in it when invited to a banquet.

Popular Chinese Alcoholic Drinks

Although wine was not very common in China in the past, red wine is now the top selling alcoholic drink in China because of the rise of a new middle class. Vineyards have sprung up all over the country. *Baijiu*, as mentioned above, is the most consumed hard liquor in the world. The most popular brand in China is Maotai. Another popular and traditional liquor in China is *huangjiu*, usually translated as yellow wine. It is made from water and cereal grains like rice, sorghum, millet or wheat. It is not distilled and has less than 20 percent alcohol content. The color varies from beige to yellowish brown to reddish brown. It is often drunk warm. The most popular beer in China is Tsingtao. It comes from the city of Qingdao, which had a strong German presence in the early 20th century.

REGIONAL CHINESE CUISINES

Chinese food is traditionally divided into four major categories. The distinct foods of each category is largely a reflection of their geographical location, the raw ingredients available and the unique methods of preparation.

SPICY CHICKEN

SICHUAN CUISINE (SICHUAN, GUIZHOU AND YUNNAN PROVINCES, CHONGQING)

The epicenter of Sichuan cuisine is Chengdu, the capital of Sichuan Province in southwest China. Sichuan is considered one of China's bread baskets as the area is very fertile. Rice is also cultivated and, as such, Sichuan is one of the main rice-eating regions of China.

Sichuan cuisine is characterized by the abundant use of chili peppers and Sichuan peppercorns (or Chinese prickly ash). Although many Sichuan dishes are spicy, many of their famous dishes are not particularly so.

Though not native to China, chili peppers are a major ingredient in Sichuan and related cuisines. The chili pepper is used in a variety of forms. Although they are used fresh in many dishes, they are often dried and used either whole, in pieces or in flake form. They are also commonly used in a paste with either broad beans or soy beans. These pastes may include other ingredients such as garlic, vinegar and sometimes small amounts of meat. Mushrooms are another important ingredient in many

Sichuan dishes. Sichuan cuisine also uses garlic and ginger quite liberally.

Sichuan peppercorns are not a true pepper or chili. They grow on bushes and when fresh look like bright red berries the size of a large peppercorn. They are almost always used dried, after they have turned a dark brownish-red color, either whole or ground. When ground, they are much hotter than whole. Sichuan peppercorns are spicy but not in the same way as chili peppers. They produce a numbing sensation in the mouth that is unique to this spice. Some people find it off-putting but the Sichuanese love the combination of fiery spice and numbing spice. The numbness seems to enhance the flavors of a dish, though some foreigners find it overpowering.

Popular Sichuan dishes include *mapo tofu*, *kung pao* chicken (or pork), spicy deep-fried chicken, Sichuan stewed fish, dry-fried green beans and shredded pork in fish-flavored sauce. Hot pot is also a favorite dish in Sichuan cuisine. It can be very, very spicy. Hot pot in Chengdu is usually served with the raw ingredients on bamboo skewers. You can either stick the whole skewer into the hot pot

or slide the ingredients off the skewer into the pot. People from Sichuan will tell you that hot pot originated there, but this is debatable.

Sichuan food can be truly spicy. I ate at a restaurant in Chengdu once that was supposedly the birthplace of the famous dish *mapo tofu*. It was so spicy that we could hardly eat it and we were sweating profusely. But we were also surprised to eat a delicious dish of smoked pork ribs that contained no spice whatsoever.

Noodles are also extremely popular in Sichuan cuisine, the most popular dish being *dandan* noodles. This is a bowl of noodles with a spicy mix of ground pork, ginger, garlic and chili pepper, often sprinkled with fresh scallions. There are dozens of different versions of this popular dish and it makes a great meal for lunch or dinner.

MAPO TOFU

SICHUAN NOODLES

EGG AND TOMATO

CANTONESE CUISINE (GUANGDONG AND GUANGXI PROVINCES, HONG KONG AND MACAU)

Guangdong Province and Hong Kong in China's far south are the main centers of Cantonese cuisine, which is generally considered the most popular Chinese food outside of China. The Cantonese are obsessed with eating and this is obvious from the number or restaurants and food stalls all over every city in Guangdong and Hong Kong. It is common for restaurants to set up tables and chairs along the sidewalks where you will find people eating at all hours of the day and late into the night. Street markets and shopping areas are also full of restaurants, cafés, food stalls and snack bars. Food carts can also be found near train and bus stations as well as at busy intersections. It is quick and convenient to grab a snack while on the run.

Southern China is also a rice-eating area where steamed white rice is served with most meals. It is also a fertile area of great abundance. Cantonese cuisine is thus characterized by the use of a lot of garlic, ginger and scallions. Cantonese food flavors are comparatively light and fresh and, because of the geographical location, there is an emphasis on seafood. Chicken is very common and countless chicken dishes can be found all over the area. Roasted poultry and pork are a mainstay and can be seen hanging on hooks at shops all over. Guangzhou offers a huge variety of dishes and the Cantonese are known to eat just about any plant or animal. Soups and stews are also an important part of Cantonese cuisine. In addition to

DIM SUM

Dim sum is an integral part of Cantonese cuisine. It consists of small dishes that are most often steamed and eaten in one or two bites for breakfast or in the late morning, similar to our brunch. It is common to order a dozen or more of these small dishes. There are large restaurants, typically called teahouses, some as big as four or five stories, that specialize in dim sum. Traditionally, dim sum was served from carts in a restaurant. Vendors would wheel their carts about, shouting out what they were offering and you simply motioned for them to come to your table to serve their dishes. With this kind of ordering and serving, the tab is calculated by the number, kind and color of the plates that are left on your table when you are done. Going out for dim sum is a great social activity and the Cantonese may spend hours at a dim sum meal eating, chatting or reading the newspaper. Whenever I am in a Cantonese area of China or Hong Kong, a dim sum meal is a must and is a great way to reconnect with old friends.

Popular Cantonese dim sum dishes include barbequed pork buns, meat with sticky rice wrapped in lotus leaves, steamed shrimp dumplings, steamed meat dumplings, beef meatballs, and a wide variety of rice noodles with beef and *congee*, a rice porridge.

A lazy Susan in the center of a table allows diners to sample a dozen or more dim sum dishes washed down with Chinese tea.

A selection of small steamed and baked dishes on offer at a dim sum teahouse.

YANGZHOU-STYLE STEAMED DUMPLINGS

BEANS AND PORK SKIN

garlic, ginger and scallions, Cantonese cuisine uses an abundance of soy sauce, oyster sauce and fermented black beans. Popular Cantonese dishes include *cha siu* (barbequed pork), salt-baked chicken, roast duck, steamed fish with ginger and scallions and, of course, dim sum. The Cantonese also have delicious pastries, including pineapple bread, cocktail bread and others.

Several years ago I was in Guangzhou doing work with some local Cantonese colleagues. We wrapped things up at about 10:30 pm. They suggested we go out and get something to eat. I was thinking it would be a light snack. We ended up at a casual restaurant where we sat at tables set up on the sidewalk. I was surprised at the quantity of food they ordered. We ended up with ten or twelve dishes and ate and talked until 2:00 am. They didn't think anything of having a late meal like this.

NORTHERN CUISINE (BEIJING, TIANJIN, SHANDONG PROVINCE, NORTHEASTERN CHINA)

China's north is a wheat-growing area and this is reflected in a preference for noodles and steamed bread, buns and pancakes over rice. The hearty, starchy food is also suitable in the harsh, cold, dry winters and hot summers. In Shandong Province, you can find literally hundreds of different shapes and sizes of noodle and a good chef will be able to create many dozens of noodle dishes.

Northern dishes, usually called Lu Cuisine, are oilier and richer in meat than in other areas because of the north's agricultural tradition. Beef and lamb are commonly used, as is duck and pork, all popular with Western visitors. Mutton is the main ingredient in the Muslim northwest, while seafood is abundant in Shandong bordering the Yellow Sea in the northeast.

Northern food is also characterized by stronger flavors than in other parts of China. There is less use of chillies and pickles and more of strong seasonings compared with the south. These include vinegars, thick salty sauces like soy sauce, fermented soy beans, leeks, onions and garlic. Dipping sauces are also popular, as seen in the plum sauce traditionally served with Peking Duck (Beijing Roast Duck).

Popular Northern dishes include *jiaozi* (dumplings) served with a vinegar dipping sauce, Peking Duck, steamed bread (*mantou*), a simmering hot pot stew into which skewers of ingredients are dipped, fried sauce noodles, lamb with cumin and red braised beef.

HUAIYANG CUISINE (JIANGSU, ZHEJIANG, ANHUI PROVINCES, SHANGHAI)

The lower Yangtze River valleys in Jiangsu, Anhui and Zhejiang provinces are another of China's bread baskets, where there is an abundance of water for irrigation and thus plentiful vegetable crops. Sometimes Huaiyang

cuisine is also called Shanghai cuisine. Huaiyang cuinese is delicate, with an emphasis on the natural taste of the ingredients, which tend to be sweeter than in other areas. Hence, sauces are kept to a minimum. There is ample use of ginger, scallions and garlic and lots of fresh vegetables. Fish, pork and poultry are the most common meat dishes. In this area, rice is more commonly eaten than noodles, but because it lies between the north and the south, noodles are also frequently eaten.

A very popular specialty Shanghai dish is soup dumplings, in Chinese called *xiao long bao*, or 'small-bamboo-steaming-basket dumplings'. They are similar to *jiaozi* but smaller and have a lightly translucent skin. In addition to pork or crab, they also contain a deliciously rich broth. When they are eaten, care must be taken not to burn yourself on the hot broth but also to not take a bite and have the broth gush out all over you. One strategy is to take a tiny bite in one corner of the dumpling and carefully suck out the rich broth, then eat it like any other dumpling. Any Chinese traveling to Shanghai will undoubtedly want to try this specialty. They are served in fancy restaurants, specialist restaurants and small noodle shops and stalls all over the city. Din Tai Feng, a famous restaurant that started in Taipei, Taiwan, specializes in these soup dumplings. Show up on a weekend evening and plan on waiting a couple of hours to be seated. Soup dumplings are

HOT POT

PEKING DUCK

BUNS

the main attraction, but they also serve appetizers, soups, noodle dishes, various buns and some desserts. When I visited the Taipei restaurant with some friends, I was impressed with the freshness of the food and the excellent service. It is a chain now and there are branches all over Asia, including three in Shanghai and some in Los Angeles and Seattle. Their food and service are often described as impeccable, even though their soup dumplings will cost about ten times what you will pay at a roadside stall. It is definitely worth a visit for excellent, authentic soup dumplings. If in Shanghai, you can get excellent soup dumplings that are much cheaper but there are also many places selling inferior ones as well.

Popular Huaiyang dishes include Yangzhou-style fried rice, soup dumplings (*xiao long bao*), steamed fish, salted duck and fresh stir-fried vegetables with garlic.

JIAOZI, CHINA'S TRADITIONAL FAST FOOD

Jiaozi or dumplings can be found all over China, though they are more popular in the north. There are even fast food dumpling restaurants that serve only *jiaozi*. These delicious dumplings are traditionally filled with a mixture of ground pork, cabbage, garlic, ginger, etc., but nowadays you can get them with just about any kind of filling, both meat and vegetarian. Dumplings are usually served with a sauce of soy sauce and dark vinegar, although the sauce will vary depending on where you are in China. They are either boiled and served on a plate, boiled and served in a broth in a bowl, or fried in a pan until crispy then steamed until they are done. Served this way they are called potstickers.

Whenever I am in Beijing, I love to get a big plate of dumplings. The skins are freshly made and are thick and chewy. A good dumpling restaurant will have a wide variety of dumpling fillings, including chicken, lamb and beef, as well as a variety of vegetarian varieties with tofu, mushrooms and all kinds of vegetables. It is always good to get a nice variety of dumplings.

They are usually sold by the Chinese unit of weight called a *liang*, which is equivalent to 1.7 ounces. One hungry adult can easily consume about four *liang* of dumplings, enough to fill a regular sized dinner plate. Make sure you dip them in the vinegar soy sauce mixture. This is simple Chinese eating at its best.

CHINESE FOOD IS CHANGING

Traditionally, the Chinese diet consisted mainly of grains (rice and wheat), vegetables and pork. As the economy has grown, dietary practices have changed. While the rural poor in China remain thin, the urban middle class are seeing rapidly rising rates of obesity.

In the past, the vast majority of Chinese shopped for meat and produce at outdoor street market stalls. Everything was very fresh, and because most Chinese did not own refrigerators, people shopped daily. Today, many urban Chinese prefer shopping in supermarkets where the meat is shrink-wrapped, the produce is carefully displayed and everything is clean and sanitary.

Several factors have led to major changes in the Chinese diet:

1. The Chinese are increasingly concerned about the quality and safety of the food they eat, especially after recent scandals involving tainted food that resulted in illness and death.

2. With official promotion of the meat and dairy industry, many Chinese are eating more meat and dairy products.

3. The Chinese are increasingly interested in exotic foreign foods, ranging from tropical fruits like bananas to exotic seafood.

4. There is a significant increase in processed foods. Urbanization has meant that many people put convenience before quality.

5. Increased global trading has opened up imports of a large variety of foods previously not available in China.

These factors have contributed to a more diverse diet but also to rising obesity rates, especially among the younger generation and urban Chinese. Chocolate consumption has risen dramatically, as has ice cream, soda pop and calorie-laden milky coffee served from Starbucks and countless Chinese knock-off chains. With China's typically tiny apartments and more disposable income, Chinese are eating out more or are using processed foods in their cooking at home. But for those visiting China, it has resulted in a greater variety of eating options, especially for Western food and not just fast food.

Where to Get the Best Food in China

This will not be found in your hotel restaurant nor at the banquet you've been invited to. The best food is what the Chinese eat on a daily basis. In my many years of visiting China, I have tested the following strategies in numerous cities:

Walk Around the Block

Get out of the commercial area and into a residential area where there are narrow streets lined with small shops and restaurants with apartments above them. This is where you will find authentic, inexpensive and delicious Chinese food.

Go to Where the People are

Often many small restaurants, lined up side by side, serve the same kinds of dishes. Pick the restaurant that is the most crowded.

Order What Others are Eating

Watch what other people are eating, often a specialty. That is what you should order, too, along with other dishes you may like. If you don't read Chinese, look around at what others are eating and simply point to the dish. Sometimes the smallest noodle shops will have pictures of the dishes on the wall.

When Ordering

When ordering, use this ratio: 1 meat to 2–3 vegetable dishes. Keep in mind that some vegetable dishes may have small amounts of meat in them. Tofu is generally regarded as a vegetable dish and egg dishes are regarded as meat. Generally, you will want to order 1–2 dishes per person. For two hungry people, you might like to order 4–5 dishes.

If you know some Chinese, here are some ordering strategies:

1. Tell the server you would like the dish that you have seen on other tables.

2. Ask the server what the specialty dishes are.

3. Look at the various sections in the menu and ask the server to recommend good dishes in each section.

4. Ask what fresh vegetables they have that day.

Watch How Things are Done

Watch what other diners are doing. Are they ordering at the counter then sitting down, or do they sit and wait for a menu to be brought to them? Pay attention to how to pay for your meal. At very small informal restaurants, you may

just toss your money into a basket on your way out, or you may be required to pay when you order. It all depends on the restaurant.

What to Drink

Tea will be served automatically. If you don't want tea, larger restaurants will typically have some soda pop, beer, maybe wine, or you can simply drink hot boiled water. The Chinese typically don't drink a lot when they are eating. Or you can simply buy a drink, such as a Coke or bottle of water, at a nearby store and bring it in with you. This is fine. In some smaller restaurants, if they don't have soda pop, they may send someone out to get it for you.

Eating Like a Native

Eating in a Chinese restaurant is a group experience. Unlike in American restaurants, diners order several different dishes and everyone at the table shares them as they are served from the center of the table, often on a lazy Susan. Sometimes a serving spoon is provided with each dish to bring a spoonful of food back to your bowl, but sometimes you simply serve yourself using your chopsticks. Chinese dishes are delivered to the table as they are prepared, so it is not uncommon to be completely done with one dish before others arrive. It is common in many parts of China, especially the south, to eat plain steamed white rice with a meal. Rice usually needs to be ordered as it is not served automatically. Each diner will have their own individual rice bowl. Plates are usually not supplied unless you are at a fast food restaurant where food is often served heaped on a large plate and eaten with a spoon or a combination of a spoon and chopsticks. This is especially true in Hong Kong and Taiwan.

It is common for the host of a group to serve guests from the dishes in the center of the table. For example, if you are visiting a friend in China, or a friend takes you out to eat at a restaurant, they might select especially good pieces of meat or vegetables and put them in your bowl with their chopsticks (or a serving spoon, if provided). This is the way a host shows you respect and ensures that you eat well. In situations like this, it is polite to thank the person who has done this and appear grateful.

Chinese Street Food

Street food in China is usually served from mobile carts. These carts can be found around subway and train stations, bus stations and college campuses, near schools, at night markets, in shopping areas and at busy intersections. Since the carts are mobile, vendors may set up for breakfast early in the morning and be gone by 8:00 or 9:00. Another set of

ANATOMY OF A CHINESE MENU

A typical Chinese menu is arranged by category, using the character 类, meaning 'category', based on the main ingredient. The Chinese character for meat is 肉 and the character for vegetable is 菜. A typical menu will have the following categories:

Special dishes 特色菜
Cold dishes 冷盘 / 冷菜
Seafood 海鲜类
Poultry 鸡鸭类
Pork 猪肉类
Beef 牛肉类
Meat dishes 肉类
Vegetable and vegetarian dishes 素菜
Rice and noodle dishes 饭面类
Noodles 主食类 or 面类
Soups and stews 汤羹类
Beverages 饮料

vendors may then show up at lunchtime and likewise for dinner. Night markets always have a wide variety of food and snacks.

You may think that eating street food will make you sick. But street food is usually prepared as it is ordered, cooked in a hot wok or other pan and served immediately. I have eaten quite a bit of street food over the years and have never had a problem.

Street food will vary depending on where you are because the offerings usually focus on local specialties. Some of the more common street food in cities includes steamed buns (sometimes with fillings of meat or vegetables), wonton soup, fried noodles, kabobs of various kinds (usually in front of Muslim restaurants), dumplings and potstickers, scallion pancakes, fried bread sticks (*youtiao*), stinky tofu, soy sauce boiled eggs, egg crepes, sugar-coated haws (hawthorn berries) and fresh fruit.

One of my favorite breakfast foods is egg crepes, called *jian bing* in Chinese. They are made with a large crepe or thin pancake cooked on a large flat pan. An egg is cracked onto it and partially cooked, then flipped over so the egg is on the pan. Once the egg is fully cooked, it is flipped over again. You then choose your condiments, which may include a sweetish plum sauce, a spicy chili pepper sauce, scallions, pickled vegetables and Chinese sausage. Usually a long piece of deep-fried bread is folded in half and wrapped up in the egg crepe. I also love scallion pancakes, called *cong you bing* in Chinese. This are pancake-like breads studded with scallions and cooked in oil until they are crispy on the outside but still tender and chewy on the inside. These are very filling and deliciously simple. They are very popular and can be found all over China.

WHAT IS REAL CHINESE FOOD?

Chinese food in China is quite different from what you get at your typical Chinese American restaurant in the United States. It has far fewer deep-fried offerings, the sauces are less sweet and sticky and there tends to be more vegetables and less meat in most dishes. And rarely does it look anything like American Chinese food. Authentic Chinese dishes in China have distinct flavors and vary considerably from region to region.

Traditional Chinese food emphasizes vegetables. Meat is primarily used to season or enhance the flavors of the other ingredients. In fact, some meat dishes may have more vegetables in them than meat. For example, fish-flavored shredded pork contains thinly sliced pork with garlic, scallions, ginger, chili pepper, wood ears (a type of mushroom), bamboo shoots and sometimes green pepper. There are as many vegetables as there is meat. Another example is the popular dish, dry-fried green beans. This dish comprises deep-fried green beans, garlic, preserved vegetable and just a bit of ground pork. The pork gives the dish more depth and a richer flavor.

Even if eaten outside the home, Chinese food is also eaten family style, that is, several dishes are ordered and shared by everyone in the group. As such, eating Chinese food is a very social experience. Usually one person in the party will order the dishes and one person typically will pay. Tables are usually round and have a lazy Susan placed in the center so that everyone has access to all the dishes. In many parts of China, particularly the south and west, people eat steamed white rice with their meals. In the north, noodles or steamed bread called *mantou* can be more popular than rice, though some northerners also eat rice, especially in restaurants.

Green vegetable dishes are an important component of Chinese cuisine, whether eaten at home or outside the home, as are nutritious and inexpensive tofu dishes. Peking duck is a more special restaurant treat.

IT'S ALWAYS TEATIME IN CHINA

China is a major tea producer as well as consumer. Tea is an important part of Chinese tradition and is typically taken with every meal. At a restaurant, the house tea, usually green, is automatically served. In some restaurants you may order your favorite tea from a variety of options. When you visit someone in their home, there is a good chance you will be served tea. Teahouses are a place to drink tea and socialize and have been around in China for hundreds of years. The Cantonese use the expression 'to drink tea' to mean to go to a large teahouse and have tea and dim sum.

There are several types of Chinese tea, which vary in the degree of fermentation and processing:
• Green tea • Dragon well tea • Jasmine tea

These three teas have a fresh aroma and are green or light green in color. Green tea, made from new shoots, is the oldest and most popular tea in China.
• Oolong tea • Steel Guanyin tea

These teas are partially fermented, have a stronger flavor and are yellow to brown in appearance.

Black tea is actually called red tea in Chinese. It has a dark red appearance, is sweeter and has a roasted flavor.

Pu'er tea is the strongest tea favored in China's southwest. It has a strong, full, earthy taste.

Not a tea drinker? Try chrysanthemum tea. It is light, refreshing and is a pure herbal tea that is widely available. Barley tea is also sometimes available.

CHINESE-STYLE FAST FOOD

Fast food has been around in China since ancient times but in the form of what we call street food. Street food is usually sold by vendors with movable carts set up alongside roads or inside very small restaurants. The typical fast food in many parts of China, particularly in the north, is *jiaozi* or dumplings. It comes in two main forms, boiled and pan-fried (called *guotie* or potstickers), which are usually served with a soy sauce vinegar dipping sauce. There are even chain fast food restaurants specializing in dumplings. One popular chain is called Guniang Dumplings. Other popular fast foods include various meats or seafood on skewers, such as squid or lamb.

Another kind of Chinese-style fast food is a plate of rice or noodles with meat and vegetables on top, eaten with a spoon or a combination of spoon and chopsticks. At some sit-down fast food restaurants, noodle dishes may include a small bowl of soup, a small side dish and a drink. Many imitate Western fast food restaurants in that you order, wait for your food, then take it served on a tray to your table.

Below Chaozhou snack. **Bottom** Potstickers.

WESTERN FOOD IN CHINA

McDonald's, Starbucks, KFC and Pizza Hut are all over China. In Shanghai alone, there are more than 100 McDonald's outlets. Eating Western food in China tells people that you have money, are young, sophisticated and international. Brazilian barbeque restaurants are becoming increasingly popular, and in cities with a more international presence, such as Shanghai and Beijing, there are restaurants specializing in fusion cuisine, both Western-influenced Chinese food or Chinese-influenced Western food.

Although tea remains the preferred drink, more people in China are drinking coffee, another Western status symbol. In 2014, there were 823 Starbucks outlets in China, and like many Western restaurants they have adapted to suit Chinese culture. The stores are bigger with more seating space because the Chinese like to socialize in such settings. Chinese teas and snacks like mooncakes are available. Other fast food restaurants have also modified their menus to suit Chinese palates: Pizza Hut serves pizza topped with slices of hot dog, mayo, shrimp tempura and squid; KFC offers Texas steak with spaghetti or garlic snails; and McDonald's sells a beef rice bowl and sweet taro pie. Most of these 'Western' dishes are pretty bland and barely Western.

There is also increasing interest in upmarket Western restaurants located in large, expensive hotels or in areas with higher numbers of foreigners, such as near college campuses. These restaurants tend to be small cafés that offer things like hamburgers, sandwiches, salads, pizza and coffee, but some have an ethnic focus, such as French, Russian or Brazilian. Don't expect the food to be authentic. Personally, I avoid Western food when I'm in China. Chinese food is so good it doesn't make sense to eat imitation Western food. However, you may have Chinese friends or colleagues who want to go out and eat Western food. In that case, ask the concierge at your hotel or other contacts for a good Western restaurant in the city where you are staying.

CHAPTER 3

CHINESE CHARACTER AND SOCIETY

The Chinese approach life differently than in the West. What the Chinese consider 'normal' behavior may seem strange to us. In order to get things done in China, it is important to understand the Chinese character and the different aspects of Chinese society. Humility, politeness and respect are an integral part of Chinese culture, and understanding how the Chinese exhibit these traits will enable you to integrate smoothly into Chinese society.

BUILDING A HARMONIOUS SOCIETY

China is a group-oriented society unlike in the West where the individual is most valued. The Chinese find it uncomfortable to be singled out from the group. They want to fit in, assimilate and work for the common good. They like being associated with a group, whether at work, at school or in their neighborhood. In contrast to the more individualistic 'American Dream', their goal is to belong to what *New York Times* columnist David Brooks calls a 'harmonious collective'.

At a basic level, the Chinese are deeply rooted to place and have strong associations with the area they come from. Each region in China has its own language (a Chinese dialect), its own food and its own cultural identity. When Chinese migrate to other parts of the country, they seek out people from their hometown or region. They find comfort in associating with a group that shares common values, goals and tastes.

Getting along with others is of utmost importance in Chinese society. In a business or work setting, this group mentality manifests itself in a number of ways in the interests of 'collectivism', where people act in the interests of the group and not necessarily of themselves. Decisions may be put off by individuals because these decisions or ideas are not compatible with what others within the group think. In fact, individuals within an organization are often not granted the power or authority to act on their own. They wait for instructions.

In business meetings, individuals are often reluctant to voice an opinion for fear that these may not be in harmony with the boss or their colleagues. They will wait for others to express their ideas so that they don't have to. Even though the boss may solicit opinions and ideas, in reality everyone is expected to agree with him and support his decisions. It is more important to go along with consensus than rock the boat. This makes China one of the most difficult countries to understand and to adapt to, especially for foreign business people who have a tendency for impatience to get things done quickly.

In everyday conversations as well, the Chinese are generally reluctant to express their personal opinions. Doing so may put them outside the bigger group. When speaking to foreigners, a Chinese person will not say 'I think' but, instead, 'we Chinese think such and such.' This does not mean, of course, that the Chinese don't express opinions privately. With China's rising Internet and cell phone culture, there are means to express opinions, albeit carefully.

MIANZI: PUTTING ON A GOOD 'FACE'

Mianzi or 'face' is a very important concept in Chinese culture. There are 98 dictionary forms of the word in Chinese. Face is the positive social image that one presents in society. It relates to a person's reputation, dignity and prestige as seen by others. Saving face simply means maintaining your image or integrity in a social context. Losing face means that your reputation or image has been questioned publicly.

Face and harmony are inextricably connected. In a group mentality, harmony must be maintained at all costs. Losing face or causing someone to lose face disrupts this harmony and causes discomfort for all present. In a public setting, even if a person is in the wrong, it will seldom be brought up for fear of causing that person to lose face. Serious issues may be raised in private between two individuals, but not in a group setting. At the other end of the spectrum, one may 'give face' in the group by praising someone in public, showing support for them, agreeing with them, complimenting them and so on. This is one of the ways that the Chinese build and maintain good relationships with others.

Saving face is of utmost importance in Chinese society. Saving or maintaining good face relations is the primary concern in any kind of meeting, talks or negotiations. The Chinese will go to great lengths to make sure no one in the group loses face. As such, the Chinese will seldom say 'no' to your face as this would cause you to lose face, which would disrupt the harmony within the group. Rather, they use strategies such as saying it is not convenient or they will think about it, or they may simply come up with an excuse.

THE IMPORTANCE OF GUANXI: IT'S NOT WHAT YOU KNOW, IT'S WHO YOU KNOW

Developing and cultivating personal relationships is of utmost importance to the Chinese in order to get things done. Although *guanxi* means 'relationships', it goes far beyond this simple definition and is better understood as 'connections'. It includes a network of people that one has connections with and can get help from.

China has a huge bureaucracy and getting things done is often nearly impossible without connections. It is a crucial part of business life in China. *Guanxi* is sometimes referred to as 'walking in the back door'. The Chinese are always looking for opportunities to cultivate relationships with people who may be able to help them out at some point. This is often done with gifts, favors or an invitation to a meal. Reciprocity is an important part of building and maintaining relationships. If someone does you a favor, you should return the favor at some point. This kind of reciprocity is taken very seriously in Chinese society and is based on mutual respect and understanding.

The Chinese are very sensitive about in-group and out-group relationships. Those in your in-group include family, friends and close associates, people who will go to great lengths to help each other. They will even call on others (outsiders) to help get things done for you.

This allows them to disagree or reject someone without actually saying 'no'. The Chinese understand this and will interpret these evasions as a 'no' response and move on.

Another way the Chinese maintain face is to go along with the crowd. By agreeing with others' ideas, especially of those in a higher position, harmony and good relations are maintained. Rather than directly confronting someone, the Chinese may make suggestions in a casual or offhand way, implying that these are what others want and not necessarily what they believe. When the boss, or someone in a higher position 'borrows' their idea, they will give credit to that person and count it as a compliment that they wanted to borrow it.

THE HUMILITY OF YAO MING

When Yao Ming began playing in the NBA in the US, he didn't fit the stereotype of the typical brash, cocky player. Many players and coaches thought he would have to change his attitude to gain respect, even though fans found his humility refreshing.

Why did Yao Ming have this kind of attitude? It goes back to the Confucian ideals he grew up with in China. It is deeply ingrained in the Chinese psyche to be deferential and humble, building up those around you while belittling yourself. This is what Chinese children are taught from an early age. You don't want to stand out; rather, you want to fit in. This is part of the group mentality that exists in China and other Asian societies.

COMMUNICATING CHINESE STYLE

To Westerners, the Chinese can seem hesitant, indirect and evasive. In the West, we are trained to be direct, say exactly what we mean, with no beating about the bush. In China, it is almost the opposite.

Children in China are trained to infer meaning from cues given by others. It is considered rude to be direct, especially if you disagree with someone. In China, it is common to decline an invitation by saying you are busy or, literally, 'I have things.' When a Chinese says this, it is the end of the discussion. No explanation or reason is given or expected. By saying 'I have things' the person politely declines an invitation while still maintaining harmony in the relationship.

With the Chinese, what is not said is often as important as what is said. In fact, the Chinese have a saying 'Meaning lies beyond words'. Communicating requires implied meanings and reading between the lines. Being vague allows a person to think about what was said and interpret it without being put on the spot. Requests are often implied rather than spoken directly. For example, if a Chinese person needs help with something, they will not directly ask. Instead, they may casually talk about what they need to do and the difficulty of doing it alone. The other person will pick up on this and offer to help. It is considered forward, or even rude, to ask directly for help.

And don't be surprised if you hear Chinese consistently denigrating themselves. It is considered polite to put yourself down and praise others. And when someone is complimented, they either deny it or downplay it. For example, if you compliment a Chinese person on their English skills, they will respond by saying, 'Oh no, it's not that good' or 'I only know a little bit' or something to that effect. This is considered the polite way to respond to a compliment. Saying 'thank you' to a compliment is too direct and not humble. Remember Yao Ming?

An office team having a discussion in their company's meeting room. Despite the relaxed and casual atmosphere, Chinese social structure and hierarchy, respect and reverence are nevertheless ingrained in communicating with colleagues.

WHO'S WHO? HIERARCHY IN CHINESE SOCIETY

Social structure was very important in ancient China, based on the Confucian system that valued hierarchy, group orientation and respect for age and tradition. Because of the importance of hierarchy in Chinese society, who you are in China in relation to others is still very important.

The primary unit of social organzation has always been the family, including the extended family. The Chinese are very respectful and deferential to older people. They are obedient to their parents even after they become adults and are expected to take care of them in their old age. Hierarchy and respect are evident in the terms of address used within the extended family. Everyone has a specific term of address that places them in a hierarchal position in relation to other family members. For example, the term for elder brother is *gege* and for younger brother *didi*. Cousins on your mother's side have different terms of address from cousins on your father's side. Older cousins are referred to differently from younger cousins. When addressing anyone older than yourself, it is important to use the proper term of address, but when addressing someone younger it is fine to use their name.

THE INSIDER EFFECT

The Chinese view relationships and treat people very differently based on their relationship with them. The Chinese generally view others as either 'insiders' or 'outsiders'. Insiders include family members, close friends and associates. Outsiders are everyone else, particularly strangers. Insiders provide a Chinese person's support group. Insiders enjoy privileges and special treatment not given to outsiders. Chinese will seldom be involved in social interactions with outsiders or even show them common courtesies. While they are extremely polite, respectful and deferential to those in their in-group, they may be rude and inconsiderate to outsiders, such as people on a bus or in the street. The Chinese are uncomfortable dealing with strangers and feel it is not their business to initiate contact with them. When they want to make contact with someone, they will use an intermediary, a mutual acquaintance, to initiate the contact.

POLITENESS? IT DEPENDS WHO YOU'RE DEALING WITH

Politeness is a key feature of Chinese communication. It signals intimacy or the lack of it. When dealing with others, the Chinese consider it important to be thoughtful, well-mannered, civil and pleasant. However, this only applies to more formal situations, such as when hosting guests, in verbal business communications and when interacting with foreigners and the elderly. The same goes for children when they communicate with their elders. They are taught to be polite to their parents and grandparents and older relatives. This politeness is readily apparent when the Chinese are offered a gift or an invitation, or something as simple as a cup of tea. It is proper to gently decline before reluctantly accepting. This is the Chinese way of showing politeness and humility.

These politeness rules change, however, when dealing with their in-group or insiders. Because the relationships are already well-established, the rituals are dropped. Polite phrases like 'thank you', 'please' and 'I'm sorry', which are part

PRIVACY (OR THE LACK OF IT)

In the West we place great value and importance on personal privacy. We are surprised, sometimes offended, when complete strangers in China ask us details about our age, weight, marital status, children, salary, etc. But personal privacy is a foreign concept in China. In fact, the sheer number of Chinese all but rule it out. Thus, lack of privacy is displayed in many of China's elbow-to-elbow open-plan squat public toilets and the 'public' treatment of patients in overcrowded hospitals. Open-plan work stations are the norm in most companies.

Personal privacy as we know it in the West is, in fact, frowned upon in Chinese society. The Chinese find it very strange if someone wants to be alone or spends long periods of time alone. It is looked upon with suspicion. It is common for workers to spend most of their time working together, eating together at lunchtime and socializing together after work. School children study together. On college campuses, students almost always have roommates and it is not uncommon for dorms to house eight students to a room.

and parcel of most Western cultures, are rarely used because these kinds of feelings have already been established through close contacts. In fact, being overly polite to those close to you is a surefire way of distancing yourself from them. It is often regarded as insulting or insincere among close friends. Likewise, a person may choose not to use such polite terms with an outsider in order to make them feel included.

Modesty and humility are also a part of politeness in Chinese society. The Chinese are very reluctant to talk about themselves or to be boastful, and will more likely be self-effacing and downplay their accomplishments.

Visitors to China are often unsure of politeness 'rules'. As a foreigner, interactions with Chinese will often be more formal. When you are complimented, downplay it by gently denying it. Unless you know an individual very well, always address people by their surname and title. Be deferential to those older than you or in a position above you. Avoid telling someone 'no' directly, and avoid confrontations by not getting angry in public. Keep your emotions under control at all times.

A SEA OF HUMANITY

China is the most populous nation on earth. It is crowded beyond most Westerners'comprehension if they have never visited. While China is physically about the same size as the United States or Europe, it has four times the population.

According to the World Bank, only 12 percent of China's landmass, primarily its grasslands, is suitable for growing crops. Its vast landscape encompasses deserts, mountain ranges, lakes and rivers and a long coastline. But because most of China's landmass is so inhospitable, about 80 percent or 1.3 billion people live in the central and eastern parts of the country, while a few million live in the west and north. The vast majority of Chinese live in major cities in the east. The population density here can be likened to squeezing the entire population of the United States into the east coast, or the entire population of Europe into France and Germany.

This all means that it is extremely crowded in China. The streets of large cities are gridlocked with cars, buses, trucks, scooters, bicycles and people. Boarding public transportation can be challenging, especially during rush hour. With all this activity, it seems like it is always noisy in China. It can be very difficult to find a quiet, out-of-the-way place to be alone.

Space is at a premium in Shanghai where individually designed skyscrapers tower over rows of uniform high-rise apartment blocks.

Above left Nanjing Road, Shanghai's prosperous commercial district. **Top** Crowds exiting one of Beijing's subway stations. **Above** Rush hour traffic, Qingdao.

WHY IS CHINA SO CROWDED?

As early as the Han Dynasty (206 BCE–220 CE) China had a population of 60 million people, which was a quarter of the world's total population at that time. China was already a well-established nation that had been in continuous existence for a thousand years. For the next thousand years, the population stayed at between 37 and 60 million before dramatically increasing during the Qing Dynasty (1644–1912) when it doubled.

Part of this increase was due to agricultural innovation resulting in increased grain production. Even more significant was the introduction of new crops from the New World, including corn, sweet potatoes and peanuts, which could be grown on hilly areas where the soil was dry or sandy. Other factors, such as improved irrigation techniques, terracing, grain storage, better tools and the use of fertilizers, also caused a spike in the population as people could afford to have more children. These children also supplied abundant labor.

China's population reached the billion mark in 1982 and at the time of the last census, in 2010, had reached 1.380 billion, the world's most populous nation.

THE 'LITTLE EMPEROR' SYNDROME

Until the 1960s, the Chinese government encouraged its people to have large families and create manpower. However, in 1979 the government introduced a one-child policy to combat growing social, economic and environmental problems caused by the burgeoning population. Couples in urban areas were allowed to have one child but in rural areas were allowed to have two if the first was a girl or was disabled. Ethnic minority groups were exempt from the policy. The policy resulted in a nation of one-child households. The term 'little emperors (or empresses)' is used to describe these spoiled, often unruly children who have grown up with the full attention of their parents and two sets of grandparents. They often get anything they want and have an attitude of privilege and entitlement. From January 1, 2016, the law was changed to a two-child policy in order to balance China's aging, increasingly male population and to resolve a diminished workforce to support this huge aging population.

EXTENDED FAMILIES

Before the introduction of the one-child policy in 1979 to control population growth, the Chinese ideal was to produce male heirs to carry on the family name. Because the family was so important, large families were common and every individual was guaranteed support, livelihood and security.

Wealthy families lived together in a large complex consisting of a central courtyard surrounded by several wings where individual families lived. The whole extended family was presided over by a patriarch. It was not uncommon to have four generations living together in one large home and for grandparents, parents, uncles, aunts, siblings and cousins to help with child rearing. Among wealthy families a patriarch often had multiple wives and concubines. This also resulted in very large families.

Urbanization has resulted in some breakdown of the extended family structure and replaced it with a more Western-style nuclear family.

Left An old Yi woman. **Below** China's ethnic minorities proudly don their distinctive traditional attire.

NOT EVERYONE IN CHINA IS CHINESE

Although the majority of China's people are ethnically Chinese, called Han, there are 55 officially recognized minority groups comprising about 9 percent of the population. These groups are ethnically diverse, speak languages not understandable by others and have distinct cultural identities. Among them are Tibetan, Mongolian, Korean, Miao (Hmong), Uyghur, Kazak, Yi, Yao, Dai and Naxi. Most live in western China and the provinces that border these areas, including, Gansu, Qinghai, Sichuan and Yunnan. These minority groups celebrate different festivals and have distinct foods, clothing, languages and customs that differ dramatically from the Han.

THE COMMUNIST PARTY OF CHINA

The Communist Party of China (CPC), founded in Shanghai on July 1, 1921 after a lengthy civil war, is the founding and ruling political party of the People's Republic of China (PRC), which has been in power since 1949. There are 85 million members of the CPC, or 6 percent of the population, making it the second largest political party in the world after Narendra Modi's Bharatiya Janata Party in India.

The red scarves worn by these school children signal their membership as Young Pioneers of the Communist Party of China.

Most Chinese believe that the government is a benevolent, paternal organization that exists solely to serve the people. The official name of China, the People's Republic of China, confirms their belief that the country belongs to the people.

The CPC has maintained a political monopoly since its founding despite shifts in its ideology from Marxism and Leninism to incorporate Mao Zedong Thought and Deng Xiaoping Theory, a succession of leaders and, more recently increasing social unrest and political destabilization as a result of China's rapid economic growth.

In the past, being a member of the CPC was highly prestigious. Membership signified allegiance and loyalty to the government, bringing with it social status and upward mobility. People would go to great lengths to ensure membership. This began at a young age with the Young Pioneers, followed by the Communist Youth League, to prepare them for membership in the party.

Since the economic reforms of the past 20 years, membership in the CPC has been declining. The prestige and status formally associated with membership in the party are now associated with wealth. Party membership brings fewer perks than in the past.

THE GREAT HELMSMAN: MAO'S LEGACY

Mao's influence in Chinese society is still very significant, regardless of how he is viewed personally. In just 25 years, he transformed China from a weak, backward nation with a life expectancy of 35 years into a modern nation with a life expectancy of 66. Although some of his policies proved disastrous, much of what he did had a positive impact on the nation.

At the height of his popularity, in the 1960s, Mao was elevated to a god-like status. Many people literally worshipped him. This loyalty and adoration resulted in a cult-like following that continues to this day. During his reign, his portrait was in nearly every home. Large statues appeared all over the country in city squares, parks and schools. Mao paraphernalia, from watches and buttons to posters and pins, was everywhere. His face continues to grace most banknotes in China.

Collecting Mao paraphernalia has become a popular pastime. Original items can be found at flea markets and antique shops. New merchandise can also be found in souvenir shops in China, particularly in Beijing. Most of what is around now are reproductions even if they are touted as originals.

Far left The 18th National Congress of the Communist Party of China in session, Beijing. **Left** A Chinese guard on duty in Tianfu Square, Chengdu, Sichuan Province.

THE POLITICAL SYSTEM

China is a one-party political system where the CPC holds absolute power. All political organizations in China fall under the direct leadership and control of the CPC.

The CPC's constitution states that the party must hold a national congress every five years. At these meetings the delegates elect a new Central Committee of 205 full members and 171 alternate members. Within the Central Committee is a 25-person Politburo, a more élite 7-member Politburo Standing Committee and a General Secretary, the top leadership position in the country. The current General Secretary, Xi Jinping, is also President of the country.

The Politburo controls three important bodies and ensures that the CPC line is upheld. These are the Military Affairs Commission, which controls the armed forces; the National People's Congress or parliament; and the State Council, the administrative arm of the government.

BECOMING A PARTY MEMBER

Over three-quarters of the members of the CPC are men and one-third are farmers. Membership in the party comes after a lengthy application process. Potential members are groomed from the ages of 6–14, before they graduate from junior high school, when they become members of the Young Pioneers. Most school children are members even though few understand the goals or purposes of the CPC. They join out of national pride and a fear of being left

out. They are easily identified at tourist sites by the red scarves they wear, the symbol of the Young Pioneers. When they turn 14, they join the Communist Youth League, an organization for 14–28 year olds, which is a more serious group. In practice, nearly all high school children are members of the Youth League, a prerequisite for membership in the Communist Party.

Today, membership in the party is seen more as a way of boosting your resume, especially for those working in state-run organizations, than a belief in Communist ideals. Party members typically are promoted more rapidly. Those who hold leadership positions within the Youth League are more likely to be accepted into the party. Many party members are recruited from the top ranks of high schools and colleges, which is often an invitation that is difficult to refuse. Others may be nominated by friends who are members. The bottom line is that it pays to be well connected.

SELECTING LEADERS

Delegates of the national congress elect new members from a pool of candidates selected by the party leadership. The

Central Committee elects the 25 member Politburo and the Politburo Standing Committee, the most senior decision-making body, and the General Secretary. These 'elections' are non-competitive, with the outgoing party leadership only nominating as many positions as available. In reality, these positions are assigned before any election takes place. The Standing Committee then nominates a Party Secretariat, which overseas the daily operations of the Politburo, the Standing Committee and the departments of the Party Central Committee. These members serve five-year terms, until the next party congress is held. With this kind of system, there are no real surprises as to who will hold what positions as it is all decided internally by the current party leadership.

The fact that Politburo members have never faced competitive election but have made it to the top shows that in China personal relations count a lot more than title or talent. A member's influence rests on the loyalties they have built up with superiors, proteges and patrons over years, even decades. It explains why elders in the party sometimes play a key role in big decisions.

CONFUCIAN VALUES AND **FAMILY LIFE**

Filial piety is a Confucian value that is defined as unquestioned loyalty and respect for one's parents and ancestors. Details on how to behave towards a senior are outlined in *Classic of Filial Piety*, a Confucian treatise dated about 400 BCE. Filial piety not only includes general obedience to elders but love and respect and courtesy for them, taking care of them in their old age and never doing anything to give parents or ancestors a bad name.

FILIAL PIETY

Filial piety is one of those values that is in every Chinese person's psyche at a subconscious level. From young, it is drummed into the Chinese that the family and social harmony, reflected in the ordinary activities of human life, especially in human relationships, are sacred. Family and social harmony results in part from every individual knowing their place in the family and social order and playing their part well.

The system of Confucian ethics has a significant effect on Chinese behavior. For instance, the Chinese tend to be much more deferential to their parents than children in the West. These attitudes follow individuals into adulthood and Chinese will go to great lengths to obey the will of their parents, even as adults. Although we may find this strange in the West, it is important in China and people take these responsibilities seriously.

THE CHANGING FACE OF MARRIAGE IN CHINA

In early times, most marriages in China were arranged by parents or through a matchmaker. Weddings were an elaborate affair with large dowries of cash and gifts paid to the bride's family. When the Communists took over in 1949, one of the first things they did was pass a marriage law stating that people were free to choose their own partner. This law also outlawed concubines, polygamy, child marriages and the sale of sons or daughters into marriage or prostitution.

Wedding expos, such as this one in Pazhou, Guangzhou, held in 2011, showcase all types of wedding products.

The current law states that men must be 22 and women at least 20 to get married. Today, the groom is expected to provide a new furnished apartment and other material things when a couple gets married, plus gifts and money for the bride's parents. This puts a terrific burden on many young men who have difficulty attracting women who have come to expect these things, especially a home. It is estimated that the cost of weddings and all that goes along with them has increased 4,000 times in the past 30 years.

In recent years, there has been a reaction to these expectations. 'Naked marriage', a term coined in 2008, refers to couples getting married without any significant assets and encompasses the Five No's: no ring, no ceremony, no honeymoon, no home and no car. This frees up couples from the huge expense of traditional weddings and dowries and allows them to find happiness outside the confines of tradition. 'Flash marriage' is another recent phenomena. It is a negative slang term for couples who get married when they have known each other for less than seven months. This often happens when parents pressure their children into getting married before it is too late. It also is a reaction to the economic pressures of traditional marriages. Unfortunately, many of these marriages end in divorce.

RELATIONSHIPS AND DATING

The Chinese tend to have fewer friends compared to Westerners whose numerous friends are slotted into groups, such as school friends, work friends and golf buddies, who may come and go, but those the Chinese have are generally deeper, longer-term relationships.

Boy–girl relationships in China tend to develop rather slowly and cautiously. Potential partners are usually introduced by a third party, such as a friend, colleague, parent or relative. Casual dating and relationships as we know them in the West are relatively uncommon. For this reason, Americans need to be careful with casual flirting and dating as it may be interpreted as more serious than it really is. Chinese couples may go out together but don't consider it dating until they get to know each other well and have developed strong feelings for each other. Then the relationship becomes very serious and usually leads to marriage. However, the younger generation is more casual about relationships and may go out with several different partners before they tie the knot.

GROWING OLD IN CHINA

Traditionally, the elderly were cared for by their children, usually their sons. With many elderly in China only having one child, this is becoming increasingly difficult. China's population is aging faster than social services can cope and there is a major shortage of rest home beds and qualified workers to care for the elderly. An aging population is also having an effect on the availability of labor. It is estimated that by 2050 a third or 450 million Chinese will be over the age of 60. China has long relied on a young, agile workforce and it is becoming very difficult to find workers for China's many factories. As workers' parents age, many are moving back to their hometowns to find work where they can also take care of their elderly parents.

A young couple spending time together.

SHOW IT, DON'T SAY IT

Students of Chinese often want to learn how to say 'I love you'. In reality, the Chinese seldom say this, even to those whom they love. They generally don't talk about their feelings, preferring to show their affection through actions. Even 'I like you' has serious connotations and is best avoided unless you really like the other person.

FAMILY LIFE IN CHINA

The Chinese are very family oriented in that they pay a great deal of attention to the Confucian values of respecting elders, revering ancestors, carrying on the family name and being obedient to parents' wishes. Even into adulthood Chinese are expected to obey the wishes of their parents and then take care of them in their old age. Traditionally, families in China were large, but in modern China they are quite small as a result of the one-child policy.

The family unit usually consists of father, mother, child and two sets of grandparents who play an active role in taking care of pre-school grandchildren. As such, children receive lots of attention. Because women are expected to work—they comprise half of the workforce—one set of grandparents may live with the family, but this is changing as housing prices rise. Almost all holidays are times when families gather and

Grandparents play a huge role in looking after their pre-school grandchildren while the parents work.

usually have a meal and spend time together. It is very important at major holidays like Chinese New Year to go home and spend time with your family, even if your home is very far away.

WOMEN AND CHILDREN IN CHINA

Marriage and family in rural and urban China are evolving with economic development and modernization. Nucelar families have increased to about 60 percent in the cities. People are marrying and having children later, while husbands are sharing more household chores and women are having an equal say in family financial affairs. More women, who form half of China's workforce, are choosing to remain single and to focus on their careers despite ingrained discrimination.

Women in China play a far less subservient role than in the past within the family and in the workplace. They form half of China's workforce and are involved in all sectors although they often face discrimination.

WOMEN IN CHINA

For most of China's history, women played a subservient role to men. They were not allowed to own property and when they married they cut ties with their own family and became a member of their husband's extended family. Women had little say in important decisions and were expected to defer to and obey their husbands or fathers. If their husband died, they were not allowed to remarry but had to remain a part of the husband's family.

When the Communists came to power in 1949, one of their central goals was to elevate the status of women. Mao famously said that women hold up half the sky. Women were given jobs traditionally assigned to men. In the early years of the People's Republic, women enjoyed more equality than they had in the previous 2,000 years, but in recent years this equality has been eroded. A small proportion of women, less than 20 percent, hold positions in the legislature, senior management and manufacturing and less then 3 percent have been chief officials in government departments, state-owned enterprises and public institutions.

A derogatory term, *sheng nu*, meaning 'leftover women', is applied to women who are not married by their late twenties. Women are trained to see marriage as their first priority and a career as their second. When women fail to conform to this ideal, they are often labeled 'leftover'. As more and more women are pursuing advanced degrees, they are postponing marriage and finding it difficult to attract men, partly because they are older and partly because Chinese men often feel threatened by a women who is more educated than they are. A recent government propaganda campaign encouraged women to marry younger. A government article states, 'As women age, they are worth less and less. So by the time they get their M.A. or Ph.D. they are already old, like yellowed pearls.'

Women in China also experience discrimination in the workplace as most management positions go to men, even if a woman has more experience. Women may also be hired for their looks or even their height. This has led to an explosion in the plastic surgery business in China.

THANKS A LOT, CONFUCIUS: THE GAOKAO AND STUDENT LIFE IN CHINA

As early as the Han Dynasty (206 BCE–220 CE), the Chinese government set up a rigorous civil service examination system based on learning the Confucian Classics, a system that lasted until the fall of the imperial dynastic system in 1911. Those who were privileged enough to be educated would spend countless hours (sometimes a lifetime) preparing for the exams, which were held at the county, provincial and national levels. Those who passed were assured government appointments and a comfortable, often lavish lifestyle, and the highest social status in China.

The term *gaokao* ('high exam') refers to the college entrance examinations held each year all over China. They play a similar role to the civil service examinations of old. Those who pass are accepted into China's universities and on graduation are more likely to obtain good jobs and enjoy a comfortable life. Those who don't are often relegated to lowly jobs, which often means long hours and low pay. Be-

cause *gaokao* is so important to a person's future, parents go to great lengths to get their children into the best kindergartens and primary schools. If they succeed, their children will be more likely to get into the best high schools and thus have a much better chance of passing the college entrance exams. Kindergartens, primary schools and high schools all have entrance exams. This puts intense pressure on China's children, often with negative effects. Because there is a limit to the number of universities in China, the competition to do well in these exams is intense. Chinese children often spend up to 12–14 hours a day studying in school, with tutors and in after-school and weekend prep schools.

SCHOOLING IN CHINA

Some 97 percent of Chinese children finish the mandatory nine years of primary and junior secondary schooling.

Pre-school Kindergartens for 1–3 year olds may be half-day, full-day or boarding. They offer structured play to prepare children for the rigors of primary and secondary school. In rural areas, many kindergartens also provide day care.

Primary and Secondary School Children attend primary school for 5–6 years and junior and senior secondary for another three years each. The school year comprises two semesters, five days a week, with some schools having half-days on Saturdays. Education is free for primary and secondary schools in China. In many impoverished rural areas, children only complete junior secondary school.

Class size in China is generally bigger than in the US with up to 45 in a single class. Classes also start earlier: primary schools at 8:00 am until 5:00 pm and secondary schools from 7:00 am to 5:00 pm. But it doesn't end there. Because of the fierce competition to get into the best schools, it is common for children in China's larger cities to attend cram schools in the evenings and on weekends, which may last until 11:00

pm for senior secondary students. This leaves little free time. Students generally start learning English in the third grade, though in some areas in may be as early as first grade and in less developed areas as late as junior middle school.

College Only about 30 percent of high school graduates get into colleges in China, based entirely on the *gaokao* test. Those wanting to get into college spend most of their waking hours studying and preparing for this one-shot exam. Lack of sleep is a serious problem for many Chinese students.

The number of colleges in China is very low for its large population. The vast majority of colleges and universities are state-run and the curriculum is controlled. Students will take *gaokao* based on subject matter. Once accepted into a university, their curriculum is set, based on their major. Students form close ties with their classmates as they take the same classes through-

out their college career. Whereas in primary and secondary school the competition is fierce and students spend most of their time studying, it's a different story in colleges and universities. The attitude is that once you have got into a college, you have it made. Courses at Chinese universities tend to be less demanding and require less homework than universities in the West. In a sense, college is a reward for surviving primary and secondary school.

> Education in China is tough. Children study all day long, then attend after-school cram schools in the hope of eventually getting into a university.

CHINA'S MILLENNIAL GENERATION

China's Generation Y, also called Millennials, are those born between 1980 and 1997 and are thus aged between 19 and 35. Two Chinese terms describe China's millennials: *balinghou*, the 1980s generation, and *jiulinghou*, the 1990s generation. These Chinese youth are growing up in the digital age. They have been described variously as optimistic, opinionated, apolitical, eco-friendly, fickle, adventurous, impressionable and individualistic.

Many of China's millennials have the means to dine at upmarket restaurants, drink wine, wear brand-name clothes and make-up and drive expensive imported cars.

GENERATION Y AND THE CHINESE WORKFORCE

Chinese millennials represent about 40 percent of China's workforce. Unlike their parents, many are asserting themselves more and demanding that their voices be heard. If they are not happy with their job, they are likely to quit and find a new one. They are also more willing than previous generations to relocate to a new city for job reasons because they are more concerned than their parents about job advancement. Previous generations were focused on the collective good, but Chinese millennials are more concerned about personal and career advancement. They are willing to express their opinions, even at work.

Transparency at work is also important to Chinese millennials and they are insisting on fair practices in the workplace and clear promotion policies. Since they form such a significant part of China's workforce, human resource departments throughout China are changing their policies to attract and retain them.

China's millennials are also more entrepreneurial and many express an interest in starting their own companies. This is partly motivated by their desire to earn a great deal of money and to have expendable income.

Most Chinese millennials are not that interested in working for the government and the job security that it can offer. A high percentage of millennials these days don't even bother to take the Chinese civil service examination.

THE DIGITAL DIFFERENCE

Growing up in the information age, China's millennials are tech-crazy and well versed in cell phone and Internet communication. About 85 percent own a smart phone, 58 percent a laptop and 41 percent report that surfing the Net is one of their favorite pastimes. In fact, China has more people online than any other country. Social media is an integral part of their lives and this influences how they socialize, work, shop and play. Generally, millennials are apolitical except when it comes to complaining about Internet censorship, China's so-called Great Firewall.

A small number of millennials are rebelling against the government, mostly through blogs and other online venues. This is done through roundabout wordplay and satirical metaphors. For example, in 2004 the Chinese government announced a campaign to construct a more harmonious society. What this meant was stricter censorship of the Internet. The word for harmonious sounds the same as the word for 'river crab'. So clever Internet users use the word 'river crab' (*hexie*) to poke fun at Internet censorship. In these ways, the Internet is being used by millennials to express themselves, even if it goes against government policies.

INDIVIDUALISM AND THE CONCEPT OF KU (COOL)

In the mid-1990s, Chinese youth, especially in the cities, began bucking the imperialist and collectivist traditions of their grandparents and parents' generations and started to define themselves as individuals. They adopted the Western notion of 'cool' or *ku*, becoming what many say is the 'me generation'. Many now eschew the 'work hard and get rich' mentality, preferring instead to live a life that suits them.

This includes the way dating and courtship are carried out. In the past, people only dated when they intended to find a partner and get married. China's Generation Y youth now date just for entertainment when they know there is little or no chance of marriage.

Generation Y are also avid consumers of everything the Western marketplace has to offer. They are far more brand conscious than their parents and will buy name brands to impress others. But although they are more materialistic, they are also more environmentally conscious and often select products that have a lower environmental footprint.

It has also become 'cool' to travel. No longer satisfied with a trip to Hong Kong or Macau, Generation Y prefer to travel to destinations further away, the more exotic the better.

Along with this new individualism comes some rebellious behavior, at least rebellious compared to previous generations. This includes looser sexual practices, such as pre-marital sex and talking and writing about sex on blogs.

A FORCE TO BE RECKONED WITH

Dramatically different from previous generations, urban Generation Y Chinese, especially in the 18–25 age group, are leading the globalization of contemporary China. With their acceptance of foreign ideas, tastes and trends, and a desire to work for themselves and to travel, they are becoming increasingly like their Western counterparts. These changes, combined with China's booming economy (albeit with problems), has led many analysts to believe that the 'capitalism friendly' Generation Y will be a force to be reckoned with in business and politics, including future China–US relations. Some of them may even become the political leaders of China by the mid-2020s.

THE STUDY ABROAD EFFECT

It is estimated that more than 200,000 Chinese, mostly from Generation Y, are studying abroad, mostly in the West. After being exposed to Western ideas and practices, many students bring these new-formed habits back to China. Exposure abroad has created more globally minded individuals who are more likely to be employed in businesses with global ties. They also tend to have more in common with millennials from other countries than with the older generation in China. Millennials who have studied abroad also tend to be more assertive, more independent thinking and more likely to share their opinions on everything, from the environment to societal ills.

China has long been a tea drinking country, but coffee is on the rise. In fact, there are more than 1,500 Starbucks coffee shops in China and rising. Even though the cost of a cup of coffee is quite high, many millennials are drinking coffee on a regular basis.

For generations the Chinese have valued white skin. It has been a sign of wealth and prosperity in contrast to those who work outside for a living (i.e. peasants) and have darker, tanned skin. There is a huge industry of skin-whitening cosmetics to support these ideals. However, many millennials returning from abroad are going against this trend and sporting a tanned and toned look. There is even a term to describe this, *mei hei*, which literally means 'beautiful dark'.

Out of concern for recent food safety issues in China and in an effort to live a healthier lifestyle, many millennials are eating organic food. Designer furniture is important for the younger generation as well, and stores like IKEA (left) are doing well. Millennials are also traveling abroad in record numbers. Exotic locations and activities, such as trekking in Nepal and snorkeling in Indonesia, are the preferred vacations. But shopping in Dubai is also on their list of destinations and activities.

INTERNET AND CELL PHONE CULTURE

The West has Google. China has Baidu. It functions much the same as Google but is a Chinese company and caters to the Chinese population. China has the highest number of Internet users in the world, approximately 700 million and rising. Internet use in China is so widespread that it is not limited to the cities. Nearly every corner of China has Internet access and Internet cafés can be found all over China. More and more Chinese also have smart phones and access the Internet with their phones.

China has similar social networking and blogging sites to those in the West, but because of the 'Great Firewall of China', a term used to refer to the Internet censorship that exists in China, the Chinese government goes to great lengths to filter online content. Popular sites such as Facebook, YouTube and Twitter are blocked in China, but the Chinese have their local equivalents.

TEXTING AND INTERNET MEMES AND SLANG

It's hard for Westerners to understand how the Chinese can text Chinese characters on their phones, but it is not only possible but very popular in China. It is done is the same way that we type on computers. It's a bit more complicated than typing an alphabetic language, but once you get the hang of it, it is relatively easy and efficient.

Chinese is full of Internet slang. Most is composed of Chinese characters or abbreviations of Chinese words or phrases in *pinyin*, and are often puns or phrases that have been manipulated to mean something different.

ALIBABA

Alibaba is the massive Internet-based e-commerce business started by Jack Ma in Hangzou, China, in 1999. Ma, a billionaire, is Asia's richest person. The Alibaba Group owns the online consumer-to-consumer retail site Taobao, the business-to-consumer retail site Tmall, the third-party online payment system Alipay and the online retail search engine eTao. The company went public on the New York Stock Exchange in September of 2014. It was the largest IPO in history with USD 25 billion raised. Alibaba's market value was estimated at USD 231 billion.

CELL PHONES IN CHINA

Cell phones are everywhere in China. They have been embraced by everyone, including the very old and the very young. It is astonishing where you can get cell service, including remote areas of Tibet and the jungles of the southwest. The government has spent a great deal connecting even the most remote areas of China. Chinese use their cell phones to talk, text, read novels, play games, for instant messaging and online banking and anything else possible on a smart phone. Apart from the many international brands, such as Apple, Nokia and Samsung, Chinese brands like Lenovo, Huawei and Zhongxing are popular. Many of these mimic the styles and features of outside brands. There are also many fake iPhones and other types of phones. They usually look like the real thing but lack the sophisticated features of the originals.

SOME COMMON INTERNET SLANG TERMS

女汉子	A masculine woman; reflects women's changing role in Chinese society (they can do things now that only men did in the past)
高富帅	Tall, rich, and handsome (the ideal boyfriend or husband)
白富美	White (fair), rich and beautiful (the ideal girlfriend or wife)
矮丑穷	Short, ugly and poor (the worst kind of guy)
杯具	Tragedy; literally means 'cups/cupware'; a pun for the word tragedy
菜鸟	Newbie, novice, rookie; literally 'vegetable bird', meaning a bird that is young and inexperienced
土豪	Nouveau riche, someone who is wealthy but uncultured; literally a 'local tyrant'; describes the many entrepreneurial peasants in China who have become wealthy
被自杀	To be 'suicided', meaning that a murder is ruled as a suicide to cover it up
雷	To express shock or to be dumbfounded; literally means 'thunder'
屌丝	A loser, douchebag; often used humorously and refers to someone who is poor, ugly, short and good for nothing
草泥马	This is a pun for 'f- your mother'; literally it means 'grass mud horse' and has been used online as a way of making fun of government censorship

Below A young man uses his laptop in a Starbucks coffee shop, Guangzhou.
Bottom People surfing the Net on fixed computers in an Internet café in Chengdu.

Taobao, China's Ebay Taobao (tabao.com) is similar to both Amazon and Ebay. Most sellers offer products for purchase by fixed price, but a small percentage of items are offered through auction. Over a billion products are for sale on the site and it is one of the twenty most visited websites in the world. Buyers can access a seller's ratings, comments and complaints just as on Amazon or Ebay. Taobao eventually overtook Ebay in China and Ebay shut down its Chinese site in 2006. Taobao holds about 60 percent of the market for online sales in China.

Tmall, eTao and Alipay Tmall (tmall.com), created in 2008, is an offshoot of Taobao. It is a separately operated company but is also owned by the Alibaba Group. It is a business-to-consumer (B2C) online store that focuses on premium Chinese brands and foreign luxury goods and is targeted at affluent Chinese shoppers. A third company, eTao (etao.com), was formed in 2010. It is a search engine for online shopping. It offers products from Taobao, Amazon China, Dangdang and other online retailers in China. Alipay (alipay.com) is a third-party online payment platform with no transaction fees. It is similar to Paypal in the US.

INTERNET CAFES AND ONLINE GAMING

Although many Chinese now own personal computers, Internet cafés are still a popular option for many people. They usually consist of a large room or rooms with rows and rows of computers. The most popular activity in these cafés is online video gaming. The PC game sector is worth 6 billion dollars in China, the largest in the world. China has produced many video games, the most popular being the *Genesis of the Century* trilogy, but they are mostly unknown outside China. The Chinese company Tencent, an Internet service portal, is China's gaming giant. Action RPG's (role play games) are the most popular genre of online games in China.

YOUKU, CHINA'S YOUTUBE

Youku (youku.com) is China's answer to YouTube, which is blocked in China. It is the largest video site in China with over 500 million active users. It is a combination of user-shared videos and commercial videos, including full-length movies and television programs. Because China does not have specific copyright laws and enforcement is limited, people worldwide are able to view videos that would be illegal on sites like YouTube.

SOCIAL MEDIA AND NETWORKING IN CHINA

Traditional social networking sites such as renren.com and kaixin.com, which are similar to Facebook, have declined in popularity in recent years. Sina Weibo (weibo.com) is a micro-blogging site, the Chinese equivalent of Twitter, and is a very popular way to spread news and gossip, but it also has lost some of its appeal, partly because of government censorship. The bottom line is that social networking platforms are constantly changing in China. QQ (qq.com) is an instant messaging software service that was hugely popular but has recently given way to WeChat (wechat.com). The latest and most popular way to connect with friends, WeChat was started by the Chinese company Tencent and is a platform for text messaging, voice messaging, broadcast messaging (one-to-many), photo and video sharing and location sharing. The app is available for iPhone, Android and several other systems.

CHAPTER 4
THE FACE OF URBAN CHINA

There are obvious differences between the way people live in China's urban and rural areas. China's urban economy and culture are moving in the direction of those in developed countries, including ways of working and of doing business, improved facilities and infrastructure, and changing lifestyles and family structures. While the rural economy shifts from pure agriculture to agriculture supported by industry, changes are afoot there, too with more people enjoying consumer goods like washing machines and televsions. But the countryside lags behind the prosperity seen in China's cities.

RISE OF THE CHINESE MIDDLE CLASS

China's rapid economic growth has spawned a new middle class. Although the Communist ideal was a classless society, it was never truly one. Prior to economic reforms in the 1970s and well into the 1990s, there were really only two classes in China: government officials who enjoyed a privileged life, and everyone else. Beginning in the late 1990s and into the early 2000s, private ownership accelerated and people began to make money outside the confines of the state-owned system.

The quality of life continued to get better and consumer goods became widely available. Up until the early 1980s, it was unusual for people to own a telephone, television or refrigerator, but these things are now commonplace, along with cell phones, personal computers, tablets and designer clothes, even cars.

Above: Forty percent of the 30–40 million fake designer watches in circulation in the world each year are made in China. *Left:* New and old vehicles vie for space in China's gridlocked cities.

CARS

China's streets used to be teeming with millions of bicycles. For decades it was the only means of transport for many Chinese. But over the years the bike lanes have shrunk as cars have taken over. There are now more cars in China than in any other country on the planet, mostly in large urban areas where Chinese wealth is concentrated.

China is also the world's biggest producer of cars. Chinese brands such as Geely, Chery, Wuling, Great Wall, Dongfeng, Changan and BYD vie for space with Toyotas, Hondas, Nissans and Hyundais as well as luxury Mercedes, Audis, BMWs, Porches, Ferraris and Bentleys. More and more Chinese are relying on private cars for transportation, travel and entertainment, and more roads are being built to cope with the increasing number of vehicles. Car clubs are also popular.

Because China's roads were never planned for this many cars, navigating city roads can be a nightmare and parking is a serious problem.

SHOPPING

Until the early 1980s it was difficult to find any Western consumer goods or food products in China. Today, there are shopping malls everywhere selling the latest Chinese and Western merchandise. High-end luxury malls full of designer boutiques such as Prada, Gucci, Louis Vuitton, Christion Dior, Zegna, Rolex and Cartier are teaming with consumers. High-end shopping centers are also ubiquitous even in smaller cities where you least expect them. Young people in China generally place a higher emphasis on the latest game console or cell phone than on democracy. Online shopping has also becone very popular.

WILL THE REAL iPHONE PLEASE STAND UP?

Pirated goods are rampant in China, from designer jeans to iPhones. Sometimes it is difficult to tell what is real and what is fake, at least without close inspection. In many street markets there is no attempt to conceal the fact that vendors are selling fake branded products. Both seller and buyer know that the product is a pirated version and everyone seems to be fine

with that. Although some pirated products are as good as the original, most are of very poor quality. Sometimes Chinese consumers may not know the difference between the original product and a good fake. Some vendors will sell fake products right alongside the real thing. The fake products may even have more features than the original. Not only are fake products available all over China but fake stores are common as well. Most of the time they are easy to spot as there may be spelling errors in the signage or the construction may not be up to Western standards. Pirated items are not limited to consumer goods. There are also television programs that copy the name and format of the original program. Movies, music, software and literature are openly pirated and sold not only in street markets but in upscale department stores.

WESTERN RESTAURANTS AND PRODUCTS

The three big fast food chains in China, McDonalds, Pizza Hut and KFC, are everywhere and the Chinese are flocking to them in astonishing numbers, as well as to countless other American and European restaurants. The first Starbucks opened in Beijing in 1999. Now there are now 851 Starbucks in China and growing. In 2010, the 100th McDonalds opened in Shanghai.

Western-brand personal computers, cell phones and other electronics are also becoming increasingly popular. Apple stores, both genuine and fake, have cropped up all over China. It is common to see people with iPhones and the latest Samsung Galaxy phones and children playing games on iPads.

PETS

In traditional China, common pets were crickets or birds. Now everyone wants a dog because it is a sign of affluence. The Chinese not only like to walk their dogs, they also like to congregate in public squares where they can socialize and let their dogs play together. Although most people prefer small dogs, especially the cute puffy poodle types, I have seen many large breeds, including Huskies, Labs, Golden Retrievers and German Shepherds.

CHINESE TOURISM

Over the last decade or so, the Chinese middle class have become the new tourists around the world because many now have the means and ability to travel. It used to be the Japanese you would see in large groups with cameras around their necks. In 1995, fewer than one million Chinese tourists traveled abroad. By 2015 that number had reached 120 million. Apart from flocking overseas, Chinese tourists are taking family or work-related holidays to the main tourist sites in their own country.

THE BLING DYNASTY

Forty years ago, there were no millionaires in China. By 2015, there were 3.6 million of them. Only the US had more. Not only are there many rich people, there is also a growing middle class hungry for consumer and luxury goods.

The Chinese have always placed great emphasis on image and face. You can see this every day on the streets of China's cities. Chinese brands may be popular in the home but outside, where others can see them, the Chinese like to flaunt their newfound wealth with luxury watches, cars and Western designer fashions, and to dine at expensive restaurants. Luxury apartment and housing complexes dot China's cities. Rents are astronomical, especially in Beijing and Shanghai.

Buying luxury goods is one of the main reasons Chinese travel abroad. Their favorite destinations are the United States, the European Union, Hong Kong, Japan and South Korea and the most commonly purchased items are jewelry, watches, wines and spirits, bags, shoes, cosmetics and perfumes, and apparel. Luxury goods in China are heavily taxed, sometimes as much as 50 percent, making them a lot more expensive than buying abroad. A wider range of luxury goods is also available overseas. And with rampant pirating and fake products in China, the Chinese are more likely to get an authentic product if it is purchased overseas.

Even with the financial crisis in Europe, luxury goods continue to sell well to tourists, many coming from mainland China. Many Chinese budget a high percentage of vacation funds to buying luxury goods. It is common to have Mandarin Chinese-speaking sales staff in high-end designer boutiques, such as Tiffany's in New York City. Most of the staff in the expensive but popular designer boutiques in New York's JFK Airport are native Chinese speakers.

SHOPPING AS A SPORT

Shopping in China has been likened to a sport. The younger generation, in particular, are crazy about clothes, shoes and accessories. Nearly every large city has a shopping district with a walking street mall where people like to congregate, meet friends, shop and have a meal. Shopping is also popular at China's many street markets where prices are very cheap. Vendors set up booths along the street, often selling second-hand goods, and bargaining is hard and fast. This can be great recreation for Chinese and foreigners alike.

Much of China's old architecture is disappearing in the name of progress. While some new buildings adopt elements of ancient Chinese architecture, most comprise modern Western-style high-rises.

DOING BUSINESS IN CHINA

At the end of 2014, based on purchasing power parities like GDP growth, exports and household savings, China overtook the US as the world's largest economy. Some 500 million people had been moved out of poverty. With a rapidly expanding middle class, the market potential in China is staggering. China already has the world's largest cell phone, computer and automobile markets.

AN ECONOMY ON THE RISE

Since Deng Xiaoping's economic reforms, the economy has been growing at an average rate of 10 percent per year, three times the global average. Apart from being the world's largest exporter, China is now the world's largest energy user, and, as a result, the world's largest emitter of carbon dioxide.

This rapid growth has resulted in a huge increase in construction, from skyscrapers, high-rise apartment complexes and shopping malls to new rail lines and other transportation infrastructure. It also means that much of the old China is rapidly disappearing. Old neighborhoods with architecturally important buildings, sometimes hundreds of years old, are being razed to build modern structures. It said that to go to the countryside in China is to go back in time. The Chinese are so obsessed with modernization that their very cultural heritage is losing out to architecture and infrastructure.

Another side effect of this is the rapid growth in air pollution, with pollution levels sometimes exceeding 40-fold the safe limit set by the World Health Organization. Sixteen of the twenty most polluted cities in the world are in China, including Beijing and Shanghai, where pollution is a serious health risk, especially to the very young, the very old and those with respiratory illnesses. Sometimes the smog is so bad, you can hardly make out buildings across the street. Most of this pollution is due to burning coal. China burns more coal than the rest of the world combined, much of it poor quality high sulfur coal.

PLAY BY CHINESE RULES

Doing business in China has its rewards as well as its challenges. To be successful, it is important to know how to play the game (or 'play by Chinese rules'). This largely involves understanding the importance of developing good relations with your counterparts. Chinese relationships, both personal and business, develop and progress much more slowly than in the West. Trust is very important to the Chinese. They feel that before you get down to any business details, it is important to get to know each other first. They want to be able to decide if they can trust you and work with you. In the West, we are more concerned with hammering out the details of a business proposal than with developing relationships with our counterparts.

We tend to be more focused on contracts and the law, whereas the Chinese are more concerned with developing good relationships. In some cases, the Chinese may not necessarily see a contract as legally binding. Business negotiations with the Chinese thus follow a different and more gradual path than what you may expect or are used to.

Formal introductions through a mutual contact go a long way in China. Connections and contacts are very important to the Chinese. Contacting a potential Chinese business partner out of the blue, with no prior contact with each other, will not work nearly as well as if you are introduced by a mutual colleague or associate. This is the preferred way to make contacts in China. This is not to say that you won't succeed by sending out feelers and inquiries because this sometimes works as well.

Upon arriving in China to meet with potential business partners, you will probably first attend a banquet. This may be followed by more social activities, including visiting tourist sites and more eating. You may not get down to business until the second, third or even fourth day. It is important that you portray yourself as a professional and remain formal even in what seems like informal contexts.

DRESS FOR SUCCESS CHINESE STYLE

The Chinese tend to be more formal than in the West and this is reflected in their business attire. Don't be surprised to see Chinese dressed formally when visiting tourist sites or doing seemingly casual activities. In public, the Chinese tend to be more concerned about their image and thus dress up to show their status, even if they don't come from a wealthy background. Chinese businesses typically don't have a casual Friday policy. When in doubt, dressing up is better than assuming you can go casual.

SUCCESS = BMW: BUSINESS, MONEY, WOMEN OR BUS, METRO, WALK

With the economic boom in China has come a new class of wealthy entrepreneurs as well as a rising middle class. In the past, success may have been defined as having Communist Party membership or a good state job. Nowadays, success is usually defined as wealth. When China's former leader Deng Xiaoping began experimenting with Western-style market reforms in the late 1970s, he said, 'To get rich is glorious.' Many Chinese took this to heart, and with private enterprise came newfound opportunities, wealth and privilege. Luxury cars have become commonplace and are status symbols of the wealthy. The Chinese joke that not only is BMW the brand of a German luxury car, it also stands for business, money and women, all signs of success in the new China. Those from the working class often counter this with the joke that for most Chinese BMW stands for bus, metro and walk, the primary means of transportation for the majority of Chinese living in busy, crowded cities.

END OF THE IRON RICE BOWL: RISE OF THE ENTREPRENEUR

Under a socialist planned economy, nearly everyone works for the government. The vast majority of jobs and nearly all businesses are state-owned (the latter also subsidized by the government). This creates a situation where there is not much incentive to innovate or even work hard because wages are not tied to production. Pay stays the same. In China, the expression 'iron rice bowl' meant that having a government job guaranteed that you always had a salary and therefore always something to eat, hence the iron rice bowl. But not any more!

In 1978, Communist Party leader Deng Xiaoping began instituting economic reforms that resulted in dramatic social and economic changes. The first wave of reforms occurred in the late 1970s and early 1980s and involved decollectivizing agricultural communes, allowing foreign investment and granting permission for entrepreneurs to start their own businesses. The second wave, in the late 1980s and 1990s, involved privatizing many state-owned industries and lifting price controls and other regulations. These reforms resulted in an explosion of private enterprise matched by an increase in personal wealth. Slowly at first, people began to give up their state-owned jobs and the security they provided for the opportunity to make more money. In the early days of economic reform, it was considered a risky undertaking, but now large numbers of Chinese citizens are happy to work in private industry and, in a sense, be in control of their own destiny.

WORKING IN A CHINESE OFFICE

For foreigners working in China, one of the biggest challenges is understanding its office politics—how the workplace and workforce operate and how you fit in. The system works in its own way, and has for a long time, and you are expected to join that system, to find your own place in it and to adapt where necessary.

HIERARCHY IN THE WORKPLACE

In Chinese organizations, nearly all the power and authority rests with a few individuals at the top of the pile. This usually means the president or owner of the organization. If it is a government organization or a government subsidiary, important decisions may be made by a high-ranking official who overseas that organization. This results in employees being reluctant to offer their own suggestions or ideas. It is considered inappropriate for lower ranking employees to question decisions made higher up. As a result, relatively straightforward business negotiations may take a number of meetings to hash out the details.

BUSINESS CARDS

Because hierarchy is such an important and integral aspect of Chinese culture, business cards play an important role in identifying your role in relation to others, particularly in government, education and business organizations. The first thing that happens when meeting others in a business setting is to exchange business cards. This then tells you not only how to address the person but also how to act towards him or her. If they are in a position above you, then it is important to be deferential toward them. Chinese business cards can seem cluttered with information because many people feel the need to add all their titles and significant achievements.

GROUP MENTALITY

In the US, the individual and individualism are valued. The Chinese, on the other hand, find it uncomfortable to be singled out from the group. The basic unit in society and in the workplace is the group and Chinese people want

Getting to know new people at meetings and conferences begins with the exchange of business cards.

to fit in, assimilate and work for the common good. In Chinese business settings, group mentality is manifested in a number of ways. Decisions may be evaded or put off by individuals within an organization because they fear being criticized by their superiors or even punished. Every effort is made to try to get others to express your ideas so that you don't have to do it yourself.

Individuals are not given a great deal of power or authority within an organization, at least at the lower levels. This is saved for those at the top. In business meetings, individuals are usually reluctant to offer their own opinions on things for fear these may not be in harmony with what others are thinking, especially their boss. They may also be unwilling or unable to make

decisions until they have a chance to meet with their superiors, thus maintaining harmony within the company's structure. Getting along with others is of utmost importance in Chinese society and within the workplace. Even though the boss may solicit opinions and ideas, in reality everyone is expected to agree with his ideas and support his decisions. Or, when suggestions are made, the boss may take the credit for coming up with them. The Chinese will very rarely question the boss's decision in a public setting. Harmony is of utmost importance and agreeing with the boss and co-workers is a clear sign that you are a team player and can be trusted.

LIFE AT THE OFFICE FOR AN EXPAT

Working in an office in China with mostly Chinese bosses, co-workers and business practices can take some adjustment, especially if you're the only foreigner there. Even if you were hired based on your credentials to help expand and improve the company's operations in order to increase profits and compete globally, it is always a delicate balancing act because of differences in culture, business practices, workplace environment and unspoken social rules. You are likely to be earning a lot more than your colleagues and therefore expectations of you will be high. You have to prove that you're a worthwhile investment through your performance and by how well you get on with colleagues.

Cultural differences between West and East can be magnified in a Chinese office environment, apart from the language barrier. Many expats chaff at the lack of punctuality, the noise level, the high turnover of co-workers, the directive 'undemocratic' management style, the length of meetings and what they perceive as a lack of accomplishment and progress. Here are a few survival tips:

• *Observe the company's hierarchy*. This is rigid and impenetrable. Be mindful and respectful.

• *Obey directives*. Bosses expect orders to be carried out without discussion or by seeking opinions. Be flexible and accepting of the situation.

• *Don't rush meetings*. This alienates co-workers and clients. Relax if meetings start a little late.

• *Maintain good relations with supervisors and co-workers*. To get anything done, you need to form friendships and alliances. Give and take is the key.

• *Don't cause a loss of face by offending bosses or co-workers*. Don't overreact or be too vocal on opinions, disputes or other office issues.

• *Join in after work entertainment*. It's an opportunity to relax and to reinforce relationships.

Colleagues hanging out at an office outing.

HANGING OUT WITH CO-WORKERS

In the West, co-workers don't often mix after office hours except on special occasions like Christmas parties and company outings. But in China's close-knit organizations, co-workers tend to spend most of their waking hours together. It is usual for co-workers to have lunch together—loners are looked down upon—and to hang out after work, perhaps going to a karaoke bar or to a restaurant. It is also common for a company to organize outings and vacations for the staff. Chinese workers believe that socializing together makes for a more harmonious and happy team. They also feel most comfortable in a group setting.

CHINA'S EDUCATION BOOM

Education has been emphasized in Chinese society since ancient times, especially for the élite. Over two millennia ago, Confucius said, 'Is it not a pleasure to study and practice what you have learned?' Today, the emphasis is on mass education as a development strategy, with the aim of improving the quantity and quality of China's graduates. This is in the face of a slowing economy and a skills gap between the needs of the economy and graduate dreams.

There is enormous pressure on Chinese students to study hard so they can get into one of the few universities in China. To help my students understand why it is so desirable to get a college education, I get them to interview people who have graduated from college and those who have left after completing high school. What they discover is eye-opening. Those with a college education typically work about 40 hours a week, go out to eat, socialize with friends on the weekends, travel locally and overseas and increasingly own and drive cars. It is a very desirable lifestyle for many. In contrast, those with a high school education often work very long hours, sometimes 6–7 days a week, and thus have little time for leisure activities. Their pay is low as they are limited to working in manufacturing, construction, restaurants, sales and the like. Life for those who aren't lucky enough to get into college is pretty tough.

INCREASED EMPHASIS ON HIGHER EDUCATION

The Chinese education system is the largest in the world. China currently invests 4 percent of GDP on education, far short of developed countries. In 1998, 830,000 Chinese students graduated from colleges and universities. In 2015, that number had increased to 7.5 million. One of the big challenges China faces is a huge population and relatively few universities, so the competition to get a place is fierce. China's population of 20–25 years olds is also increasing.

China is also concerned about the reputation of its universities compared with other countries. In the early 2000s, China began recruiting US- and Europe-based faculty for relocation to Chinese universities. This was also seen as an effort to increase China's chances of scoring a Nobel Prize in the sciences. Most recruits were ethnic Chinese. They

FOREIGN UNIVERSITIES IN CHINA

Increasing numbers of Chinese students are going to American universities to study—305,000 in the 2014–15 academic year. They are by far the most visible international presence and account for almost one-third of foreign students in the US. This influx is big business for many universities. In 2014–15, Chinese students pumped $9.8 billion into the US economy through tuition and fees. It is not surprising, then, that some universities actively recruit Chinese students from mainland China.

But it works both ways. Many Chinese feel that getting a degree from an American university will not only give them a better education but will also make them more marketable. Their middle-class families place a high value on education and are able to pay for it.

In the past decade or so, foreign universities, realizing the educational potential in China, have entered into contracts with Chinese universities to build campuses or learning centers. Their academic programs are at least part owned by the foreign university. They offer face-to-face instruction, access to academic resources at the home campus and, in some cases, credentialed degrees or certificates.

One of the earliest of the foreign ventures in China was the Johns Hopkins Nanjing Center, which opened in 1986. Its School of Advanced International Studies offers a graduate-level program to both American and Chinese students. Some 30 other foreign universities have followed suit and have campuses or research centers in China. One of the most high profile is New York University's campus in Shanghai, affiliated with East China Normal University. This was the first Sino-US joint venture university approved by China's Ministry of Education. It offers degree programs in English for Chinese and international students. Other universities with campuses in China include Duke University with a campus at Wuhan University; Carnegie Mellon University at Sun Yat-sen University; and University of Michigan at Jiaotong University in Shanghai. Universities from the European Union, the UK, Australia and other countries are also establishing a presence in China. All offer Chinese students an alternative to the rigid educational system prevalent in their country, adding a liberal touch to their educational training.

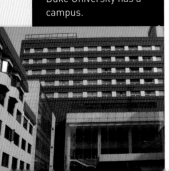

Johns Hopkins Nanjing Center. Wuhan University where Duke University has a campus.

Students taking an examination in a hall at a university campus.

were given fat salaries and nice accommodations in the top universities, such as Peking University and Qinghua University in Beijing. Some of these faculty members settled in well while others were disenchanted with the education system in China.

Many universities in China are now building additional campuses to meet the increased numbers of students desiring advanced degrees. In some cases, whole student villages are planned and built with multiple university campuses, housing and commercial space. Some have separate campuses for undergraduate and graduate students linked by bus routes or subway lines.

PRIVATE EDUCATION

Because of the intense competition to get into China's universities—9.42 million students took China's National Higher Education Entrance Examination in June 2015—there has been a significant increase in private and online education, which is growing at a rate of 20 percent every year.

Private school organizations such as Montessori and Waldorf are popular options for parents who want their children educated in a less rigid and more open environment. These schools use Western education models and are attractive to wealthy parents who realize that a Chinese education may not be the best option, especially if they want their children to study abroad in the future. Waldorf now has more than 200 pre-schools and 20 elementary schools

in China and there are well-known and established Montessori schools in Beijing and Shanghai. Fake Montessori kindergartens have also popped up in China charging high tuition rates. Many Chinese are fooled by these schools, thinking they are genuine international bilingual schools.

International schools, which in the past catered to the children of diplomats and expatriates, are also an option for Chinese children. English is usually the language of instruction and most offer an international baccalaureate degree that is recognized around the world. Most large and mid-sized cities in China have international schools. Tuiton fees run to thousands of US dollars per semester. As such, international schools are limited to the wealthiest in China.

Tutoring is also big business in China. Thousands of 'cram' schools offer after-school and weekend programs for

kindergarten through high school, but the main focus is on helping students prepare for the dreaded college entrance exams (*gaokao*) in a variety of subjects. These programs mean that many urban Chinese children spend long hours studying beyond the normal school day, often up to 12 hours a day all in.

ONLINE EDUCATION

Internet-based online learning has become a viable option in rural areas where students don't have access to quality high school and university education. Some of this comes in the form of Massive Online Open Courses (MOOC), where generally university-level course content is offered for free through instructional videos, then students are charged for certificates showing they have completed the course satisfactorily. Four universities in China—Xi'an Jiaotong University, Peking University, Fudan University and Shanghai Jiaotong University—have teamed up with the US-based company Coursera to offer such online classes. Coursera has also partnered with the Chinese company NetEase so that there is a Chinese platform to deliver the content in order to avoid YouTube, which is banned. There is now a start-up company in Beijing called One-Man University (www.wanmen.org) that also provides online university level education. While not an official university, it offers online instruction and now has over 130,000 registered learners.

A foreign instructor teaches Latin dance to young children at the Baxiang County Youth Center in Sichuan Province.

ARCHITECTURE AND INFRASTRUCTURE

In the last 30 years, China's flourishing economy, massive migration to urban areas, government housing initiatives, private property speculation and infrastructure programs have driven construction to record levels. Traditional and modern architecture now co-exist in cities and villages as older buildings are torn down to make way for newer ones, and the slow, unreliable transport systems of the past are superceded.

As China has modernized, an astonishing building frenzy has taken the country by storm. It is sometimes joked that China's national bird is the crane, referring to the construction crane. Although not all of China's new buildings are exotic and groundbreaking, the skylines of nearly all large Chinese cities are changing rapidly as skyscrapers are built at an incredible pace.

THE 'BIRD'S NEST'

PUDONG'S MEGA SKYSCRAPERS

CHINA'S NEW ARCHITECTURE

China's architectural boom began with the lead-up to the Beijing 2008 Summer Olympics when several new buildings were built as sporting venues.

Beijing National Stadium

Affectionally known as the 'Bird's Nest' because of its exposed, intertwining steel structures and saddle-shaped roof, this iconic building, situated in Olympic Green Village, was the main stadium for the 2008 Beijing Olympics and Summer Paralympics opening and closing ceremonies and for track and field events. Accommodating 80,000 fixed seats, the stadium is now used for domestic and international sports competitions and recreational activities. Its architecture is a major tourist attraction.

Beijing National Aquatics Center

Colloquially known as the 'Water Cube' because of its steel cuboid frame, which is covered with a membrane of bubble-like 'cushions', it was used for swimming and diving events during the 2008 Olympics. Since then, part of the center has been turned into a water amusement park, with wave machines, speed slides and aqualoops.

National Center for the Performing Arts

This stunning building in Beijing, nicknamed the 'Giant Egg', is an ellipsoid titanium and glass dome surrounded by a man-made lake. Entrance is via an underground hallway. Its three halls, for opera, music and theater, seat 5,452. The inaugural concert was held in 2007.

CCTV Headquarters

This 44-story skyscaper in Beijing, home of China's largest media company, China Central TV, is not your traditional tower. The structure consists of a loop of six horizontal and vertical sections that link all TV-making activities. Completed in 2012, locals refer to the building as 'Big Pants'.

Linked Hybrid Building

This large apartment complex in Beijing, comprising several towers connected by indoor walkways, houses 750 apartments for over 2,500 residents, public green spaces on its multiple layers of roofs, commercial areas, a hotel, a theater, schools and underground parking. Completed in 2009, its environmental design, which uses underground geothermal wells for cooling and heating, has won several architectural awards.

HALLSTATT, HUIZHOU, GUANGDONG

CHINA'S COPYCAT ARCHITECTURE

Not only is China known for pirating DVDS and making fake iPhones, there is also a thriving scene of communities replicating famous cities and icons around the world. Outside Shanghai there is a Little Paris community complete with a replica of the Eiffel Tower, as well as Thames Town, which resembles an English town with cobbled streets, pubs and a clocktower. There is a replica of Hallstatt, Austria, in Huizhou, while Florentia Village outside Tianjin is a copy of Venice, with canals and gondolas. Also under construction outside Tianjin is a copy of Manhattan, complete with a Hudson River. These fake towns are an attractive draw for Chinese who can experience a taste of Europe without ever leaving China.

Shanghai World Financial Center

This 101-story, multi-use skyscraper in the Lujiazui Finance and Trade Zone in Pudong, Shanghai, forms part of the amazing Pudong skyline from the Bund. It houses offices, conference rooms, observation decks, ground-floor shopping malls and the Park Hyatt Shanghai. When it was completed in 2008, it was the tallest building in China, but in 2015 was surpassed by the adjacent Shanghai Tower.

Shanghai Jinmao Tower

This landmark 88-story skyscraper, the third tallest in the Pudong district of Shanghai, contains office space, a shopping mall and the Grand Hyatt Shanghai. Completed in 1999, its design combines elements of traditional Chinese culture. It is said to be one of the best constructed skyscapers in China.

Shanghai Tower

The tallest of the group of three adjacent megatall buildings in Pudong, Shanghai Tower was completed at the end of 2015. The 128-story building is formed of nine cyclindrical buildings stacked on top of each other forming a 120-degree twist, all enclosed by a glass façade. It houses offices and retail spaces.

Oriental Pearl TV Tower

The Oriental Pearl TV Tower is also located in the Lujiazui area of Pudong and is part of the skyline seen from the Bund. The tower's unique architectural design, often described as 'twin dragons playing with pearls', combined with its history museum, futuristic space city and revolving restaurant, attract thousands of visitors all year round.

Canton Tower

This multipurpose tower in Guangzhou, the fifth tallest free-standing structure in the world, has a twisted shape that is narrower in the middle than at the bottom and top, earning it the moniker 'slim waist'. Completed in 2010, it houses TV and radio transmission facilities, observatory decks, revolving restaurants and computer gaming centers.

Other mega skyscrapers currently under construction are the Ping An Financial Center in Shenzhen and the Suzhou Zhangnan Center in Suzhou.

Above Shanghai's cityscape of highways and high-rises.
Right A high-speed train arriving at Zhuhai Railway Station.

SUBWAYS

The first and biggest advance in intercity travel in China began with the building of the first Beijing subway line in 1969. It has since expanded to 18 lines, 269 stations and 527 km of track. Ridership is over 10 million a day. Other cities have followed and the pace of building new subway lines is growing. The subway systems in China's big cities have partially addressed the congestion found on the streets. Most of the subway systems are relatively new, clean and efficient.

CHINA'S BULLET TRAINS

China's high-speed rail began operation in 2007, with average speeds of 200 km/h (124 mph). China now has the world's largest network of high-speed rail lines with more than 15,000 km of track. A network length of 30,000 km is planned for 2020. China also boasts the longest high-speed rail line, the Beijing–Guangzhou rail line at 2,298 km. The high-speed rail system is now also the most heavily used system in the world. China's bullet trains are called G-class trains and travel up to 350 km/h. They are clean, comfortable and pleasant and an attractive alternative to air travel. The 1,318 km route from Shanghai to Beijing only takes 5–5.5 hours compared to the 15 hours it used to take by train. You can travel the 2,000 km from Guangzhou to Beijing in only 8 hours. New routes are being added each year.

CHINA'S BOOMING HIGHWAY SYSTEM

In 1985, there were only 19,000 private cars in China. In 2014, there were an astonishing 154 million for 244 million lisensed drivers. All those cars have to go somewhere and China is engaged in a colossal highway building program called the National Trunk Highway System. The project began in 1990 and by 2011 85,000 km of highways were built. By 2020 the Chinese government plans to have 3,000,000 km of highways and expressways. Ninety-five percent of China's highways are toll roads that cost a driver an average of 7 cents per mile. It actually costs more in tolls than in gas to travel longer distances in China. You simply cannot set your GPS to 'no tolls' and expect to get by; you have to drive on toll roads to get anywhere. These highways connect all the major cities in China, along with 12 major trunk roads. Five of the trunk roads are oriented from north to south and seven from east to west.

BEING A FOREIGNER IN CHINA

Being a foreigner in China has changed dramatically in the past 2–3 decades. For most of China's history, the country was insular, with little contact with the outside world. The first significant contact between China and Europeans began in the 13th century, with visits by the Venetian explorer Marco Polo, followed by missionaries and traders. By the end of the 1800s, several foreign powers had established a presence in China to further their commercial and economic interests, but that was not to last for more than a few decades.

A foreign visitor choosing a hand-held fan from a street vendor in Tianjin in northern coastal China. Bargaining is normal. It helps to know a few shopping phrases in Chinese.

From the early 1900s until the early 1980s, very few foreigners were allowed to visit China. In the early 1980s, the government began allowing foreigners to travel to China for tourism and for educational and business purposes. However, foreigners are still relatively rare in most parts of the country outside Beijing, Shanghai, Guangzhou, Shenzhen and a few other large cities.

HERE COMES A LAOWAI

The term for a foreigner in China is *waiguo ren*, which literally means 'outside country person'. The Chinese term for China means 'central kingdom' as the Chinese believed China was the center of the civilized world and all other people, including Westerners, were considered barbarians. Anyone from outside China is still considered an 'outside country person'. The more common term used for foreigners these days is *laowai*. This is a little tricky to translate directly, but means something like 'old outsider'. It is often used as a derogatory term for any foreigner, but it can also be used in a playful way and is not always considered insulting. The term *laowai* typically refers only to non-Asians. This means that Chinese who live outside China, such as in the United States, are never referred to as *laowai* or even *waiguo ren*. Because the term refers not to geographical location but to ethnic identity, even a *waiguo ren* is used for a non-Chinese person. Other more formal terms for foreigners include *waibin* (foreign guest) and *waiguo pengyou* (foreign friend).

STANDING OUT IN A CROWD

China is a very homogenous country. For most of its history, nearly all its inhabitants were Chinese, or at least Asian. This meant that everyone had similar physical features, such as black hair. No one really stood out, everyone physically fit in. When Westerners began arriving, brown, blonde or red hair and pale skin were something most Chinese had never seen before and therefore attracted a great deal of attention. Outside the big cities, and sometimes even in these cities, the presence of foreigners is still uncommon. Most Chinese people have never seen more than a few foreigners in their life, let alone actually talked to one. Most everyone has seen foreigners on television, but to see one in real life is quite unusual. When a foreigner walks into a store or restaurant in an area not frequented by foreigners, they often attract attention. This may come in the form of Chinese staring at you, wanting to talk to you or wanting to take their picture with you. If you have red or blonde hair, you may attract even more attention. It is not uncommon for children to want to touch your hair to see if it is real. It may seem strange at first that young people also want to have their picture taken with you.

For these reasons, some foreigners feel like celebrities in some parts of China. People will go out of their way to talk to you or be associated with a foreigner. It is considered quite prestigious to have a foreign friend, as being seen with a foreigner is a sign of importance to some Chinese. Some Chinese companies, may even try to hire a foreigner just for the prestige factor. They may not have much for you to actually do, but having a foreigner working there says to others that you are important, international and forward-looking.

Tourists riding bicycles in Beijing. Bicycles can be rented from shops around the Drum and Bell towers and also from most hotels and hostels.

Banquets are a good way for foreigners to build up relations with their Chinese colleagues or business partners. The food served is usually more exotic than that found in side street restaurants.

DEALING WITH CULTURE SHOCK

Culture shock is the difficulty one experiences adjusting to a new culture. This often starts when encountering things that go against one's expectations. In a place like China, this would include dealing with things that you are not used to, such as the food, the climate, the behavior of people and how things are done. It can also be caused by missing loved ones, being overly tired (jet lagged) and being faced with the unknown—not knowing what to do in a given situation. The language barrier can significantly increase the chances of experiencing culture shock, especially if you are traveling by yourself.

Culture shock can be quite severe and can result in physical illness. Most everyone, even experienced China hands, experience culture shock to some degree. Culture shock is usually experienced almost immediately but it can be delayed for some time. Below are some tips on how to minimize your culture shock:

• Go with an open mind. Remember that things will be different. Try to adapt to the changes, keeping in mind that things are not inferior, just different. Trying new things won't hurt you.

• Get proper rest. Try to acclimatize to the new time zone as quickly as possible.

• Avoid isolating yourself and sleeping too much. Get out there and get into a normal routine as soon as possible.

• Stay healthy by eating well. Chinese menus can be intimidating and you may find that you are ordering the same things all the time because that is what you know how to say. Learn how to say, and read if possible, many different kinds of foods.

• Make friends as soon as possible. Having a support group early on will help with unforeseen problems. This may include fellow classmates or colleagues in your office.

• Study the language. The more Chinese you know and can use, the more integrated into society you will be.

CHINA'S CHANGING VIEWS TOWARD FOREIGNERS

In China's big cities, the novelty of foreigners is beginning to wear off. When foreign business people began coming to China, most worked for large international or foreign corporations. Their companies usually provided generous salaries (including hardship pay), nice accommodation, often in housing complexes that look just like suburban America, education stipends for their children and a personal driver. These expatriates led pretty comfortable lives in China and many didn't mingle much with the Chinese population. They lived in foreigner compounds, socialized with other expatriates and hung out at bars and restaurants frequented by other expatriates. These kinds of positions were sometimes looked at negatively by the Chinese because many of these expatriates were getting paid quite a lot more for doing the same thing as their Chinese counterparts.

There are about 71,000 Americans living in China, mostly in Beijing, Shanghai and Guangzhou, with triple that number of foreigners living in the country. This number is on the rise. What is different now is that the fat cat expat lifestyles are not as common as they were in the past. Many Americans working in China do not work for large international corporations but moved to China to find work. Some work for Chinese companies. They have to find their own housing in apartment complexes alongside average Chinese. They go to work on public transportation and eat at casual restaurants and noodle shops filled with average Chinese citizens.

Because there are so many foreigners now in China's big cities, they often don't get a second glance.

DEALING WITH CHANGE

The happiest foreigners in China are those who have adapted to their new environment. For this to happen, you need to go in with a positive attitude, be open to new things and be flexible. Below is a list of tips that will help with adjustment to life in China:

• The air pollution in large cities can be very bad. Buy a good face mask, avoid being outdoors on the worst days and try to take it in your stride.

• Shop where the locals shop. You'll get things for much cheaper. Avoid the touristy shopping areas. If you are not sure what to pay for an item, hang around and watch what the locals are paying.

• Always carry tissues or toilet paper. Restrooms in China often don't supply toilet paper.

• The Chinese seldom drink cold or ice water. If they are not drinking tea, they often drink hot water. You'll get used to it.

• Get off the beaten path. Some of the best experiences you'll have won't be in the guidebooks.

• Don't expect people to speak English. In the big cities, some young educated people speak pretty good English but don't count on it. Most Chinese are reluctant to speak English.

• Stop and talk to old people. They have the best stories and the most time to chat.

• Make Chinese friends. They will be invaluable resources to you.

• If you want to understand China, get to know its history and culture. Read some books.

• Watch out for spit on the streets. Spitting is common.

• Get used to people telling you how to dress, what to eat and so on. The Chinese are genuinely concerned for your welfare and will be open with their advice on how to make you more comfortable.

• Be cautious when crossing the street. Look left, then right, then left again, then right again, etc. Vehicles do not yield to pedestrians.

• Be adventurous in your eating. Chinese food is wonderfully varied and you may really like something that at first seemed a little strange.

NO CLOCKS OR CALENDARS, PLEASE

Getting things done efficiently in China depends on your connections with others. As noted earlier in this book, the Chinese call this *guanxi*, meaning 'connections'. When someone has developed a relationship with another, they are expected to help each other out in any way they can.

Sometimes relationships are developed and maintained with an elaborate system of gift giving. When you visit someone, it is expected that you will take a gift to show your appreciation, admiration or general goodwill. Small items like books, music CDs, candies and cigarettes are best. The Chinese are superstitious about receiving certain gifts because they are associated with bad luck, so take care. For example, clocks or calendars are associated with death, knives or scissors are symbolic of a break-up, and cups are not good because in Internet language the word for cup sounds like the word for tragedy. The number four is particularly inauspicious as it is associated with death and funerals, so don't give gifts that have anything to do with four.

Wrap a gift in red or other festive colors, not black or white, and present (and receive) it with both hands. The Chinese don't usually unwrap a gift on the spot but will open it after you leave. When you receive a gift from a Chinese, don't open it unless they insist, or until you have sat down and asked them if you can open it.

GETTING ALONG WITH THE CHINESE

An important thing to remember is that the Chinese are the way they are from a couple of thousand years of culture, traditions and customs. Don't ever think you will be able to change Chinese behavior through your actions. You are the one that needs to adapt and change. To get Chinese people to like you, you need to behave in ways they expect people to behave. This doesn't mean that you have to like everything they do, but at the very least you should try to understand how they do things and accept it. The goal is for you to not attract too much attention to yourself and to mesh well with your surroundings, whether that be in the classroom or the workplace or at a tourist site. Below are some strategies to help you get along with the Chinese and to blend in:

▪ **Avoid loud, flashy clothing**
Wear clothing that is similar to the clothes of people you work or study with. Err on the side of conservative dress. Women should avoid overly revealing clothing. Extreme clothing styles will only be a distraction and attract attention. This is especially true in professional settings. Shorts, sandals, loud flowery shirts and baseball caps don't go over very well in China and will make you stand out like a sore thumb.

▪ **Dress appropriately for the occasion**
If everyone at the office is wearing shirts and ties or skirts and blouses, then you should also. Be aware that Chinese may dress up when you would least expect it, such as for outdoor activities.

▪ **Keep your voice down**
Americans can be very loud, even boisterous, especially in groups. When in public, try to keep your voice down. Avoid yelling, screaming and loud laughter.

- **Don't assume everyone loves Americans**

You may feel like the world revolves around the United States and that everyone is enamored with American pop culture and lifestyle, but most Chinese are very proud of their heritage, ideals and lifestyle. Be respectful of Chinese ways, even though they may be very different from what you're accustomed to.

- **Avoid criticizing and complaining**

You're not going to win many friends if all you can do is complain about the pollution, the traffic, the humidity, the food, people spitting on the street and so on. It is especially bad to compare everything to the United States and constantly mention how much better things are back home.

- **Don't overreact when asked personal questions**

Chinese often ask personal questions not because they're nosy but to seek common ground.

- **Don't insist on American-style goods and services**

This is especially true in rural areas or smaller cities. Sometimes Western goods are not available or are at least hard to find. Remember, potatoes are not common in most areas of China.

- **Eat what is placed before you**

At least pretend that you appreciate the food and nibble on it. Shunning food given to you, especially at a banquet, can be very offensive to your hosts.

- **Observe Chinese table manners**

Never place chopsticks upright in your bowl as this symbolizes death. And don't tap your bowl with chopsticks. Watch how others deal with bones. When drinking a toast, it is more formal to stand up.

- **Learn at least a few phrases in Chinese**

Learning a few phrases in Chinese and using them when you can will go a long way in China. The Chinese understand how hard their language is and appreciate it when foreigners make an effort to speak Chinese.

- **Always remember that you are the guest**

The Chinese should not have to adapt their behavior to accommodate you. You should adapt your behavior to fit in with them.

- **Make friends with the locals**

Sometimes Americans tend to hang out together in groups. Branch out and try to make friends with local Chinese. You will see and do things that most Americans will not have access to.

- **Avoid common stereotypes**

Not all Chinese are good at math, are humble and are martial arts experts.

- **The Chinese are neither quaint nor cute**

With over a billion people, the Chinese can hardly be considered quaint. Some tourists make a big deal about the Chinese and Chinese things being 'so cute'.

- **Be discreet with your camera**

Nothing screams 'tourist' more than a large expensive camera around your neck, except maybe pushing into everyone's faces and taking pictures. Keep your camera in an inconspicuous bag when not photographing. I will often leave my camera in my apartment or hotel unless I am specifically going out to take pictures. Be respectful when taking photographs. It is best to chat with someone before asking to take their picture.

- **Don't always hang out at expat bars, hotels and Western fast food restaurants**

Eat like the locals. Hang out with locals. Unfortunately, many Americans spend a semester or two in Beijing or Shanghai and spend the bulk of their time eating American food and fraternizing with other foreigners. That's not why you are in China.

- **Smile**

Even if you are confused, frustrated and don't know what is going on, smile. It will ease the tension for both you and others.

- **Take it easy**

Avoid public displays of anger or frustration. Keep your cool and be patient, especially when dealing with government officials. Logic and reason don't always work. Trying to force your way seldom works. Try to understand the situation, be open to alternatives and generally try to be pleasant no matter how ugly things get.

- **Don't flirt**

American-style flirting is often misunderstood in China. While you may think it is innocent and not that serious, Chinese usually interpret this behavior as serious affection.

- **Pay attention to mannerisms**

This is especially true with non-Chinese minority groups. They have different behaviors and mannerisms. If you are traveling to the western provinces, such as Gansu, Xinjiang, Tibet, Yunan and Western Sichuan, pay close attention to how people interact with each other.

- **Be humble**

Look people in the eye when you talk to them and acknowledge their humanity. Treat people with respect and dignity.

- **Go slower but go deeper**

Become a regular by frequenting the same places repeatedly. Get to know local people, like your neighbors, the lady who sells breakfast items from a cart on the street, the bicycle repairman on the street corner.

- **Have patience with yourself and those around you**

China can be a difficult place. Allow yourself some time to and adjust and adapt to the differences.

- **Be punctual**

Although on average the Chinese are 10 minutes late for engagements, being on time shows respect for others.

- **Embrace the culture**

Remember that you have a unique experience that may be over before you know it.

- **Don't expect things to be the same all over China**

Each area of China has different food, cultural icons and ways of doing things. This makes your experience rich, exciting and varied.

STUDYING AND **LIVING IN CHINA**

The number of students studying in China has increased dramatically since they were first allowed to go for studies in the early 1980s. There are now more than 500,000 foreigners studying in China, mostly from South Korea, Japan and the United States. Business is booming at Chinese universities for foreigners studying Chinese. Because of the increased interest and demand, the quality of these programs varies considerably. Just because a program exists in China and is affiliated with a Chinese university doesn't mean it is a quality program.

Left A Westerner working in a Chinese office in Beijing. **Below** A generation Y girl working in an office.

WHEN TO GO TO CHINA

Based on the research available, the best time to study Chinese in China is after you have about four semesters of Chinese study under your belt. This will allow you to hit the ground running. There will be much that you will be able to do, and you will be able to progress at a much faster rate than if you are a true beginner who has little or no prior foreign language proficiency, or any knowledge of the culture. Another advantage to having this base is that you will have a solid foundation in the structure of the language; you will have a sound knowledge of Hanyu pinyin and the tones of the language, a solid understanding of the writing system and character formation, a basic knowledge of Chinese grammar and, hopefully, an understanding of basic Chinese communicative conventions, including behavior that is associated with interacting in Chinese. Based on research in second-language acquisition, for effective learn-

ing to take place there must be a great deal of comprehensible input. That is, the learner must be hearing a great deal of Chinese that is understandable or just slightly above their level of comprehension. When true beginners go to China, there is an overload of incomprehensible input that can slow down the process. In other words, the amount of comprehensible input available to a beginner is quite limited. For these reasons, the optimal time to study Chinese in China is after you have developed a solid base in the language.

WHERE SHOULD YOU STUDY?

There are numerous programs offering a study abroad experience in China. Some are very good and some are very poor, with everything in between. You basically have four options: studying with a formal study abroad program affiliated with your university; study abroad programs that are part of a university consortium that can often transfer the credit back to your university; through private study abroad organizations; and going independently.

If you are studying at a university in the US and they have a China study abroad program, this may be the easiest option as the university will provide all the logistical support and credit for your studies. If your university does not have a program, a consortium such as the Associated Colleges in China (ACC) or the Inter-university Program for Chinese Language Studies (IUP), accepts students from any university. They will likewise provide all the logistical support to study at one of their programs in China. Many private organizations, such as CIEE, offer comprehensive programs in various parts of China. Most universities in China also offer programs for individuals. This will take quite a bit more effort on your part to set up, but it is possible and may allow you more freedom of location and individual study. Most students of Chinese are in the big cities of Beijing, Shanghai and Guangzhou, but many other cities have excellent programs with the added benefit of there being fewer foreigners around.

MAKING THE MOST OF YOUR STUDY EXPERIENCE

To make the most of your studies in China, you will have to put in some effort. It is easy to fall into the trap of hanging out with other foreigners, frequenting expat restaurants and bars, and generally not using your Chinese very much. The following strategies will help you make the most of your time:

▪ **Take advantage of your environment.** If you already have some Chinese, you have an instant language lab right outside your door every day, all day. Speak as much Chinese as you can. Be bold and try to communicate the best you can. Take every opportunity to use Chinese, even if you could use English. Try to hang out with Chinese students and friends and don't depend on your classmates to speak for you.

▪ **Be a keen observer.** Watch carefully how Chinese interact with each other. Pay attention to what they say and how they say it. Observe how Chinese haggle over prices in a market. Watch how the Chinese greet each other, how they take leave of each other, how they pay for items at a department store, and so on. If you are ever unsure about what to do in a given situation, watch and listen to what the Chinese do, then imitate their behavior.

▪ **Use a language-learning notebook.** Get in the habit of carrying around a small notebook. Jot down things that you see and hear. Write down vocabulary items that you have studied and want to use. Write down characters on a sign that you don't recognize or items on a Chinese menu. Later, you can look these words up in a dictionary or ask a friend what they mean. When you encounter a situation that you don't understand, jot down

Left The main gate of Nanjing University. **Below** A dormitory on a Chinese university campus.

a few notes so you can ask someone later what was going on. This simple notebook can be a great language learning tool.

▪ **There isn't always an English equivalent.** Get used to the fact that in language learning, especially learning Chinese, there is often no one-to-one equivalent of words and expressions as in English. Rather than asking 'How do you say "hi" in Chinese?' you are better off saying 'How do Chinese greet each other?' Understand and accept that the Chinese do things differently and they say things differently than we do in the US. Ordering a meal in China is done very differently from in the US. Learn to play by the Chinese rules of the game. That is, learn how the Chinese get things done and follow suit.

▪ **Consider hiring a tutor.** Hiring a tutor can be a very effective way to learn Chinese, maintain what skills you already have or go beyond what you have learned in the classroom by tailoring your learning to your exact needs and aspirations. Keep in mind that just because a person is a native speaker of Chinese doesn't automatically qualify them to be a good tutor or teacher. To effectively use a tutor, it is important that you have clear objectives in mind and that those objectives are understood by your tutor. Tutors can be found on or around any university campus. Ask your friends or colleagues for recommendations. If you pay for your tutor, you are likely to have a better learning experience and you can call the shots on how and what you want to learn.

WHERE SHOULD YOU LIVE?

As a student in China, you have a few options of where to live. If you go on a formal study abroad program, your university or program may provide housing for you. This is usually in foreign student dormitories on the campus in China where you are studying. The disadvantage of this kind of housing is that you will be surrounded by other foreigners, not an ideal situation if you really want to be immersed in Chinese society. If you have the option of choosing your own housing, there are a couple of other choices. Homestays are where you live in the home of a Chinese family. Most of these arrangements will need to be through a study abroad program unless you have some personal contacts and can make the arrangements yourself. Another option is to rent an apartment in the university area. This can be a daunting but very rewarding experience. If you don't speak Chinese well, it is best to take a Chinese friend or colleague along when looking for housing and negotiating a rental contract. The advantage to living in an apartment is that you will be able to experience a real Chinese neighborhood and live like the Chinese do.

CHAPTER 5
THE CHINESE AT PLAY

With the explosive growth of China's middle class, 110 million adults have more money that ever before for recreation and travel. The travel industry, both domestic and international, is booming, art and literature are flourishing, the Chinese film industry is expanding rapidly, with many Chinese films being lauded abroad, and the music industry is also increasing.

SPORTS AND LEISURE ACTIVITIES

The most popular sports in China are badminton and table tennis. They are played for fun and at the highest levels of professional competition. Most children learn how to play these sports in school, and most schools and housing complexes have table tennis tables. Many Chinese will play badminton in a park without a net or court, just hitting back and forth for exercise.

Badminton and table tennis are hugely popular in China thanks to their relative simplicity and inexpensive equipment.

The Chinese are also keen on soccer and basketball. There are professional leagues for both and they have big followings. Most schools, from primary through to university, have basketball courts. It is common on college campuses for people to go to the courts to play pick-up basketball. Televised NBA games have fueled the interest in basketball in China. Soccer is also very popular, but it is harder to find a playing field. More often than not, pick-up games are played on an open piece of concrete. Grass is hard to come by in China except on dedicated playing fields such as those at college campuses. Some larger, more affluent high schools may also have soccer fields.

BUSINESS 101: LEARNING TO PLAY GOLF

Although the Communist Party of China imposed a ban on building new golf courses in 2004 and more recently banned its 88 million members from joining golf clubs (considered places for cutting shady deals), golf is undoubtedly the sport of the rich in China today. There are over 600 golf courses with 3 million players, up from zero 25 years ago. Golf is not cheap anywhere in the world and especially in China. But it is increasingly associated with big business in China. The ultra rich and up-and-coming businessmen are following Western practices and doing business on the links. Country clubs offer lessons and golf courses are often flanked by conference centers and shopping malls. China has also been producing some young golfers who are making a presence on the pro scene, such as Zhang Lian-Wei. In 2014, PGA Tour China, a China-based men's professional golf tour, made its debut, with a 12-event season.

Golf is becoming more popular and golf courses are being built all over China. They mostly cater to the wealthy and are typically located outside of city centers.

Other activities the Chinese enjoy are playing mahjong, Chinese chess (*xiaqi*), cards, reading and karaoke, called KTV in mainland China. Most large restaurants have rooms with karaoke machines for private parties. The Chinese love to get together and sing karaoke. It is well-liked among both young and old.

Gaming, particularly at Internet cafés, is a great favorite among the younger generation, especially with boys. Internet cafés are all over China and are mostly filled with young men playing Internet games. Some of them spend huge amounts of time and money playing games.

Reading is also a very popular activity in China. China is a nation of newspapers, books, magazines and comic books. Newspaper and magazine stands are spread out all over China's cities. The number of different newspapers and magazines available at these kiosks is staggering. The

Chinese also love bookstores. Branches of the famous state-run bookstore Xinhua Bookstore are in every Chinese city. Some bookstores are enormous with multiple floors. It is common for these stores to be packed with shoppers browsing and reading. Book malls are also common where individual book dealers have booths set up side by side in a large warehouse-type space.

Eating out and going out for tea are also immensely popular with the Chinese. The Chinese love to eat and there is no better place to socialize than at a local restaurant or teahouse. In the south, going out for dim sum in large and small teahouses can last hours.

China's elderly favor spending time with friends playing games such as Chinese chess or mahjong on tables set up in the street.

BALLROOM IN THE PARK: WHAT THE CHINESE DO FOR EXERCISE

For much of China's history, working hard was all the exercise most people ever got, or needed. China's economic development has meant better jobs, shorter working hours, more leisure time, more and better food and, with it, an increased risk of obesity. Thirty years ago, it was rare to see any overweight Chinese. Now, with all the newfound prosperity, the Chinese waistline is growing. Exercise, which has always been a favorite way to pass the time among the elderly, is becoming more common, and necessary, among younger people as well.

Although exercise may take the form of various sports, ballroom dancing, literally 'friendship exchange dancing', is particularly popular among the elderly, who gather in public spaces like squares or parks early in the morning or at dusk to do Western-style ballroom dancing to the sound of a huge boom box. Several groups sharing the same area may have to cope with competing music. It doesn't matter who they dance with, male or female. Admiring bystanders, including foreigners, who watch the dancers strut their stuff, be it a waltz, quickstep or foxtrot, are sometimes invited to do a turn or two.

Taichi has a long history throughout China as both a form of exercise and a competitive sport. It is a popular form of exercise very early in the morning in green spaces such as parks, along canals, in courtyards between residential buildings and in open spaces like town squares. Large groups of people of all ages, but mostly the middle-aged and elderly, follow the same routines led by a teacher.

PETS THEN AND NOW: CRICKETS, BIRDS AND DOGS

In China's imperial past, the most common pets kept by ordinary people were birds and crickets. Both were small, didn't eat much, and thus could be reasonably cared for even if you were not wealthy. Today in China, crickets are raised mostly for fighting. But birds are still a popular pet, especially among elderly men. It is common to see bird cages hanging in the trees at parks all over China. Older men like to hang out in the parks with their birds to socialize with others. You may also see people walking the streets with their birds in bamboo cages covered with blue cloth. Once they get to the park, they take the cover off so their birds can enjoy the outdoors, sort of.

Dogs are the most popular pet of the rising middle class. You'll see all breeds of dogs out on the streets. People like to take their dogs to public squares to play with other dogs and to socialize with other dog owners. Some go to great lengths to indulge their dogs with toys, treats, even clothing.

Red lanterns and fireworks are traditional symbols of the Chinese New Year or Spring Festival.

CELEBRATING CHINESE STYLE

The Chinese know how to celebrate, and this is nowhere more obvious than during popular annual holidays. The largest and most important celebration of the year is Chinese New Year, also called the Spring Festival. It falls at the beginning of the new lunar year, which is usually sometime from early January to early February depending on the year. It is very important at this time of year for the Chinese to be together with family. This is when schools have their winter break, which usually lasts three weeks. It is also common for businesses to shut down and give their employees time to visit family. This may involve long-distance travel, meaning that this is a very busy time for travel as millions of people are on the move.

SPRING FESTIVAL

Chinese New Year is traditionally a time to honor deities as well as ancestors. Celebrations, which include feasting, setting off and watching fireworks and visiting relatives and close friends, start with a family reunion dinner on the evening preceding the first day and continue until the Lantern Festival on the 15th day. Traditionally, families eat dumplings or *jiaozi* at New Year. It is also popular to watch the New Year's celebration variety show on television (CCTV). This show includes traditional as well as contemporary music, dance, acting and other entertainment.

LANTERN FESTIVAL

The Lantern Festival is celebrated on the 15th day of the new lunar year, also the first full moon, between February 5 and March 7. It traditionally ends the official Spring Festival. The main activity of the Lantern Festival is to make, light and appreciate lanterns of various sizes featuring traditional Chinese images such as fish, fruit and dragons, which may be fixed, held or even floated in homes and public places. People also solve riddles written on the lanterns, eat sweet sticky rice balls and enjoy entertainment such as lion dances (to ward off evil) and stilt walking.

QINGMING FESTIVAL (OR GRAVE SWEEPING DAY; EARLY APRIL)

Qingming means 'pure brightness', signifying that the days are becoming warmer and brighter. Traditionally, this was a day when people would go to the graves of their loved ones and sweep them clean, pull out weeds and replace soil as a way of showing respect to their ancestors. A sampling of the deceased person's favorite food, tea and wine were presented, incense and joss paper representing money were burned, willow branches were put on the grave, and prayers were offered.

MID-AUTUMN FESTIVAL

This festival, also called the Moon Cake Festival, falls on the 15th day of the 8th lunar month, usually in the middle of September. It is exactly in the middle of the autumn season and coincides with the full harvest moon. Traditionally, this was a time to take a break from the fall harvest and enjoy a leisurely day with family. Now, it is a romantic time to enjoy the full moon with a loved one. Round cakes filled with sweet or savory fillings, called moon cakes, are commonly given as gifts during the festival. Most people aren't that crazy about eating moon cakes but they are obligatory at this time of year.

Although many Chinese still visit the graves of their ancestors on this day to pay their respects, with cremation increasingly replacing burial, especially in cities, Qingming customs have been simplified and many people often just bring flowers for their dead relatives and pray for their blessings.

Spring outings and flying kites are also popular activities on this holiday. Kites are often decorated with tiny lanterns and flown in the evening so they resemble stars. Sometimes the string is cut so the kite can fly free. This is said to bring good luck.

HUNGRY GHOST FESTIVAL (MID–LATE AUGUST)

This festival, also called the Ghost Festival, is a traditional Buddhist and Taoist festival held on the 14th night of the 7th month, the same time as a full moon. Unlike the Qingming Festival, in which living descendants pay homage to their deceased ancestors, during the Ghost Festival the deceased are believed to visit the living. People prepare an array of food offerings, often a veritable feast laid out on a table, burn incense, joss sticks and papier maché replicas of items such as cars, houses and TV sets, to please the visiting spirits of the ancestors, and also offer prayers.

Another activity may include releasing miniature paper boats and lanterns on water 14 days after the festival to provide directions to the hungry ghosts and spirits of the ancestors and other deities to find their way back home.

NATIONAL DAY (OCTOBER 1)

In China, National Day is celebrated every year on October 1 to celebrate and commemorate the founding of the People's Republic of China. This is a time when people usually are given three days off work. The day is celebrated with flag-raising ceremonies, parades, song and dance shows, variety shows on television, fireworks displays and painting and calligraphy exhibitions. Every five or ten years, an impressive military parade is held along Chang An Avenue between the Forbidden City and Tianan-

THE DRAGON BOAT FESTIVAL

The Dragon Boat Festival is celebrated on the 5th day of the 5th lunar month (double 5th day), usually around the summer solstice (June 21). The festival is celebrated with river parades, dragon boat races and rice offerings called *zongzi* to China's earliest known poet Qu Yuan, who lived in the 3rd century BCE. He tried to advise the king but fell out of favor with the court and was banished to the south. When he learned that the capital city had been destroyed by war, he wrote a moving elegy, then threw himself into the Milo River and drowned. People got into boats and raced out to try to find him. When they realized he had drowned, they threw rice into the water as a sacrifice or, according to legend, to prevent fish from eating his body. Dragon boats and eating rice dumplings are symbolic of this story.

men Square in Beijing. The week of National Day, called 'Golden Week', is also a very popular time for Chinese to shop as many malls offer big discounts, and to travel, so train and bus stations and airports can be very crowded.

INTERNATIONAL LABOR DAY OR MAY DAY (MAY 1)

This is a holiday many countries observe to celebrate the worker. It is especially popular in socialist countries where the common worker is venerated. In China, assemblies and ceremonies are held in parks, theaters and public plazas. Entertainment programs are aired on television in the evening and sometimes model workers are celebrated.

CHILDREN'S DAY (JUNE 1)

Children's Day is celebrated on June 1 every year in many countries and in many ways to honor children. In China, Children's Day is an official holiday for primary pupils although schools often have a cultural program with children participating. The day is filled with activities especially for children. Parents take their children to parks to participate in games and to watch shows, as well as to museums, amusement parks and movies. Entrance fees for cultural sites, such as the Forbidden City, are usually free and discounted for adults on this day. Sometimes children will receive small gifts from their parents or grandparents.

Far left A photojournalist in Tiananmen Square, Beijing. **Left** The river Thames and the Tower of London are must-see sites for Chinese traveling to the UK. **Below** A Chinese girl gets ready to take a photo in Jiuzhaigou, Sichuan Province.

CHINA'S NEWFOUND LOVE OF TRAVEL

Since the beginning of reform and the opening up of China in the late 1970s, the country has become one of the world's hottest and most watched inbound and outbound travel markets. The emergence of a newly rich middle class and an easing of restrictions on movement by the Chinese authorities have fueled this travel boom. The Chinese are now eager to go outside to explore other parts of the world, while others, along with foreigners, are keen to see the many wonders that China itself has to offer.

THE NEW CHINESE TOURIST

Domestic tourism has grown dramatically with the increase in wealth and the development of a middle class in China. It has also benefited from a large population. Tourism used to be limited to trips planned by the work unit, such as a visit to a local or regional site as part of a company-sponsored trip. Private tourism was not common until about 15 years ago and although tourist sites were crowded with foreign visitors, there were hardly any Chinese.

In recent years, more than a billion trips are taken every year by Chinese tourists within China, especially during the 'two golden weeks' of the National Day holiday (October 1–7) and the Spring Festival (January or February). This has greatly enhanced employment, consumption and economic devopment in the country. Domestic business travel is also fueling the tourist industry. As a result, new high-speed rail lines have been built, new airlines set up and air routes dramatically increased. Hotels, restaurants and shopping centers have also sprouted in great numbers in the vicinity of tourist attractions.

The most popular destinations for mainland tourists include Beijing, Shanghai, Guangzhou, Xi'an, Guilin, Hangzhou, Sanya, Lhasa, Chengdu, Lijiang, Hong Kong and Macau. Chinese tour groups are obvious as they often wear matching hats or vests and their tour guide may carry a bullhorn or flag. Traveling together is a classic example of the Chinese group mentality. Their preferred lesiure travel activity is shopping for products with local characteristics as well as luxury items.

OVERSEAS TRAVEL

In 2015, 120 million Chinese traveled overseas. Most were aged 25–34 and 64 percent of them were women. They spent a whopping US\$104.5 billion, much of it on high-end shopping. Travel is now the top luxury category of choice for China's affluent consumers.

Eight of the ten most popular overseas destinations are in Asia, with Japan, South Korea and Thailand high on the list. In Europe, France, Italy, Switzerland and Germany are also popular for their romantic culture and art, while the United States attracts Chinese to its National Parks and other well-known tourist sites around the country. Encouraged in part by a new US–China visa extension policy, more than three million Chinese tourists visited the US in 2015. Although we normally associate Asian tourists with large organized groups, more and more Chinese, especially the wealthy, are traveling independently. I have run into Chinese tourists in Yellowstone National Park as well as the national parks in Utah.

This newfound love of travel is not only great news for China's domestic travel agents but is having an impact on the tourism industries in the countries where the Chinese are traveling. Many Chinese are sophisticated and seasoned shoppers able and willing to pay, who believe luxury shops outside China offer better customer service and product selection.

DOMESTIC TRAVEL

Twenty years ago, you didn't see many Chinese nationals at sites like the Great Wall, the Forbidden City and the Terracotta Warriors. These sites were dominated by foreign tourists, including overseas Chinese. Now, most of the tourists at these sites are Chinese nationals. As with international travel, more and more Chinese are traveling independently, though many still travel in organized groups. The Chinese take great pride in their cultural heritage and it shows in the number of tourists visiting everything from Buddhist temples to ancient villages in China. The Chinese are also taking a great interest in areas of natural beauty, such as national parks. Popular destinations include Tibet, Yunnan Province where there are a number of minority groups, Beijing, Shanghai and Xi'an. Chinese bookstores are full of travel guidebooks for international locations as well as local travel. There is also a growing interest in adventure vacations that involve trekking, camping, whitewater rafting, cycling and other such activities.

Left A Chinese tour group assembled at the town hall, Palazzo Vecchio, of Florence, Italy, in front of a copy of Michelangelo's famous statue of 'David'. **Below** Many Chinese tour groups are recognizable by their matching caps and flag-bearing guide.

TIPS FOR FOREIGN VISITORS

- **Avoid visiting China during Chinese New Year** as many businesses are closed and transport is packed.
- **Don't visit sites** mid-morning or mid-afternoon when bus tours are there.
- **Show respect** for China's customs, traditions, religion and culture.
- **Dress decently**. Don't walk around half-naked. Avoid wearing vests, shorts and skimpy tops.
- **Behave appropriately**. This includes not showing affection to your partner in public.
- **Ask permission** before taking photos of people, especially the elderly.
- **Learn some Chinese**, even if simple greetings, and don't be afraid to use it.
- **Shop for locally made products** to help keep traditional crafts alive.
- **Don't bargain aggressively**. Be reasonable and keep a smile on your face.
- **Don't drink water from taps**. Fill a resuable bottle with filtered water.
- **Be wary of scams** and too-good-to-be-true 'bargains'.

THE EVOLUTION OF CHINESE MUSIC

As in most other countries, Chinese music has always been integrated with the social and cultural life of the people, be they Han Chinese or ethnic minorities. Music ranges from the traditional to the modern and is played on solo, group and orchestral instruments.

PLAYING THE *GUZHENG*

Chinese music has a long history, dating back to the Shang Dynasty (1650–1045 BCE). The first musical instruments used were bone and clay flutes and bronze bells. In the following Zhou Dynasty, music became an important part of the court, with ceremonial music composed and played on important occasions. Instruments included flutes of bamboo and clay; the *pipa*, a four-stringed guitar-like instrument; the *guzheng*, a large five-stringed instrument; the *erhu*, a two-stringed violin-like instrument; drums and bronze bells.

Music flourished during the Tang and Song dynasties, and many poems were composed to music. Several forms of Chinese opera also developed, reaching their apogee with Peking Opera in the Qing Dynasty.

At the end of the dynastic period in the 1910s, China began opening to the outside world and during the late 1920s and early 1930s Western music was introduced. In 1935, the American jazz trumpet player Buck Clayton and his big band arrived in Shanghai for an extended engagement at the Canidrome Ballroom, which catered to wealthy Chinese and foreign businessmen and diplomats. He found enthusiastic crowds and respect that he did not receive in the United States because of his race. Gramophone records of Duke Ellington and other jazz artists had already arrived in Shanghai, sparking a rage for black bands in the city's nightclubs and dance halls. These jazz musicians, with the help of Chinese musicians, also learned to play popular Chinese music to suit their audiences. This evolved into a kind of hybrid music, mixing the styles of popular Chinese folk music with American jazz and Hollywood film music. Although people loved it, China's leaders considered it vulgar and pornographic.

After the Communist victory in 1949, revolutionary music became the order of the day, and remained so up to the early 1970s. This music was carefully composed and disseminated by the Communist leaders in an attempt to encourage patriotism and loyalty to the regime. One of the most popular of these revolutionary songs is 'The East is Red', its lyrics clearly patriotic in spirit:

THE EAST IS RED

The east is red, The sun is rising.
China has brought forth a Mao Zedong.
He works for the people's happiness,
Hu er hai ya,
He is the people's saving star.

Chairman Mao loves the people,
Chairman Mao, he is our guide.
To build a new China,
Hu er hai ya,
He leads us forever forward.

The Communist Party is like the sun,
Bringing light wherever it shines.
Where there's the Communist Party,
Hu er hai ya,
There the people will win liberation.

KARAOKE

Karaoke, or KTV as it is called in China, is hugely popular. Going to a karaoke bar with friends is a widespread leisure activity in a country where drinking at a bar is less common. KTV bars can be large, elaborate and expensive or small, intimate and cheap. Private rooms are rented by the hour. The rooms have comfortable chairs or couches and a karaoke machine and food and drinks can be ordered. There will typically be a large-screen TV with the music video and lyrics and two microphones. The music can be very loud, so most rooms have padded walls. Some rooms may be large enough for a small dance floor. There is usually a large selection of music to choose from, including modern and classical Chinese music. Some English pop music may also be provided but the translations are not always that good and the selection may be pretty limited. Karaoke bars are popular places to celebrate birthdays. Some people will spend a great deal of time practicing, either at home or alone at a KTV bar, working on their repertoire so they can impress their friends.

CANTOPOP

Cantopop, a contraction of 'Cantonese popular music', emerged in Hong Kong in the early 1970s and was popular into the 2000s. Dominated by ballads and love songs, it can best be described as soft pop-rock. Cantopop has a huge following in Southeast Asia, especially in Malaysia, Singapore, Indonesia and Thailand, as well as in Guangdong Province of mainland China and Taiwan. Hong Kong is the epicenter of the genre. Cantopop stars like Samuel Hui, Anita Mui, Leslie Cheung, Andy Lau and Faye Wong are household names.

The Four Heavenly Kings In the early 1990s, four Hong Kong pop stars, Jacky Cheung, Andy Lau, Aaron Kwok and Leon Lai, dominated the music scene as well as television, advertising and magazine coverage. They became known as the 'Four Heavenly Kings' and were the highest grossing artists of the 1990s.

Faye Wong (1969–) Born on the mainland, she moved with her family to Hong Kong while still in her teens. She first became famous for singing ballads in Cantonese. At the height of her career, in the late 1990s and early 2000s, she was the best-selling Cantopop female. She is considered the queen of Chinese pop, only second to Teresa Teng. She was also the first female Chinese pop star to appear on the cover of *Time* magazine.

Beyond was a four-member Hong Kong band formed in 1983. It had a progressive rock sound with more experimental sounds and lyrics than the usual romantic love ballads. The group often sang about the grittier side of life and included songs that had been adopted by political activists. Considered the most significant and successful Cantonese band to come out of Hong Kong, the group disbanded in 2005 to pursue solo careers.

EASON CHAN IN CONCERT, SHANGHAI.

Eason Chan (1974–) is the next generation of Hong Kong Cantopop stars. He is considered Hong Kong's third 'God of Song' after Samuel Hui and Jacky Cheung. He has won numerous awards in the Asian music industry. He is considered one of the top singers of his generation and has been credited with breathing fresh life into the Hong Kong music scene.

Khalil Fong (1983–) was born in Hawaii but moved to Shanghai, then Guangzhou and finally to Hong Kong when he was still young. Although he got his start in Hong Kong and is based there, he sings primarily in Mandarin rather than Cantonese and therefore has a large following in mainland China as well as in Taiwan. A talented singer and songwriter, he regularly writes songs for other well-known singers. He has released nine albums so far.

G.E.M. (short for 'Get Everybody Moving') is the stage name of Hong Kong singer Tang Tsz-kei. Born in Shanghai, she is a popular singer, songwriter, dancer, musician and actress. She is known for writing her own songs and is highly skilled on the piano and guitar. Her YouTube channel has received over 75 million views.

MODERN CHINESE MUSIC

In 1977, popular music from Hong Kong and Taiwan was introduced to mainland China through Guangzhou in China's far south, near Hong Kong. The Guangdong Audio Company, founded in 1979, controlled all the music coming from Hong Kong and Taiwan into the mainland. This genre of music was called *gangtai feng* from the Chinese words for Hong Kong (Xianggang) and Taiwan (Taiwan).

With the development of the cassette tape, popular music became widely listened to by ordinary people in China. The two most celebrated early pop stars in China were Teresa Teng (Deng Lijun, 1952–95) and Steven Liu (Liu Wenzheng, 1953–), both from Taiwan.

A TERESA TENG ALBUM

Teresa Teng became a superstar in the 1960s for her romantic ballads and folk songs, sung in a sweet, soft, almost whispery voice. After Deng Xiaoping opened up China in the 1980s, Teresa Teng became very popular. It was said that Deng Xiaoping ruled during the

day but Teresa Teng, nicknamed 'Little Deng', ruled during the night. She died of life-long asthma at the age of 43.

Liu became a superstar in the 1970s and 1980s, releasing close to 40 albums and acting in a dozen movies. His distinctive singing style and good looks quickly propelled him to stardom. He and fellow Taiwanese singer and songwriter Lo Ta-yu (Luo Dayou) were pioneers of what came to be known as 'campus folk music', a style of folk rock popular on college campuses in Taiwan. Lo was best known for his witty lyrics that addressed social problems and political issues, especially between China and Taiwan. In 1983, at the age of 30, Liu retired from the entertainment industry to become a businessman.

Left Jay Chou, one of Mandopop's biggest stars, has sold more than 30 million albums. **Above** S.H.E. is one of the first successful girl bands in a male-dominated industry.

S.H.E. is an all-girl Taiwanese band formed in 2001 that takes its name from the first initial of its members, Selina Jen, Hebe Tien and Ella Chen. Their music is a pop style that includes light melodies, simple drumbeats, piano or synthesizer and harmonized vocals. They have released 12 albums with sales totalling 15 million and their concert tours have set sales records. They have also acted in television dramas, hosted variety shows and endorsed products for more than 30 companies. They were one of the first successful girl bands in an industry dominated by male bands.

MANDOPOP

Mandopop, short for 'Mandarin popular music', originated in Shanghai but is important also in Taiwan and Hong Kong. Some Mandopop songs are versions of Cantopop songs sung by the same singers but with different lyrics.

One of the biggest stars singing in Mandarin is the Taiwanese *Jay Chou* (1979–). Chou's first album was released in 2000. He has since become a household name in many Asian countries and the US and Australia. He has sold more than 30 million albums and has won numerous awards in the Asian music industry. His music is described as a fusion of R&B, rap and classical with a distinct Chinese flavor.

Leehom Wang (1976–), another big star, was born and raised in Rochester, New York. He was trained at the Eastman School of Music, Williams College and Berklee College of Music. He had his first break in the music industry when he was in Taiwan visiting his grandparents in 1995 and entered a talent completion. He was signed by a recording company and released his first album. He is generally considered an R&B artist but he is also known for his experiments into jazz, rock, gospel, acoustic, hip-hop and world music. He is also an actor.

Emil Wakin Chau (1960–) is a Hong Kong-born Taiwanese singer and actor. He has released more than 40 albums, several of which have gone Platinum. He has recorded in Mandarin, Cantonese and English. He is very popular in mainland China, Taiwan, Hong Kong and parts of Southeast Asia.

Jolin Tsai (1980–) is a dance-pop vocalist and entrepreneur from Taiwan. Best known for her famous dance routines and elaborate stage costuming, she is called 'Asia's Dancing Queen'. She has released over 20 albums and is recognized as one of Asia's top-selling recording artits.

JOLIN TSAI AT THE *HITO MUSIC AWARDS*

THE RISE OF C-POP

C-pop is a broad term referring to Chinese popular music, including the subgenres of Cantopop, Mandopop and Taiwanese pop. Whereas Cantopop and Mandopop had their early beginnings in Hong Kong and Taiwan, C-pop encompasses the many new stars coming out of mainland China. Beginning in the late 1990s and early 2000s, many mainland singers rose to prominence in the Chinese-speaking world.

Na Ying (1967–) was born in northern China and won several singing contests in the 1980s. She began her commercial career in Taiwan and Hong Kong but is now one of the most acclaimed pop singers in mainland China. In recent years, she has been a judge on the famous *American Idol*-type television show, *The Voice of China*.

Liu Huan (1963–), considered China's 'King of Pop', is one of the most successful pop singers in mainland China. He is also a prolific songwriter and has written hundreds of songs for television shows, many of which are well known among the Chinese. In 2008, he sang with Sarah Brightman in the opening ceremony of the Beijing Olympics.

Xu Song (1986–), who goes by the English name Vae, began uploading covers of famous singers like Jay Chou in 2006 on the Internet. He would add one

song a month as he was a busy college student. He began to get a loyal following. He later won an award as best male singer. After graduating from college, he focused on his singing career. His first CD sold more than 10,000 copies in just ten days, all through the Internet. He later signed with an international music company, Ocean Butterflies.

Popular television shows such as *The Voice of China* and *Super Girl*, a national all-female singing competition in China, as well as the Internet, have been key to the rise of several stars.

Jane Zhang Lianying (1984–) got her big break on *Super Girl*. Although she was placed third in the 2005 season, she was 'discovered' and it launched her career. She is known for her high whistle register, which gained her the nickname the 'Dolphin Princess'. She sings in English, Spanish, Cantonese and her native Mandarin. Her vocal style has been compared to Mariah Carey, Christina Aguilera and Sarah Brightman.

Xiang Xiang (1984–) gained widespread popularity in 2005 after posting her song 'Song of Pig' on a free music download site on the Internet. Shortly after, she signed a contract with a recording company. She is the first female Chinese pop star to acquire success through postings on the Net.

TANG DYNASTY

Tang Dynasty, formed by two Chinese Americans and two Beijing natives in 1988, is considered the first Chinese heavy metal band. Initially, the band combined traditional Chinese music with British heavy metal. In 1990, they played at a Beijing music festival in front of a crowd of 18,000 and were soon signed up by a Taiwan music label. Their first album, 'A Dream Returns to Tang Dynasty', sold 2 million authentic copies along with countless pirated copies. Their style evolved into a type of progressive rock and artistic metal with lyric poetry intended to be similar to the poetry and music of the 10th-century Tang Dynasty. They became icons of the Chinese hard rock scene. Although they were heavily influenced by Western rock bands such as Yes, Genesis, Judas Priest, Metallica, Pink Floyd and Black Sabbath, they insist that they are Chinese and their music is infused with Chinese influences, particularly their vocals. Other popular mainland hard rock bands include Black Panther, AK 47 and Cobra.

Dao Lang (1991–) started his singing career as a bar-hopping musician in various cities around China. But he became an overnight star after his first album, 'The First Snows of 2002', was released in 2003. He was considered the best pop singer and artist of the year for 2002 by the Beijing Music Society. His repertoire ranges from adaptations of folk songs to famous revolutionary songs.

ROCK AND ROLL IN CHINA Cui Jian (1961–), the 'Father of Chinese Rock'

Beijing-born Cui Jian was originally trained as a classical trumpeter and played with the prestigious Beijing Philharmonic Orchestra. In the early 1980s, he was introduced to Western rock and roll through smuggled tape recordings from tourists and foreign students. After hearing musicians like Simon and Garfunkel and John Denver, he taught himself to play the guitar and began performing in public. He formed a band with other classically trained musicians and played in small restaurants and hotels. He is considered the first Chinese artist to write rock songs. By the mid-1980s, a great deal of Western rock had found its way into China. Cui Jian was influenced by the Beatles, the Rolling Stones, the Talking Heads and the Police. His lyrics departed from the typical syrupy romantic ballads of Chinese pop music with songs about individualism, sex and other topics not part of the Chinese music repertoire. In 1986, Cui played at a Beijing music festival and stunned the crowd with his unique brand of music. He reached the height of his popularity during the Tiananmen demonstrations of 1989 when he wrote and performed 'Nothing to my name'. He fell out of favor with the government and for a time was banned from playing in public. But he remains popular in China and has gained the moniker 'Old Cui'.

MODERN CHINESE ART AND ARTISTS

China has been called art's new superpower, with Beijing and Shanghai joining Hong Kong as the hottest spots on the international art circuit, especially for modern art. These emerging cultural capitals have thriving art scenes that encompass painting, photography, film, video and performance arts.

In 2015, China was second only to the United States in the global art auction market, with a nearly 38 percent share and with six of its best-selling Old Masters and contemporary artists—Zhang Daqian, Qi Baishi, Xu Beihong, Wu Guanzhong, Fu Baoshi and Li Keran—among the world's top ten by auction revenue. This is a far cry from the 1980s and 1990s when Beijing's burgeoning avant-garde art was frowned upon by the government and existed in scattered enclaves on the fringes of the city.

THE BEIJING ART SCENE

Beijing has a vibrant contemporary art scene focused on several creative hubs and entertainment areas:

798 Art Zone or Dazhanzi Art District is Beijing's best-known art zone. Located in a former military electronics area filled with 1950s Bauhaus-style brick factory buildings, it was previously occupied by Beijing's Central Academy of Fine Arts until it was gentrified in 2000. It now comprises a cluster of Chinese and foreign galleries and studios, exhibition spaces, cafés and restaurants. It is a popular spot for locals and tourists to see and buy new and often provocative Chinese art.

Beijing 318 International Art Village High rents and over-commercialization of their art at 798 led some Chinese artists to move to the nearby funky and up-and-coming Caochangdi district in northeast Beijing, where well-known artist Ai Wei Wei has a studio. Apart from its galleries, there are spaces for public art installations, live events, educational programs and workshops.

Further away from Chaochangdi are a number of urban village communities where artists live, work and create, among them Feijiacun, Heiqiao and Huanquie.

THE SHANGHAI ART SCENE

Shanghai's contemporary art scene, housed in world-class museums and small art spaces, is also flourishing:

Moganshan Road or M50 in the Jing'an district is Shanghai's answer to Beijing's 798 Art Zone. A former textile mill area, it is a short walk from the train station and not far from the downtown Bund area. The area began as an artist community in 2000 and the former factories now house art galleries, studios, design agencies, cafés and restaurants. More than 100 Chinese artists have studios here, including Zhou Tiehai, Ding Yi and Xu Zhen, with most studios open to the public.

ShanghART Gallery Located in the cultural hub of Moganshan Road, this is one of the best places for Chinese art. It displays paintings, sculptures, photography and multimedia by over 40 artists in a large whitewashed refurbished warehouse. It also houses an extensive library and archives.

EastLink Gallery is also located in Moganshan Road. One of the first art galleries in Shanghai, opening in 1999, it is also one of the most critically acclaimed in China, supporting both established and emerging contemporary art talent.

Island6 is an artist-run gallery founded in 2006 and managed by a volunteer staff. It includes a production site and adjoining gallery for the artwork of the Liu Dao Art Collective.

Shanghai also has numerous outstanding art museums, most of them located in the downtown area:

China Art Museum Predecessor to the Shanghai Art Museum, this is housed in the former China Pavilion of Expo 2010 in the Pudong district. It has large exhibition halls and an impressive collection of Chinese modern art.

Power Station of Art is housed in an old power station. Opened in 2012, it is the first state-run contemporary art museum in Shanghai. It hosts prestigious international touring exhibitions.

Rockbund Art Museum opened in 2010 as part by the Rockbund Urban Renaissance project whose aim is to renovate important historical buildings. Located in a beautiful Art Deco building, it is dedicated to supporting contemporary art production and creativity. It shows Chinese and international artists.

Museum of Contemporary Art Shanghai is conveniently located in the People's Park near downtown Shanghai. It has beautiful gallery space with panoramic views through the museum's floor-to-ceiling glass walls. It focuses on international exhibitions.

Inside the Beijing 798 Art Zone.

Far left Yue Minjun, 'A-maze-ing Laughter'. **Left** Zhang Huan, 'Six Realms of Rebirth'.

LEADING CONTEMPORARY CHINESE ARTISTS

While centuries-old traditions, such as ink-wash painting, remain deeply ingrained in Chinese culture, a new generation of Chinese artists are influenced by recent events in the country:

Ding Yi is a pioneer of colorful, abstract, geometric painting in China. He builds up his paintings with individual 'x' and '+' brushstrokes on plaid fabrics. Although the results look minimalist, it is a painstaking and time-consuming technique. Based in Shanghai, he has exhibited internationally.

Fang Lijun is one of the founders of the 1990s 'cynical realist' movement. He is best known for his illustrative and distorted bald-headed figures, which have what he calls 'stupid' heads that represent the loss of direction of youth in China after the Tiananmen Square protests in 1989. He is also known for his massive woodblock prints.

Wang Guangyi is a Beijing-based artist known as a leader in the new art movement that began in China after 1989. His work can best be described as 'political pop' as he uses revolutionary images, well-known from Cultural Revolution propaganda posters, superimposed on Western consumer logos such as Coca-Cola, Gucci and Starbucks, to encapsulate the juxtaposition of China's political past with its current consumerism.

Xu Zhen is a Shanghai-based artist who works in multiple mediums, including painting, mechanical installation, video, photography and performance, sometimes all in the same piece. His works, which emphasize human sensitivity and the humdrum of urban living, are both humorous and provocative. He has exhibited all over the world.

Yue Minjun is an artist based in Beijing and is best known for his cartoonish self-portraits frozen in laughter. He is classified as one of the 'cynical realist' artists in China who emerged after 1989. He works in oil paints, watercolor, sculpture and prints. His 1995 painting 'Execution' fetched US$5.9 million at auction in 2007.

Zhang Dali is a Beijing-based artist known for his graffiti art and portraits. In the 1990s, he was the only graffiti artist working in Beijing. He spray-painted over 2,000 giant profiles of his own bald head on buildings scheduled for demolition. He is also known for his various sculptures, mostly of the human form. One notable work is 'Chinese Offspring', portraying 100 immigrant workers in various poses in life-sized resin casts.

Zhang Huan is a Shanghai-based painter, sculptor and performance artist. His performance art usually consists of the use of his body in some way, usually naked, to express veiled statements against repressive rule and other issues. He also involves the body in his sculptures, which are composed of giant copper hands and feet.

Zhao Zhao works with paintings, sculptures and videos to address realities in China and document his life and those of his friends, including Ai Wei Wei. One of his most popular pieces is a large concrete bust of a policeman lying broken on the ground. Like Ai Wei Wei, this Beijing artist has been arrested and harassed for his outspoken views against the government.

Zhou Tiehai has exhibited his work in all over Europe and Asia. His style satirizes art and the art world. Although he has a degree in fine art, he hires assistants to create art that he has conceptualized digitally under his supervision. He is best known for using the Camel advertising character, which he calls Joe Camel, airbrushing the head onto 'copies' of classical European paintings. He lives and works in Shanghai.

AI WEI WEI: A-LIST POWER ARTIST

Ai Wei Wei is China's most famous contemporary artist and activist. In Western eyes, he is considered the world's 'most powerful artist'. He is best known for his large-scale, often daring and politically charged sculptural installations and for his unrelenting criticism of the Chinese government. He was famously detained for months in 2011, then released to house arrest. His work, for which he has received numerous awards, also includes performance art, painting, photography, architecture and video. He lives and works in Caochangdi art village, Beijing.

Ai Wei Wei's installation 'Straight', in memory of the Sichuan earthquake, Royal Academy, London.

CHINESE BOOKS, MAGAZINES AND COMICS

Printed books in China have been around since the 9th century, and even though only a small percentage of the population was literate a large number of books were in circulation. Education and reading have always been valued in Chinese society, and since the early 20th century there has been a great push for universal literacy. About 95 percent of Chinese are now considered literate and books, magazines and comics are an important part of contemporary Chinese life.

A COUNTRY OF READERS

Books and the written word are revered in China. The popularity of reading in China can be traced back to the Confucian Civil Service Exams of the past. Traditionally, books such as the Confucian Classics were memorized and considered authoritative. By the Ming Dynasty (1368–1644) many books were published in a variety of genres, including primers, fiction, plays, encyclopedias and poetry. It was during this time that large libraries began to appear. Education and reading were a person's ticket to a better life. When Chinese writing was reformed in the early 20th century to reflect the spoken language, literacy became more accessible and more people began reading than at any time in Chinese history. After the simplification of Chinese characters in the early 1950s, readership again surged.

Because education has been so important in Chinese society for thousands of years, reading is a natural outcome. In fact, reading is a very popular leisure time activity in China. It is not uncommon to see many Chinese reading in parks, on the subway, on buses and at airports. The large number of bookstores all over China is also testament to the popularity of reading in China.

BOOKSTORES IN CHINA

Chinese bookstores range from large multi-level stores with reading areas and coffee shops to carts at night markets selling used books. Book malls are also popular. They are usually set up in a warehouse with groups of stalls selling specialized books, such as children's books, travel books or medical texts. Bookstores are almost always crowded with people browsing, reading and socializing, sometimes late into the night. The electronic digital age has not affected print culture too much in China, except that it is now very common for people to read novels, short stories and poetry on their smart phones. The most popular bookstore chain in China is the state-owned Xinhua Bookstore. You can find a branch in nearly every Chinese city, whether large or small. There are also countless privately owned smaller bookstores.

MAGAZINES

Although more Chinese are spending time on online news and social networks, they still love browsing through magazines or reading them religiously. They usually buy magazines from small kiosks on the street where dozens are displayed for passersby to see. Chinese magazines cover just about every aspect of life in China, including politics, the economy, the military, fashion and many other topics. There are also magazines specially for children. Western magazines translated into Chinese are also quite popular in China, among them *National Geographic*, *Time*, *Vogue*, *Elle* and *Outside*.

Here are some of the most popular Chinese magazines:
Duzhe (Reader)
China's best-known magazine, it has been called a Chinese version of *The New Yorker* magazine. It contains stories, jokes, book excerpts and others.
Qingnian Wenzhai
This is a semi-monthly magazine similar to *Duzhe (Reader)* but geared toward adolescents.

Rayli
This is China's no. 1 monthly female fashion magazine. Apart from fashion, it includes articles on cosmetics, beauty and skin care, interior design, luxury goods and horoscopes.

Zhiyin
This is a highly popular magazine that focuses on traditional family values and includes true stories about love and marriage, sometimes bordering on the sensational and sentimental.

Zhoumo Huabao (Modern Weekly)
This is a very popular lifestyle magazine and includes stories and information about celebrities, news, wealth, etc.

Zhongguo guojia dili (Chinese National Geography)
Similar to *National Geographic Magazine*, it includes indepth stories on Chinese geography, history and culture.

Caijing
This is a leading weekly business and financial issues magazine. It also includes information on economic reform and major events in China's markets.

Jiating (Family)
This magazine covers love, marriage and family stories, including exclusive stories.

COMIC BOOKS

Although the Japanese borrowed comics (*manga*) from China, comics never caught on in China in the same way. *Manga* is wildly popular in Japan but has a much smaller following in China where the genre is called *manhua* ('impromptu sketches'). A 1925 series of cartoons entitled *Zikai Manhua* by Feng Zikai (1998–75), a painter, children's book illustrator and cartoonist, pioneered the comic form of art. Today, there are four main categories of *manhua*: satirical and political, comical, action (*kung-fu*) and children's *manhua*. Comic versions of Chinese stories, novels and classical poetry, complete with Romanization to aid in pronouncing the words, are particularly popular with children.

Sanmao the Orphan One of the longest running comic strips in the world, drawn without words for the benefit of China's illiterate population at the time, is the adventures of Sanmao, a young orphan living in the slums of Shanghai. Created by Zhang Leping in 1935 as a way to depict the plight of children during the Sino-Japanese War, Sanmao became an anti-hero for China's upper class. The artist continued to create Sanmao comics into the 1980s although his tone became more political. Many movies and TV series have been made based on the adventures in the comic books.

Old Master Q (Lao Fuzi) Another popular comic in China is *Old Master Q*. Created in Hong Kong in 1962 by Alfonso Wong, it features a lanky elderly man dressed in traditional Chinese attire, his main sidekicks, Big Potato, Mr Chin, Mr Chiu and Miss Chan, and a cast of other characters. Each comic typically contains four, six or twelve panels. The main focus of the comics centers around humor but from the 1960s onwards they also portrayed social and political trends. Numerous films have been made featuring Old Master Q. The comic is still in publication and is based in Taiwan.

Right *Old Master Q* comic book. **Below** Classical *Sanmao the Orphan* comic book.

CHINESE CINEMA **IN CHINA**

Over the last 100 years, Chinese cinema has faced invasion, civil war, censorship, shutdown and competition from the West. But the Chinese film industry is now big business, with many Chinese films reaching international audiences.

CHINESE CINEMA TO 1949

The first projection of a motion picture in Beijing, a recording of the Beijing opera in 1905, marked the beginning of the Chinese film industry. Domestic film then moved to Shanghai and by the 1920s Chinese film companies were producing nearly 50 films a year, a luxury entertainment for the masses. Despite this, about 90 per cent of the films viewed in China were from America.

The 'first generation' of truly important Chinese films were produced from the 1930s and focused on the common people, class struggle and external threats. *The Goddess* (1934), about the tragic life of a prostitute trying to raise her son, made Lily Yuen (Ruan Yuying) China's first film star. The Japanese invasion and takeover of Shanghai ended film production, but important 'second generation' films after 1945 dealt with these war years. *Crows and Sparrows* (1949), about corruption in the KMT government, is a classic of Chinese socialist realism and was the most acclaimed film of the 1940s and 1950s.

CINEMA UNDER MAO

When the Communist Party gained power in 1949, it took over the film industry, making it a propaganda and educational tool. It invested heavily in the film industry (some 600 feature films, 8,000 documentaries and a few 'revolutionary model operas'), but because the 'third generation' films of this era had heavy propaganda influences, the film industry stagnated.

THE POST-MAO ERA

In the aftermath of the Cultural Revolution, the film industry again flourished as a medium of popular entertainment. 'Fourth generation' filmmakers had plenty to say as they came to terms with the emotional traumas left by the Cultural Revolution. Production rose steadily, with a focus on more critical, innovative and exploratory films, often dubbed 'scar dramas'. Among the better known were *Hibiscus Town* (1986) and *The Blue Kite* (1993). Foreign films also began again to be imported into China from the 1970s and tickets for foreign film festivals were snapped up. The Beijing Film Academy reopened its doors.

In the mid to late 1980s, 'fifth generation' filmmakers, mostly graduates of the Beijing Film Academy, began experimenting and pushing the limits of the state censorship board. They rejected the socialist realism tradition of earlier directors in favor of free-thinking films about the lives of ordinary people, many reaping the rewards of international attention and acclaim.

An advertisement for a typical action-packed Jackie Chan movie.

Left to right *The Flowers of War* (2011), *Red Sorghum* (1987) and *The Banquet* (2006).

IMPORTANT FIFTH GENERATION DIRECTORS

With China opening up to the rest of the world, and with their more liberal style of filmmaking, several 'fifth generation' film directors brought Chinese cinema to the attention of international audiences:

Zhang Yimou (1951–), an actor, cinematographer, director and producer, made his directorial debut in 1987 with the acclaimed film *Red Sorghum*. His films generally deal with Chinese cultural issues, often injustices to the unfortunate, people facing hardship and the role of women in traditional society. His best-known early films are *Judou* (1989), *Raise the Red Lantern* (1991), *The Story of Qiuju* (1992) and *To Live* (1994). Other films include *Not One Less* (1999) and *Happy Times* (2000), and the martial arts films *Hero* (2002) and *House of Flying Daggers* (2004). His most recent movie is a historical war film, *The Flowers of War* (2011). His films have won several prestigious awards, including at the Cannes Film Festival, Berlin International Film Festival and Venice Film Festival. He also directed the opening and closing ceremonies of the 2008 Beijing Olympics, receiving international acclaim.

Chen Kaige (1952–) is a leading member of the fifth generation of filmmakers. His films are known for their visual flair and epic storytelling. His first film, *Yellow Earth* (1984), is notable for its powerful visual imagery and is con-

sidered one of the most important films of his generation. His most famous films in the West are *Farewell My Concubine* (1993), which was nominated for two Academy Awards and won the Palme d'Or at the 1993 Cannes Film Festival, and *Temptress Moon* (1996). His other well-known film is the story of a father and his son, *Together* (2002).

Tian Zhuangzhuang (1952–), a classmate of Zhang Yimou and Chen Kaige at the Beijing Film Academy, started off making avant-garde documentary type films, such as *On the Hunting Ground* (1985), *The Horse Thief* (1986) and *Li Lianying: The Imperial Eunuch* (1991). In *The Blue Kite* (1993), he addressed sensitive and dark periods in China's modern history. The film was banned in China and Tian was banned from making films for ten years, but the film received international acclaim, winning the Grand Prix at the Tokyo International Film Festival and the Best Film at the Hawaii International Film Festival, both in 1993. After his ban ended, Tian continued to make important films, such as *Springtime in a Small Town* (2001), *The Go Master* (2006) and *The Warrior and the Wolf* (2009).

Feng Xiaogang (1958–) is known for his highly successful commercial films, most notably his comedies. Produced in a new genre dubbed 'New Year's Celebration Films', his films are light, entertaining and accessible to a wide audience in China. His most popular films include *Dream Factory* (1997), *Big Shot's Funeral* (2001), *The Banquet* (2006) and *Aftershock* (2010).

THE SIXTH GENERATION AND BEYOND

The post-1990 era saw the rise of amateur filmmakers responding to censorship clampdowns following the 1989 Tiananmen Square demonstrations. Because these films lacked state funding, they were shot quickly and cheaply, often with 16 mm film or digital video. The films look closely at contemporary life in China and are anti-romantic views of life. They also tend to highlight people on the fringes of society. Many of the actors in the films are not professionals and were thus unknown to film audiences. The most prolific and important directors of this period are Wang Xiaoshuai (*The Days, Beijing Bicycle*), Zhang Yuan (*Beijing Bastards, East Palace West Palace*), Jia Zhangke (*Xiao Wu, Unknown Pleasures, The World*), He Jianjun (*Postman*) and Lou Ye (*Suzhou River, Summer Palace*).

Xu Zheng (1972–) is a 'newborn' director, as those of the latest generation are called. Prior to 2012, he was a popular actor in comedies. His 2012 film *Lost in Thailand*, which he co-wrote and starred in, was a big hit, making 300 million yuan in the first five days. He has also acted in half a dozen other films.

FAMOUS ACTORS AND ACTRESSES

Most of the top ten celebrities in China are actors and actresses, leading stars of comedies, dramas, horror movies, action-adventures and other genres.

CHOW YUN-FAT

In 2012, she was ranked number nine in *Vanity Fair*'s International Best Dressed list and was awarded 'The Most Beautiful Woman in the World' by the Chinese edition of *Esquire* magazine. In 2015, she was named the fourth highest paid actress in the world.

Ge You

A native of Beijing, Ge You (1957–) is one of the most recognizable and acclaimed actors in China today, especially for his comedy roles. He has acted in more than 40 films, including *Farewell My Concubine* (1993) with Gong Li. At the 1994 Cannes Film Festival, he won Best Actor Award for his role in the Zhang Yimou film *To Live*.

GONG LI

Chow Yun-fat

Born in Hong Kong in 1955, Chow Yun Fat is called the 'God of Action'. He first became a household name in Hong Kong with the 1980 gangster TV series *The Bund*, which spawned numerous sequels and film adaptations. Well known in Asia for his roles in the John Woo action movies *A Better Tomorrow* (1986) and *The Killer* (1989), he is also one of the first Chinese actors to achieve international fame, also for his roles in action movies such as *Crouching Tiger, Hidden Dragon* (2000) and *Pirates of the Caribbean: At World's End* (2007).

Fan Bingbing

An actress, singer and producer and considered a fashion icon in China, Fan Bingbing (1981–) rose to stardom with her role in the mega hit Chinese TV series *My Fair Princess* in 1998–9. Popular films include *Cell Phone* (2003), *The Matrimony* (2007) and *Chongqing Blues* (2010), which premiered at the 63rd Cannes Film Festival. She is known for her extravagant gowns on stage and at film festivals.

FAN BINGBING

Gong Li

Gong Li (1965–) first came to international attention for her roles in several Zhang Yimou films, including *Ju Dou* (1990), *Raise the Red Lantern* (1991), *The Story of Qiu Ju* (1992), for which she was named Best Actress at the Venice Film Festival, *To Live* (1994) and *Shanghai Triad* (1995). In 1993, she won a New York Film Critics Circle award for her role in *Farewell My Concubine* (1992). She made her English-speaking debut in *Memoirs of a Geisha* (2005). In 2006, in a newspaper poll she was voted 'The Most Beautiful Woman in China'.

Huang Xiaoming

Born in Qingdao in 1977, actor, singer and model Huang Xiaoming studied at the Beijing Film Academy. He got his first big break in the TV series *Da Han Tian Zi* (2001–5). He later played the

GEISHA

ZHANG ZIYI

lead role in the TV series *The Return of the Condor Heroes* (2006) based on the famous Jin Yong novel of the same name. His most critically acclaimed role was in the 2007 TV series *Shanghai Bund*, a remake of the original Hong Kong series starring Chow Yun-fat. He also starred in *Ip Man 2* (2010) and *American Dreams in China* (2013). He is endorsed by many international brand companies and appears in their advertisements.

Jackie Chan

Hong Kong actor, director, comedian, choreographer, singer and martial artist, Jackie Chan (1954–) is best known for his acrobatic kung-fu fighting style in the more than 100 Hong Kong and Hollywood movies he has starred in or produced (see page 42 above). He is the recipient of numerous Hong Kong and international acting awards.

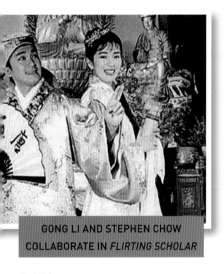

GONG LI AND STEPHEN CHOW COLLABORATE IN *FLIRTING SCHOLAR*

Jet Li

Jet Li (1963–) is best known for his roles in martial arts (wushu) films, both in China and the West (see page 43 above), having become a wushu expert in his teens. His first film was *Shaolin Temple* (1982), followed by the mega popular *Once Upon a Time in China* series where he plays the legendary *kung-fu* master Wong Fei Hung. He also played the lead in Zhang Yimou's famous film *Hero* (2002). His first Hollywood role was as a villain in *Lethal Weapon 4* (1998).

Stephen Chow

Hong Kong actor, comedian, film director, producer and martial artist, Stephen Chow (Zhou Xingchi, 1962–) got his start acting in comedies for Hong Kong's TVB. He made his name in the 1990 film *All for the Winner*, which put him in high demand in the Hong Kong film industry. Other popular movies include *Shaolin Soccer* (2001) and *Kung Fu Hustle* (2004). He has appeared in more than 50 films.

Yang Mi

Born in Beijing, actress and singer Yang Mi (1977–) has been in front of the camera since she was four years old, appearing as a young princess in two award-winning historical drama series for children. Since the early 2000s, she has starred in numerous movies and television shows and is one of China's wealthiest actresses, ranking 7th on Forbes China Celebrity List in 2014. Some of her acclaimed roles were in the television series *Palace* (2011), the film *Painted Skin: The Resurrection* (2012) and the *Tiny Times* (2013–15) series of films.

Zhang Ziyi

Chinese actress and model Zhang Ziyi (1979–) gained Western recognition for her starring role in the popular films *Crouching Tiger, Hidden Dragon* (2000), *Rush Hour 2* (2001), *Hero* (2002), *House of Flying Daggers* (2004) and *Memoirs of a Geisha* (2005), earning critical acclaim. She has been nominated for a Golden Globe Award for Best Actress and three British Academy Film Awards.

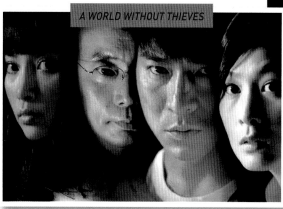

A WORLD WITHOUT THIEVES

疯狂的石头
CRAZY STONE

CRAZY STONE

热血×欢笑×

2010 爆笑公路喜剧
6月4日火爆上映
两个倒霉蛋的一段疯狂纠结旅程

LOST on JOURNEY

人在囧途

徐峥
王宝强

LOST ON JOURNEY

CHINESE FILMS YOU SHOULD WATCH

Although many Chinese films have achieved international commercial success, as of January 2016 five of the ten highest grossing films in China were local productions. Bigger and better homegrown films, expanding audiences and more cinemas have created a huge movie market in China that rivals Hollywood. The Chinese are passionate about watching movies, including the ten most popular listed below.

A World Without Thieves (2004)
This is a fast-paced action drama addressing in a humorous way the theme of thievery on public transport. It stars Andy Lau in the lead role as a con man and Rene Liu as his girlfriend accomplice who travel around western China by train scamming people.

Crazy Stone (2006)
This black comedy is about someone who finds a precious jade stone on his property and plans to display it to the public. However, three different groups set out to steal the stone with increasingly desperate attempts as the film progresses.

A cinema at the New World Emporium, Nanjing Road, Shanghai.

If You Are the One (2008)
In this romantic comedy, a well-off but lonely and insecure inventor is looking for love. He tries Internet dating without much success. He unexpectedly strikes up a friendship with an air stewardess, which eventually blossoms into love.

Lost on Journey (2010)
This comedy deals with the transportation mayhem that occurs every Chinese New Year as everyone tries to get home to spend the holidays with loved ones. It tells the story of a wealthy, arrogant businessman and a poor, gullible migrant worker both trying to get to Changsha and the many obstacles they face on their journey together.

YOU ARE THE APPLE OF MY EYE

GO LALA GO!

Go Lala Go! (2010)

This romantic comedy is about a spunky secretary who quickly climbs the corporate ladder but eventually runs into trouble with the sales director's ex-lover who throws obstacles in her way.

TINY TIMES

The Flowers of War (2011)

Directed by Zhang Yimou, this historical drama was nominated for several international awards. It stars Christian Bale as an American trying to protect a group of Chinese students and prostitutes from Japanese soldiers during the 1937 Rape of Nanking in the Second Sino-Japanese War.

You Are the Apple of My Eye (2011)

This romantic Taiwan film, based on a novel of the same name, is about a mischievous young man who falls for the smartest girl in class. The film follows their off–on relationship from junior high school though university studies.

Tiny Times (2013)

Although it received mostly negative reviews, this romantic drama, based on a best-selling novel, was a commercial success in China. The film follows the lives of four young girls living out their dreams in Shanghai.

So Young (2013)

Based on the novel of the same name, this dramatic film is about a college freshman with boy troubles who discovers that university life is not quite like what she imagined.

Finding Mr Right/Anchoring in Seattle (2013)

This romantic comedy is about a Beijing diva who goes to Seattle to give birth to her child. She tries to win over her married boyfriend, but nothing goes right. The only person willing to spend time with her is her driver.

TEN MORE CHINESE FILMS WORTH WATCHING

Devils on the Doorstep (2000)
Internal Affairs (2002)
Mountain Patrol (2004)
Waiting Alone (2005)
The Assembly (2007)
Ip Man (2008)
The Message (2009)
Aftershock (2010)
Love Is Not Blind (2010)
A Simple Life (2011)

FINDING MR RIGHT

TELEVISION IN CHINA

In the last 30 years, growing prosperity in China has created an enormous demand for media products and popular culture. No longer do families, sometimes entire neighborhoods, gather around the only television set available. Now, more than half of Chinese households own a television and over 3,000 channels are available, most offering entertainment programs.

THE EARLY YEARS

Chinese television began in the late 1950s with the help of Soviet Union technicians. The industry fell on hard times with the political and economic break with Soviet Russia in 1960, making spare parts hard to get. This was followed by disastrous economic policies and the Cultural Revolution. Only five TV stations survived. Most of the programming in these early days consisted of Mao-centered news, political education and a few revolutionary operas tightly controlled and approved by the state. By the early 1970s, TV was revived with more than 30 stations, at least one in each of China's provinces and autonomous regions and principalities. In 1978, China Central Television (CCTV) was launched as the new national broadcaster and was relayed by local stations.

THE 1980S: TELEVISION TAKES OFF

The 1980s was the decade of China's television revolution. Whereas in the 1970s only two percent of Chinese owned televisions, by 1988 half of Chinese households owned a set. Watching TV became a national pastime, with families gathering to hear the evening news and watch variety shows. CCTV also began broadcasting a Chinese New Year celebration variety show, which is immensely popular to this day.

THE 1990S AND BEYOND: CABLE, SATELLITE AND FOREIGN TELEVISION

The 1990s in China ushered in the era of cable and satellite TV. Made in China TV sets became increasingly affordable as people's disposable income increased. It became common for nearly every household to own a TV. Until 2006, it was illegal to receive a satellite broadcast into a personal home. After 2006, satellite channels had to have government approval. Approximately 30 foreign cable stations were also approved, though subject to censorship. These included stations such as CNN, BBC World, HBO, ESPN, National Geographic and MTV. However, these foreign stations were only approved for large luxury hotels and some private residential compounds where large numbers of expatriates lived. The Chinese government does not want ordinary people watching news or other programs that may present unfavorable views of China.

CHINESE TELEVISION CHANNELS

In China, there are four levels of TV programming—national, provincial, municipal and local—and over 3,000 television broadcast stations, most at the city or local county level, and most mimicking the format of the national stations. TV in China is still seen as the mouthpiece of the Communist Party, with propaganda as a central goal. CCTV is the biggest television network, with 21 public channels and 19 pay channels ranging from news to sports, movies and music. Many young Chinese avoid CCTV channels, which they consider bland and boring.

POPULAR CHINESE TELEVISION DRAMAS

Chinese viewers are the largest consumers of television dramas (period, costume, soap, family, teen, palace, fanstasy, etc.) in the world, watching an average 52 minutes of drama per day over 20–35 episodes. Below are some of the more popular TV series dramas: *The Bund (Shanghai Tan)* (1980) is a Hong Kong period drama dubbed the 'Godfather of the East' about gangster life in Shanghai. It starred the young Hong Kong star Chow Yun-fat. *Journey to the West (Xiyou Ji)* (1986) is adapted from the classic novel of the same title and is about the adventures of a monk and his three disciples. *Dream of the Red Chamber (Hong Lou Meng)* (1987) is considered the best of many adaptations of this famous mid-18th century Chinese novel about the rise and fall of four notable feudal ruling-class families. *Aspirations (Ke Wang)* (1990), one of the most successful TV shows in the history of Chinese TV drama, dominated television ratings in the 1990s. Although it was designed primarily to entertain, it also addressed many important social issues facing the Chinese during the Cultural Revolution.

Princess Pearl (Huan Zhu Ge Ge) (1997) is a costume drama set in the 18th-century Qing Dynasty. Based on the novel of the same name by Chiung Yao, it follows the story of a semiliterate vagrant and the illegitimate daughter of the emperor. It was the most successful Chinese television series ever made.

Demi-Gods and Semi-Gods (Tian Long Ba Bu (1997) is based on a novel by Jin Yong (Louis Cha) about the eight races of non-human beings in Buddhist cosmology. It is considered China's best martial arts television series.

Soldier Sortie (Shi Bing Tuji) (2007), dubbed the Chinese version of *Forest Gump*, follows the transformation through numerous trials and tribulations of a shy village boy into a brave special force soldier.

PRINCESS PEARL

POPULAR TELEVISION SHOWS TODAY

Although increasing numbers of middle-class Chinese are fascinated by Western television shows like *House of Cards*, *Big Bang Theory*, *Sherlock* and *Gossip Girls*, many locally produced talk, game and singing shows remain firm favorites for light entertainment:

Super Six Plus One (Feichang Liu Jia Yi) is a humorous talk show originally hosted by the famous CCTV personality Li Hong, now by Gao Bo. He uses humor to help three people discover their potential and achieve their dreams. The audience votes for the winner who gets a big prize.

Tell Your Stories with Lu Yu (Lu Yu You Yue) is another popular talk show on the Hong Kong Phoenix channel. The hostess interviews people from all walks of like to hear their personal stories.

Big Happy Camp (Kuaile Dabenying), one of the most popular TV shows in China, has been aired on the Hunan Province channel for the past 16 years. It has five hosts, called 'the happy family', who interview well-known Chinese and international stars. It is usually a top 5 TV show.

Happy Dictionary (Kaixin Cidian) is a popular CCTV game show. The host asks the contestants a series of questions. If contestants answer them correctly, they are asked progressively harder questions and the prize builds. If they answer a question incorrectly, they lose all their money.

Serious Inquiries Only (Feicheng Wurao) is a reality dating program. Twenty-four single girls appear on stage and single men come up, one by one, and show three videos about themselves. If the girls are not interested, they will light out. If all the girls' lights go out, the man loses.

Super Girl (Chaoji nusheng), literally 'super female voice', is a singing talent show. It is the mainland Chinese version of the UK's *Pop Idol* or *American Idol*, but it is limited to girls. It became the most popular entertainment show on TV with millions of viewers. Some Chinese pop stars were discovered on this TV show.

The Voice of China (Zhongguo hao shengyin) is a reality talent show based on the Dutch show *The*

Voice of Holland. Four judges/coaches listen to blind (unseen) auditions and decide which contestants they want on their team. Each team is then mentored and developed by their coach. Further singing battles and live performances decide the winner.

The Legend of Concubine Zhen Huan (Zhen Huan Zhuan) (above) is a popular drama that premiered in 2011. It is about the many wives and concubines of an ancient emperor. It is full of plot twists and historical background that is fascinating to the Chinese. It is being edited into six TV movies for the US market.

Struggle (Fendou) follows the love stories and dreams of a group of young people in contemporary China. It is very popular among young Chinese because of its accurate portrayal of life in China today.

Pleasant Goat and Big Wolf (Xi Yangyang yu Hui Tai Lang) is a popular cartoon in China about the conflict between a group of goats led by Pleasant Goat, and Big Wolf. Through creative storylines, it teaches children how to deal with difficulties in life. Nearly every child in China is familiar with this show.

VISITING CHINA

Whether you go to China as a tourist, for business or to study, there is a great deal to see and experience. Because of its vastness, China is an incredibly diverse country geographically, culturally and ethnically. There are numerous significant cultural and historical sites, an abundance of natural beauty and distinct differences between city and country life. Whether you are planning a short trip or an extended stay, you will find something of interest anywhere you visit.

WHAT TO SEE IN BEIJING

Located in northern China, Beijing, the capital of China, is a massive city with a huge population and a long history. Renowned for its ancient sites, art treasures and universities, it is now also known for its modern architecture and transport networks.

Beijing, the political, cultural and educational capital of China, has a population of 21.5 million people. It is one of several municipalities in China (neither a province nor a city) and as such is very large, covering 6,336 sq miles (16,410 sq km). Beijing has an extensive subway system and public bus system. To accommodate the traffic in Beijing (there are more cars in Beijing than any other Chinese city), there is a network of six ring roads that circle the city in successively larger rings. The Second Ring Road is the innermost ring road forming a rectangular loop around central Beijing, roughly equivalent to the old city. The Sixth Ring Road is the outermost road and runs around the far reaches of Beijing and is 9–12 miles (14–19 km) from the city center.

As the cultural capital of China, there is a great deal to see in Beijing. It has been the home of the central government for the past eight centuries. Unfortunately, many of the older historically significant and interesting buildings have been torn down in the face of modernization. Below are the top sites to see and things to do in Beijing.

THE FORBIDDEN CITY

This enormous palace compound, home and playground of the emperors, is at the historical heart of Beijing on the northern edge of Tiananmen Square. It contains nearly 1,000 buildings as well as a huge collection of imperial museum pieces. Plan on spending at least half a day here and make sure to wear comfortable walking shoes. It is usual to enter from the south side across from Tiananmen Square and walk through to the exit on the north side. (See Chapter 1, pages 15 and 26 for more information.)

THE TEMPLE OF HEAVEN

The Temple of Heaven, literally the 'Altar of Heaven', is a religious complex that was visited by the emperors of the Ming and Qing dynasties for annual ceremonies of prayer to ensure successful harvests. It was built between 1402 and 1420. It is located in the southern Dongcheng district of Beijing and can be reached by public transportation or taxi. The site can be accessed by any of the four gates, North, South, East or West. The East Gate is on the Line 5 subway. (See also Chapter 1, page 27.)

HUTONG NEIGHBORHOODS

A visit to Beijing's *hutong* neighborhoods gives a wonderful glimpse of the old way of life and of Beijing culture and highlights the dramatic changes in living created by high-rise apartment buildings. *Hutong* means a 'lane' or 'alley', about 30 ft (10 m) wide, formed by rows of *siheyuan*—four-sided, single-story residences built around a central coutyard—on either side. The alleys form a kind of maze. The larger *siheyuan*, occupied by aristocrats, had elaborately carved and painted roof beams, pillars and windows, with landscaped gardens. Those occupied by commoners, merchants and laborers were much smaller and the alleys around them narrower and more chaotic. Unfortunately, most of the original *hutong* neighborhoods have been torn down. But there are a few remaining north of the Forbidden City near the old Drum Tower and Clock Tower areas. There are also a few nicely preserved *hutong* near what was once the old Fox Tower in the south near the Beijing train station.

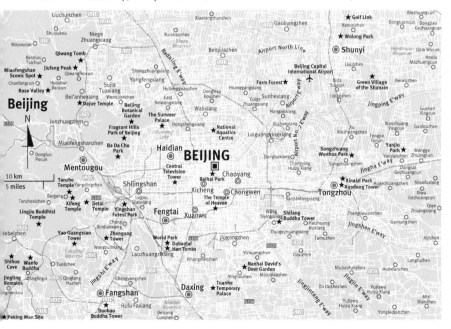

THE SUMMER PALACE

The Summer Palace (see also page 28) was once where the Qing Dynasty emperors and their families spent the hot summer months. The park is dominated by Kunming Lake and Longevity Hill. It is located in the Haidian district northwest of Beijing, about 9 miles (15 km) from Beijing's city center. It has a large number of palaces, walkways and temples with impressive architecture and a laid-back vibe. It is a relaxing place to spend an afternoon.

WANGFUJING SHOPPING STREET

Wangfujing, not far from the Forbidden City, is a shopper's paradise for locals and tourists seeking high- and low-end items. It is a pedestrian mall closed off to traffic, offering everything from designer boutiques to bookstores and souvenir stands. There are also restaurants and sidewalk cafés of all sizes and prices. It is located on a street that has been a commercial district since the middle of the Ming Dynasty.

LIULICHANG CULTURE STREET

Liulichang is one of downtown Beijing's oldest traditional quarters. Dating back to the 10th century, it was formerly a popular gathering place for scholars, painters and calligraphers who met to write, paint, compose poetry and compile and purchase books. At one point, it was the site of the country's largest book fair. During the Qing Dynasty (1644–1912), most government officials lived in the area. Today, it is an elegant neighborhood with traditional stone houses-cum-stores selling antique books, calligraphy, paintings and handicrafts, including traditional masks and puppets, pottery, silk, kites, swords, shoes and the scholar's four treasures of the study (calligraphy brush, ink stick, ink stone and paper). Some of the stores have been there for hundreds of years. It's a great place to wander around and shop, especially if you have a fascination for Chinese curios and antiques. Even if you aren't into shopping, it's a pleasant place to view traditional architecture and do some people watching as many locals frequent the area. There are also a number of small restaurants and cafés in the street.

WHAT TO SEE IN SHANGHAI

Shanghai, located on China's central coast, is the country's largest city and a global financial hub. At its heart is the Bund, a famous promenade lined with colonial-era buildings on the west bank of the Huangpu River, in distinct contrast to the futuristic skyline of Pudong across the river and glamorous Nanjing Road.

Left Shanghai's Bund promenade by night, flanked by the old city's historic commercial buildings and the Huangpu River. **Below** The Shanghai Museum has one of the best collections of Chinese historical artifacts in the world.

While Beijing is the cultural capital of China, Shanghai is the commercial capital. As such, there is a large Western presence in Shanghai, not only visible among its 24 million people but also in the architecture and availability of Western goods and services. It doesn't have the cultural landmarks that other Chinese cities have, but the street life is teeming with interesting contrasts.

THE BUND

The Bund is a waterfront area along the western bank of the Huangpu River. It lines the old International Settlement where dozens of stately 1930s Western commercial buildings once housed banks, trading houses, hotels, clubs and restaurants. It is a pleasant place for a stroll and to see the old architectural styles in the middle of modern Shanghai. It is one of the few places in the city where building height is restricted.

FUXING PARK

This quiet park, designed in the French style in 1909, lies in the middle of the old French Concession near Nancheng Road. It is crowded with old men and their pet birds, ballroom dancers, people practicing taichi and old grandmas singing Chinese opera. Nearby is the former residence of China's modern founding father, Sun Yat-sen. Inside the house you can see period furniture and books.

There are many elegant mansions along the lanes bordering the park, a hangover from the foreign presence of the early to mid-20th century.

THE SHANGHAI MUSEUM

Unlike many museums in China, this one is well presented with good lighting and displays. It sits in People's Square in the Huangpu district of Shanghai. It is considered one of China's first world-

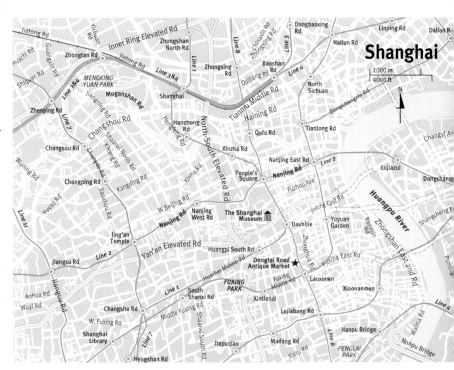

Left Pudong's rapid transformation across the Huangpu River is reflected in a multitude of extraordinary skyscrapers. **Above** Shanghai's famous *xiaolong bao* steamed dumplings.

class modern museums. It has one of the best collections of Chinese historical artifacts in the world, covering everything from ancient bronzes and jade to sculptures and paintings. There are over 120,000 artifacts to see here, so it is advisable to only try to cover a couple of galleries at each visit.

EAT SHANGHAI'S FAMOUS DUMPLINGS(XIAOLONG BAO)

Xiaolong bao are as much a part of Shanghai as barbeque is in Texas. They are small dumplings filled with tender pork and rich broth. You can't leave Shanghai without trying them. They are quite addictive. You can buy them all over the city in places ranging from tiny roadside stalls to large, expensive restaurants. One of the most famous places to try *xiaolong bao* is the Taiwanese chain called Din Tai Fung.

DONGTAI ROAD ANTIQUE MARKET

This street in the Huangpu district is an outdoor flea market selling tourist trinkets, antiques and Chinese knick-knacks that are pedaled as genuine antique items. It's a fun place to wander around, but be aware that many of the antiques are not really antique but modern replicas. If you buy, drive a hard bargain as the prices are grossly inflated.

ART GALLERIES ON MOGANSHAN ROAD

This is the place to head if you are interested in contemporary Chinese art (see page 104). The street is full of galleries as well as art studios, some open to the public. There is plenty of art for sale as well. One of the oldest and most respected galleries is Shang-ART run by Lorenz Hebling, a Swiss.

SHOPPING ON NANJING ROAD

Nanjing Road in central Shanghai is one of the city's most important commercial and tourist spots. It is a pedestrian mall lined with over 600 designer boutiques, restaurants and small shops along its 3.4 mile (5.5 km) length. You can buy anything from a Gucci handbag to traditional Chinese silk clothing.

CUANDIXIA VILLAGE

GUYAJU CAVES

WHAT TO SEE OUTSIDE BEIJING AND SHANGHAI

For those who want to get away from the crowds, pollution, concrete and chaos of China's two biggest cities, day trips (or overnight stays) to ancient mountain villages and water towns and areas of natural beauty offer not only a respite but also an insight into China's past and a different way of life.

OUTSIDE BEIJING
Ancient Villages

There are a number of ancient villages set in the hills surrounding Beijing. They are accessible by bus or by hiring a private car and are equipped to handle tourists with bed and breakfast-type accommodation in local homes.

Cuandixia Village is an historic village dating from the Ming Dynasty (1368–1644) about 56 miles (90 km) northwest of Beijing. Situated on the slopes of the surrounding mountains,

it is best known for its well-preserved but closely packed rows of courtyard homes built from stones from the nearby mountains and linked by stone-paved lanes and steep staircases. Most of the homes have traditional lattice windows and *kang*-style beds (brick beds with a place to build a fire underneath to keep people warm during the winter). Many have been converted into guest houses for those who want to stay overnight. It is a lovely place to wander around.

Diaowo Village to the east of Beijing is surrounded on three sides by mountains and on the fourth by a river. It is known for its artistic atmosphere; there are seven art studios in the village. Although there are only about 50 households, visitors can stay in farmhouses and enjoy home-cooked meals. Whole roasted lamb is the area specialty. The village is also known for its beautiful natural surroundings, with a reservoir and Stone Forest Gorge, which has many unusual rock formations.

Yanqing County Ancient Town dates back 2,000 years and is located in the Longqing Valley 53 miles (85 km) northwest of Beijing. Over 100 families live in this area and have adapted their village to entertain tourists. Visitors can pick fruit and vegetables or go fishing or horseback riding. They can stay in what is called an Agritainment Hotel, sleeping on a heated *kang* bed, enjoying a campfire outside and eating corn cakes, potato cakes and corn noodles.

Guyaju Caves are located on both sides of a secluded gorge about 50 miles (80 km) northwest of Beijing. They form the largest site of an ancient cliff dwelling community in China, and are at least 1,500 years old. There are over 170 stone rooms carved into the cliffs, from tiny spaces to suites, creating the appearance of a multistoried building. Archeologists are not sure who built them and for what reason, though it is clear they were once used as residences as there are stone beds, closets, lamp stands, cooking stoves and horse mangers. It is an interesting place to explore via stone stairs and narrow walkways.

THE GREAT WALL

Several parts of the Great Wall of China are accessible from Beijing. The easiest way to get there is to join a package tour available in most hotels. *Badaling* and *Juyongguan* are the closest sections but also the most crowded as the wall here has been specially restored for tourism. Both sections are about an hour outside Beijing if traffic is light. *Mutianyu* is slightly farther away and is less crowded with greener surroundings. It also has a ski lift to take you up to the wall and a toboggan that you can ride back down. *Jinshanling* and *Simatai* are probably the best places to visit the Great Wall. They are also the farthest away, about 80 miles (130 km) outside Beijing. Here you will find the original construction and many sections that are crumbling and in disrepair. An excellent trip is to begin at Jinshanling and hike the 6 miles (10 km) to Simatai along the wall.

HUMBLE ADMINISTRATOR'S
GARDEN, SUZHOU

XITANG WATER TOWN

Parks and Gardens

Mangshan National Forest Park is located 25 miles (40 km) from Beijing. Mangshan, which means 'python mountain' because of its undulating shape, is the largest forest park near Beijing. The area is a vibrant green with hills, forests and over 170 species of trees and flowers. It also contains hand-carved stone tablets, an artificial pool and the largest stone carved Buddha in northern China. This is a pleasant place to go for a hike through the woods.

Fragrant Hills Park is an imperial garden just 17 miles (28 km) northwest of Beijing, at the foot of the Western Mountains. It covers almost 400 acres (160 ha). Formerly known as Jingyi Palace, it was built in 1186 CE and later expanded numerous times. The area is covered with a pine-cypress forest and maple, smoke and persimmon trees. Landscaped areas feature traditional Chinese architecture, such as restored palaces, pagodas and temples that were damaged in 1860 and 1900 by foreign troops. The most popular time to visit is in the autumn when the leaves turn red.

OUTSIDE SHANGHAI
Ancient Water Towns

Whereas the outskirts of Beijing are known for ancient mountain villages, west of Shanghai and southeast of Suzhou is a maze of waterways—canals, lakes and rivers. This area is home to several water towns, some as old as 1,700 years, built on canals where boat traffic is just as common as vehicle traffic. These towns offer a nice getaway and are easily accessible via bus from Shanghai or Suzhou. Although there are about ten of these ancient water towns, below are three of the better ones.

Zhouzhuang is 18 miles (30 km) southeast of Suzhou and is China's oldest water town. Its history goes back to the Spring and Autumn Period (770–476 BCE), although most of the existing buildings, which have been beautifully preserved, were built during the Ming and Qing dynasties, making them only a few hundred years old. The town is surrounded and divided by lakes and rivers and linked by canals, and the most common way to get around is by gondola-type boats that can be hired. The arched stone bridges are impressive. Ancient homes can be visited as well as the Chengxu Taoist Temple built during the Song Dynasty (960–1279). Zhouzhuang can get very crowded with tourists, especially on the weekends.

Tongli is also located southeast of Suzhou and is about 90 minutes by bus from Shanghai. It is a smaller town and is thus less crowded and quieter, especially on weekdays. The town is divided into seven islets linked by more than 40 bridges. Almost all the houses are built along canals with a network of 15 footpaths. Many of the canals are tree-lined and shady, making it a pleasant town to wander around. As with other water towns, boats can be hired.

Xitang is one of the most attractive of the water towns with a history going back more than 2,000 years. It is located a bit further south than Zhouzhuang and Tongli, equidistant from Shanghai, Suzhou and Hangzhou, about 90 minutes from each of these cities. The town is criss-crossed by nine rivers linked by many picturesque stone arch bridges and narrow lanes. It is known for its many covered waterside streets called *langpeng*. Because of its popularity, it can get very crowded on weekends.

Lesser known water towns worth visiting are Nanxun, Zhujiajiao and Luzhi.

Parks and Gardens

The classical Chinese gardens of Suzhou, located in the historic city of Suzhou in Jiangsu Province, about an hour and half inland from Shanghai, are regarded as masterpieces of 'mountain and water' gardens. Most were constructed by scholars between the 11th and 19th centuries and were designed to recreate natural landscapes in miniature with rocks, hills and rivers and strategically placed pagodas and pavilions. Once there were more than 200 private gardens in Suzhou, but only about 50 remain of which nine are on UNESCO's World Heritage list.

West Lake in Hangzhou is a man-made freshwater lake in the charming city of Hangzhou, only about an hour away from Shanghai by train or 2–3 hours by bus. A UNESCO Cultural Heritage Site, West Lake is small (2 miles/3 km long and 1.7 miles/2.7 km wide) and is divided into five sections by three causeways. It is surrounded by mountains on three sides. Walkways surround the lake, which is dotted with small islands with teahouses and two famous pagodas. The Su Causeway, constructed under the guidance of the great poet Su Dongpo (1037–1101), crosses six bridges and is lined with willow and peach trees. The five-story Leifeng Pagoda, 230 ft (76 m) high, was originally built in 975 CE and is another place worth visiting at West Lake. The best times to visit are spring and autumn.

The bamboo forests of Moganshan, located in a mountaintop area north of Hangzhou about 3 hours by car or 4 hours by bus from Shanghai, make a good weekend retreat. The whole area is criss-crossed with hiking and biking trails, some of them quite challenging, that pass by or through dense forests of bamboo and pine, tea plantations and old stone villas built in the 1900s, some restored, some abandoned. It is an ideal place to get away for a night or two to enjoy the cool, tranquil forested surroundings.

MAIN SITES IN **OTHER PARTS OF CHINA**

Outside China's large, ancient cities and its stunning man-made attractions, there are many other beautiful places to visit in this massive and geographically varied country, including natural wonders to rival any in the world, and significant cultural sites.

POTALA PALACE, LHASA

DUNHUANG CAVES (GANSU)

This cultural site, located in northwestern Gangsu, is also known as the 'Caves of the Thousand Buddhas' (see page 28). In the 4th century BCE, caves were carved out of the cliffs for Buddhist meditation and worship. By the Tang Dynasty (618–907 CE) there were over 1,000 caves and a thriving Buddhist community. The caves were elaborately painted and statues of the Buddha were constructed inside. The most important discovery came in 1900 when a Chinese Taoist name Wang Yuanlu discovered a sealed-off room in one of the caves containing as many as 50,000 written manuscripts and paintings dating to the 5th through the 11th centuries. Most of the manuscripts were written in Chinese but some were written in Tibetan, Uyghur, Sanskrit, Sogdian and other languages. This is a popular tourist site where several caves are open to the public.

THE THREE GORGES OF THE YANGTZE RIVER

The Three Gorges is a scenic area along the Yangtze River between Chongqing Municipality upriver and Hubei Province downriver (see page 29). It spans about 120 miles (193 km) through deep and dramatic gorges. Although the Three Gorges Dam, completed in 2008, raised the water level in the gorges, they are still an impressive sight. River cruises typically take 3–4 days and can be done upriver or downriver, usually between Yichang and Chongqing.

TERRACOTTA WARRIORS OF XI'AN (SHAANXI)

The famed Terracotta Warriors are located outside the city of Xi'an surrounded by farmer's fields (see page

CHONG SHENG TEMPLE, DALI

OLD LIJIANG CITY

Chinese landscape paintings. The jagged peaks seem to rise unexpectedly from the vast flat plain around them, bisected by the broad Li River. It is this stark contrast that makes Guilin's peaks so magnificent. Apart from climbing the better known peaks, visitors can view them from boats on the Li River.

POTALA PALACE (LHASA, TIBET)

For much of Tibet's history, the Potala Palace was the political center of Tibetan rule and its spiritual center. Built in the mid-17th century, it is a huge complex, 16 stories high, comprising residences, monasteries, temples, worship halls, kitchens, etc. It has over 1,000 rooms, 10,000 shrines and 200,000 statues. In the past, 300–400 monks lived in the palace. Today, it is kept as a museum open to visitors with only about 20 monks maintaining it.

DALI AND LIJIANG (YUNNAN)

Dali and Lijiang are ethnic minority cities in Yunnan Province in China's southwest. Dali, on the shores of Lake Erhai, was the ancient capital of the Bai kingdom that flourished during the 8th and 9th centuries, while Lijiang was the political, commercial and cultural center of the Naxi people from the 7th to the 11th centuries; its old town is known for its cobblestone streets, canals and bridges. Many ethnic minority groups live in and around both walled cities. Although now predominantly Muslim, most buildings conform to the traditional Chinese style with tiled roofs and brick, plaster or white-washed walls. Both towns are also surrounded by spectacular natural scenery.

YELLOW MOUNTAIN (ANHUI)

Often touted as the 'loveliest moutain in China' with its many granite peaks, oddly shaped rocks and pine trees emerging out of a sea of clouds, Yellow Mountain (Huangshan) is a perennial favorite of poets, landscape artists and photographers (see page 27). Visitors can enjoy hiking routes along concrete stepped routes, low-level scenic walks, hot springs and waterfalls.

26). They are part of the tomb complex of Emperor Qin Shi Huang, the first emperor of China. The actual tomb has not yet been excavated but about a mile away several thousand life-sized warriors built of terracotta were discovered in underground vaults in 1974, buried with the emperor for the purpose of protecting him in the afterlife.

MT EMEI (SICHUAN)

Mt Emei is the highest of China's four sacred Buddhist mountains and is regarded as a place of enlightenment (see page 29). It is also the sight of the first Buddhist temple built in China in the 1st century. There are 76 Buddhist monasteries located near the top. It is a popular place to watch the sunrise and observe cloud formations. The area is known for an abundance of wild monkeys (Tibetan macaques) that often steal food from tourists. One can access the mountain area by cable car, bus or on foot up steep, winding mountain paths.

THE KARST MOUNTAINS OF GUILIN (GUANGXI)

The naturally forged karst (limestone) peaks, caves and sinkholes in Guilin in south-central China are one of China's most popular tourist attractions (see page 27) and the subject of countless

CHENGDU RESEARCH BASE OF GIANT PANDA BREEDING (SICHUAN)

This is the place to go to get a close-up look at the endangered giant panda. Located 6 miles (10 km) from Chengdu, it is the largest panda breeding research facility in the world and houses more giant pandas than any other place. The large park-like facility has walking paths, gardens, a museum and areas to view pandas of all ages and sizes, including newborns in incubators.

OFF THE BEATEN TRACK IN CHINA

China is full of opportunities to get off the beaten track and explore the country beyond its main cities and well-known tourist sites. With increased opportunities to travel and more disposable income, the Chinese, as well as foreign tourists, are flocking to China's 'wild west'—Xinjiang and Tibet in the far west and Sichuan and Yunnan further inland—for more adventurous vacations.

EXPLORING XINJIANG

Officially the Xinjiang Uyghur Autonomous Region, the vast Xinjiang Province in northwestern China borders Mongolia in the north and the central Asian republics of Kazakhstan, Kyrgzstan and Tajikistan in the west. Predominately Muslim, it is inhabited by Uyghurs, Kazaks and other Muslim groups. Xinjiang is home to the ancient Silk Road, the overland route between China, the Middle East and Europe. Some of the best scenery, hiking and ancient sites in China are in Xinjiang, and Urumqi, the capital, is the ideal starting point.

Urumqi The largest city and a major transportation hub, Urumqi was a major stop on the ancient Silk Road Route. One of the must-see sights in the city, especially for Silk Road enthusiasts, is the *Xinjiang Uyghur Autonomous Region Museum*, which houses an impressive collection of Silk Road-related items, including a collection of Causasian mummies. The *Grand Bazaar* or Erdaoqiao Market is a lively place to spend summer evenings if you like shopping and eating.

Turpan About 93 miles (150 km) from Urumqi, Turpan is another Silk Road city with roots going back 6,000 years. It is largely inhabited by ethnic minority groups, most notably Uyghurs. It is

Above Tuyok is a living museum of Uyghur history.
Left Riding camels up Flaming Mountains.

considered the junction of East and West. Located near an extremely hot and arid desert, the Taklamakan, the weather can be extreme. Around Turpan you can see the red sandstone *Flaming Mountains* (and ride up them on a camel) and visit the ancient city of *Jiaohe*, the oldest and best-preserved earthen city in the world.

Tuyoq The town of Tuyoq, an ancient oasis village in the Taklamakan Desert 43 miles (70 km) east of Turpan, is full of traditional Uyghur architecture and ancient Buddhist meditation caves with frescoes, while the nearby town of *Mazar* is a major Muslim pilgrimage site. This valley is also home to many vineyards, famous for seedless grapes.

Kashgar The westernmost city in China, Kashgar lies near the border with Tajikistan and Kyrgystan. Another oasis city, it was a strategically important stop on the Silk Road. It has been ruled at various times in its long history by the Chinese, Tibetan, Turkic and Mongolian empires. Han Dynasty (206 BCE– 220 CE) records indicate as many as 20,000 people lived there. The old part of the city is a maze of narrow lanes and mud and brick homes, some dating back five centuries. It is a fascinating place to explore for its history and architecture.

The Grand Bazaar can be traced back to 120 BCE. It is a shopper's paradise

TREKKING AND CAMPING IN THE TIANSHAN MOUNTAINS

Close to Urumqi, the Tianshan Mountain range offers outstanding opportunities for trekking and camping. The lower valleys are inhabited by Kazak sheep herders. Two spots are popular destinations. Heavenly Lake Scenic Spot, 42 miles (68 km) east of Urumqi, is a beautiful high alpine lake where you can hike, camp, fish and boat. South Pasture, 37 miles (60 km) from Urumqi, is a wide open landscape where sheep, horses and yaks graze, cared for by Kazak shepherds. You can stay in yurt-style accommodation and interact with the local Kazak people.

Right Karakul Lake is surrounded by snow-covered mountains all year round. **Below** Traders at the Kashgar Livestock Market.

where you can buy just about anything, from exotic rugs and jewelry to musical instruments, tea and all kinds of delicious food. It can be very crowded, especially on Sundays, but is well worth a visit.

Livestock Market On Sundays, Uyghur farmers and shepherds drive herds of camels, horses, donkeys, cows, goats and sheep to a square on the outskirts of the city to buy, sell and trade. It is lively and exiting, if not rather smelly.

Trekking to Shipton's Arch Named after the mountaineer Eric Shipton who discovered it, this natural rock arch, situated 25 miles (40 km) from Kashgar, is considered one of the world's top 20 natural wonders. At 1,500 ft (460 m) high with a 1,200 ft (370 m) opening, it is the world's tallest known natural arch and so large that the Empire State Building in New York City could fit inside it and an airplane could fly through it. It is known by locals as Toshuk Tagh, meaning 'mountain with a hole', and in Chinese as Tianmen or 'heavenly gate'. To get there, you'll need to hire a 4WD vehicle. It is about a two-hour drive, the last hour being along dry river beds. The hike in takes another 30–45 minutes up steep rock and ladders. Massive red rock walls tower all around you. Once you arrive at the arch, there is a 1,000 ft (300 m) drop on the other side. Camping is also an option in the area. It is not a well-traveled area and chances are you won't see anyone else out there.

Karakul Lake, 124 miles (200 km) outside Kashgar, is a stunning lake surrounded by high mountains that are reflected in its crystal clear waters. At 11,812 ft (3,600 m), it is the highest lake on the Pamir plateau. Two Kyrgiz villages are situated along the shoreline. This makes a nice day trip or overnighter from Kashgar.

ADVENTURE TRAVEL IN TIBET

There are numerous travel agents (easily found online) that specialize in trekking, cycling, motorcycling and river rafting in Tibet. A variety of popular trekking routes, which last from 3 to 15 days, include the Everest Base Camp, Ganden to Samye monasteries over ancient pilgrimage routes, and the Mt Kailash pilgrim route (*kora*). Many travel companies also offer a variety of mountain biking trips, ranging from a few days to several weeks, including an epic three-week trip from Lhasa to Kathmandu in Nepal over the Friendship Highway. Many of the mountain bike trips follow the same pilgrimage routes as the treks. These outfitters typically provide all the equipment necessary, including bicycles and camping gear. Some companies will ask you to bring your own sleeping bag and warm clothing but will provide everything else, including most meals. While you are out on the trail, your guides will go ahead and set up camp so that when you arrive everything is ready. Whitewater rafting is also becoming popular in Tibet and outfitters provide trips from one day to three-week-long expeditions. They run on seldom seen rivers and through spectacular canyons. Remember that when traveling in Tibet foreigners are required to have a guide with them, so booking an adventure trip with a travel company is the best option. Many of these outfitters offer custom-made trips that allow you to do much of the planning, which means that you can go just about anywhere open to foreigners.

EXPLORING TIBET

Tibet, officially the Tibet Autonomous Region of China, covers a huge area (one-eighth of China's territory) and is the highest region on earth, with an average elevation of 16,000 ft (4,900 m). Its main attractions are its spectacular mountain and plateau landscapes, its likeable Tibetan and other ethnic peoples and its Buddhist religious traditions, including its magnificent monasteries. Most people live in just a few cities in central Tibet, including Lhasa, Shigatse, Gyantse and Qamdo.

There are three ways of getting to Tibet—by air, train and overland. Air is by far the fastest and most convenient. The drawback is that there is no time to acclimatize to the altitude before you start exploring. Going from sea level to more than 11,000 ft (3,600 m) in Lhasa can be pretty hard on the body. Most people will get a headache upon landing in Tibet, which may persist for days. Breathing is also difficult in the thin air. There is now a train route from Beijing to Lhasa. It takes two and half days. The trains have sleeping compartments and are quite comfortable. Traveling by train allows more time to acclimatize and see the country along the way. Traveling overland by bus or hitchhiking

on trucks is pretty rare for Westerners although it can be arranged through a group travel organization.

There are numerous opportunities for exploring in Tibet. However, travel is strictly monitored by the Chinese government and you must have a guide with you at all times. Independent travel is prohibited. The easiest way to arrange a trip is through a travel agency that specializes in Tibetan travel and can arrange the permits needed. Despite the hassle, it is a wonderful place to visit.

Lhasa This is the spiritual and cultural heart of Tibet and is home to the Potala Palace and the Jokhang Temple, the center of Tibetan Buddhism and both UNESCO World Heritage sites. Much of modern Lhasa looks like any other Chinese city, with drab concrete buildings and unimaginative architecture. The best place to explore on foot is the old Tibetan part of the city. It is a maze of alleys full of shops and restaurants.

Jokhang Temple, built in 647, is said to be at the very heart of Tibetan Buddhism. For most Tibetans it is the most sacred and spiritual temple in Tibet and a major pilgrimage destination. It is a small temple in the center of the town, in the old Tibetan quarter. One can walk around the temple through winding alleys on a prescribed route, and observe countless pilgrims doing prostrations in front of the temple.

Drepung Monastery, built on a mountainside overlooking the Lhasa valley, is one of several monasteries in the deeply religious city. It was built in 1416 and housed as many as 7,000 monks in the past. It is one of the university monasteries where young monks go to be educated in the method of reciting sutras and debating.

Sera Monastery, also in the foothills north of the city, was built in 1419 and is one of Tibet's university monasteries. At one time it housed as many as 5,000

Debating monks at Sera Monastery in the foothills of Lhasa.

monks. It is most famous for its debating monks. Each afternoon, monks gather in a shaded courtyard outside the main hall and practice their debating skills. Young apprentice monks sit on the ground and field questions from more senior monks on various aspects of Buddhism. It is quite theatrical as the monks gesture, clap, spin around and wave their prayer beads.

MT KAILASH: A TREK ON SACRED GROUND

For the more adventurous, a 32 mile (52 km) three-day trek around the base of Mt Kailash in far western Tibet is both a challenge and an amazing experience. Mt Kailash is sacred not only to Tibetan Buddhists but also to the Tibetan Bon religion and to Hindus. It is said to be the center of the earth and produces the headwaters of three great rivers of Asia—the Brahmaputra, Indus and Ghaghara, which is a tributary of the Ganges. It is said that walking around (circumambulating) the mountain will erase your sins, while 108 circumambulations will guarantee that you reach nirvana. Pilgrims from all over Tibet and India make this trek every year. Very devout pilgrims will do full body length prostrations all the way around the mountain. The trek begins at 15,000 ft (4,600 m) and crosses an 18,400 ft (5,600 m) pass. There are primitive guest houses in the form of large tents where you can stay, although the preferred method is camping out. A few years ago, I made this trip which took five days driving overland from Lhasa just to reach the mountain.

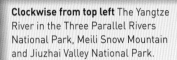

Lake Manasarova, 25 miles (40 km) from Mt Kailash, is a famous and holy freshwater lake at an elevation of 15,000 ft (4,600 m). It is a pilgrimage destination for devotees from Tibet, Nepal and India. It is believed that bathing and drinking the water will cleanse all sins. After Mahatma Ghandi died, his ashes were spread over the waters of this lake.

EXPLORING SICHUAN

Sichuan Province in southwestern China consists geographically of two very different parts—mountain ranges to the west, the source of breathtaking landscapes, and a fertile agricultural basin to the east. Although Sichuan is famous for its spicy, hot, fresh and fragrant cuisine, many parts of Sichuan, particularly the west, are inhabited by large populations of Tibetans and other ethnic minorities who enjoy a different lifestyle and diet.

Litang The small, remote town of Litang in western Sichuan sits at 13,123 ft (4,000 m), making it one of the highest cities in the world. It is a major center of Tibetan culture, offering a chance to see first-hand the life and culture of Tibetans. Litang is also home to the *Ganden Thubchen Choekorling Monastery*, built in 1580, a very interesting place to visit. The surrounding countryside is inhabited by nomads and yak herders. Litang also hosts a famous horse racing festival in late August or early September. Its nearest city is Kanding, 8–9 hours to the east over several heart-stopping passes.

Jiuzhai Valley National Park This spectacular national park, a UNESCO World Heritage Site, is located on the edge of the Tibetan Plateau in northern Sichuan Province. It is home to more than 200 species of birds and many endangered animal species, including the giant panda, golden monkey and Sichuan takin. There are also nine high-altitude Tibetan villages scattered around the park. Many of the major features of the park, such as its blue and green lakes, waterfalls and karst formations, can be reached via tour bus from Chengdu. Visitors are not allowed to camp in the park. The one exception is an eco-tourist trek through the Zharu Valley following a Tibetan pilgrim route.

EXPLORING YUNNAN

Yunnan, the most southwestern province in China, is a largely mountainous region bordering Vietnam, Laos and Burma. The average elevation is 6,500 ft (1,980 m). For a relatively small area (4 percent of China's landmass), it has enormous biological diversity. It also has a very high level of ethnic diversity (40 percent minorities). Its beautiful landscapes, mild climate and cultural variety make it attractive for both Chinese and foreigners who want to experience adventure tourism.

Shangri-la Situated in the far northwest where Tibet, Sichuan and Yunnan meet, Shangri-la (formerly known as Zhongdian) is a distant 400 miles (660 km) from Yunnan's capital Kunming to the south. It is difficult to reach Shangri-la except by long-distance bus. But its remoteness and location amidst snow-capped moutains, several considered sacred, add to its appeal for visitors. A 50-minute drive away is *Pudacuo National Park*, with mountains, lakes with raised wooden walkways and grasslands.

Deqin Some 5–6 hours west of Shangri-la is the small Tibetan town of Deqin, the jumping-off point for excellent trekking in the nearby *Meili Snow Mountain*, including the pilgrim circumambulation of holy *Mt Kawakarpo*. Half of the 150 mile (240 km) 12-day trek is in Yunnan Province and the other half in Tibet. Because of the high altitude, you need to be in good physical condition. Small guest houses line the route, but many trekkers opt to camp out along the way. The mountains around Deqin are dotted with Tibetan villages as well as temples, lakes and waterfalls.

Three Parallel Rivers National Park

The upper reaches of three of the great rivers of Asia, the Nu (Salween), Lancang (Mekong) and Yangtze (Jinsha), run parallel north to south through northwestern Yunnan Province, flowing through incised canyons up to 6,000 ft (1,830 m) deep between 12,000 ft (3,660 m) high glaciated peaks. This is wild, rugged country that holds an astonishing diversity of plant and animal life. This protected UNESCO Heritage Site is home to several ethnic minority groups. Trekking here is spectacular.

Nu River Valley Further south of the Three Rivers area, the Nu (Salween) River Valley is a very remote place inhabited by various ethnic minority groups. One of the longest free-flowing rivers in the world, the Nu flows through deep valleys. Because of the steepness of the canyon walls, all treks in this area run north and south.

LABRANG MONASTERY, GANSU

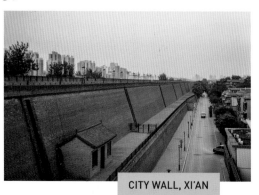

PRAYER WHEELS AT
LABRANG MONASTERY

MY FAVORITE PLACES IN CHINA

There is much more to China than famous sites like the Great Wall, Forbidden City and Terracotta Warriors. These are some of my favorite places off the beaten track.

TIBET

The appeal of Tibet for me lies in its remoteness, its pure, natural scenery and the many opportunities for being outdoors, its villages and people and their culture, including their religious devotion and their monasteries. The best time to go to Tibet is April and May when it is warmer and before the summer travel tourists arrive. Travel permits need to be obtained well in advance.

Langmusi

Langmusi is a small Tibetan village situated in a valley at 10,800 ft (3,000 m) which straddles the border of Sichuan and Gansu provinces. It is surrounded by majestic mountains and alpine forests. The people are a mix of Amdo Tibetans, Han Chinese and Chinese Muslims. There are two Tibetan Buddhist monasteries in the village, *Serti Monastery*, home to about 350 monks on the Gansu side, and *Kirti Monastery*, which houses about 750 monks on the Sichuan side. Both attract numerous pilgrims during important festivals. A short hike behind Kirti Monastery is a gorge with several old meditation caves. In addition to visiting the monasteries, the other big draws in this area are hiking and horse trekking in the surrounding mountains and nomadic grasslands. Horse treks of 1–3 days with English-speaking Tibetan guides, during which you stay overnight in Tibetan nomad tents, are particularly popular.

LABRANG MONASTERY (GANSU)

Labrang Monastery, situated about four hours by car from the provincial capital Lanzhou, is one of six great monasteries of Tibetan Buddhism. Founded in 1709, it is home to the largest number of Tibetan Buddhist monks outside of Tibet. It contains 18 halls, six institutes of learning and houses nearly 60,000 sutras (Buddhist scriptures). It is also the gathering place of numerous religious and cultural celebrations.

CITY WALL, XI'AN

XI'AN'S OVERLOOKED CULTURAL SITES (SHAANXI)

Xi'an, the ancient terminus of the Silk Road, is a culturally rich city. Besides the Terracotta Warriors (page 125), there are a number of other attractions, including the historical city wall, the Big Wild Goose Pagoda (page 29) and the less often visited Qianling Mausoleum 53 miles (85 km) northwest of Xi'an. Built in 684 CE, the tombs of the mausoleum house the remains of Emperor Gaozong (r. 649–83) and several members of his family. The mausoleum is known for the many stone statues around the complex and the murals on the walls of the subterranean tombs.

CHENGDU (SICHUAN)

Chengdu, the capital of Sichuan Province, is home to one of China's most important cuisines. If you like your food hot and spicy, Chengdu is a great place to hang out. Apart from its acclaimed giant panda breeding facility (see page 125), Chengdu also has many parks, shopping areas, restaurants of all kinds and a thriving Tibetan community.

THE BUS FROM PANZHIHUA (SICHUAN) TO LIJIANG (YUNNAN)

It takes 7–8 hours to travel from Panzhihua in the far south of Sichuan to Lijiang in northwest Yunnan. But it is a trip of epic scenery over high mountain passes. Make sure to take some snacks and cold weather clothing as it can be quite chilly, even in summer. The driver will stop occasionally for bathroom breaks and for one meal. Panzhihua is a 13-hour train ride from Chengdu.

SPRINGTIME IN KUNMING

SHANGRI-LA

KUNMING, CITY OF ETERNAL SPRING (YUNNAN)

Kunming, the capital city of Yunnan Province and its transportation hub, is well known for its moderate climate. When other parts of China are baking with 90+ degree temperatures and high humidity, Kunming will be in the 70s. Winters here are also moderate, never getting too cold. For this reason it is called the City of Eternal Spring. It is also a major source of fresh flowers for export. The Bird and Flower Market, a busy bazaar, is worth a visit. The city has a laid-back, easy-going vibe. South of the city is the Yunnan Ethnology Museum, which provides excellent exhibitions on Yunnan's many ethnic minority groups.

SHANGRI-LA (YUNNAN)

Located in the northwest of Yunnan Province, Shangri-la sits at about 10,000 ft (3,000 m) and is surrounded by snow-capped mountains and lush meadows where yaks graze. Considered a frontier town, it is about 80 percent Tibetan and 20 percent other ethnic minority groups. Nearby is the famous Songzanlin Monastery, constructed in 1679 and home to approximately 700 Tibetan Buddhist monks (from a high of 2,000). This is an interesting town to explore, especially the old Tibetan part, which is a maze of narrow alleys, shops, restaurants and residences. The mountains and pasture-land outside Shangri-la offer spectacular trekking and camping, such as in the Niru River valley. Nearby Deqin (see page 129), about 5 hours by bus depending on traffic, also has spectacular scenery and trailheads to waterfalls, forests, glaciers and river valleys and is also about 80 percent Tibetan.

EATING IN GUANGZHOU (GUANGDONG)

Guangzhou is one of the food capitals of China. Cantonese or Yue cuisine is considered one of the tastiest and most refined of all Chinese cuisines. Guangzhou is a large city in southern China situated along the Pearl River and only about 75 miles (120 km) northeast of Hong Kong. Cantonese cuisine is known for its roasted meats, such as barbequed pork, roast duck and white-sliced chicken. These delicious foods can be seen hanging in front of shops all over the city. Cantonese dim sum—bite-sized dumplings and other dishes usually eaten for breakfast or brunch—is the other culinary highlight in Guangzhou. Going out for a dim sum meal is usually referred to as going out for tea. Large teahouses all over the city serve many different varieties of dim sum. Popular dishes include barbequed pork buns, chicken feet, shrimp dumplings and rice porridge.

CANTONESE ROASTED MEATS

GUARDIAN STATUE, XIALONG MAUSOLEUM

CULTURALLY RICH NANJING (JIANGSU)

Nanjing, on the south bank of the Yangtze River, was the site of many Chinese dynasties throughout China's history and has been a culturally rich and politically important city for more than a century. It is a pleasant city known for its beautiful tree-lined, shady streets. A short distance outside the city is Purple Mountain, the site of the Ming Dynasty Xiaoling Mausoleum, one of the biggest imperial tombs in China. It contains a long walkway flanked by large stone animals and a peaceful park-like setting. Purple Mountain is also the location of the mausoleum of Sun Yat-sen (see page 27), the father of modern China.

China's rapid transit systems, called metros, currently in 23 mainland cities with many more under construction, have revolutionized the way people get around.

GETTING AROUND IN CHINA

In the past decade, the construction of high-speed rail lines, highways and many new subways as well as improved flying options have transformed China's transportation system. These have not only changed the daily lives of the Chinese but have made it easier for foreign visitors to get around.

AIR TRAVEL

Airplanes are the fastest and most convenient way for visitors to travel between cities in China, saving you time and energy. There are four main hubs: Beijing, Shanghai, Guangzhou and Hong Kong. An appealing part of flying in China is that there are generally no penalties for booking flights close to your departure date. Nor does changing flights incur a fee. I have flown into Shanghai and before leaving the airport booked another flight for the next day and it didn't cost any more than if I had booked it months in advance. There are numerous websites in Chinese and English where you can book flights, and it is increasingly easy to book domestic flights from outside China.

SUBWAYS

There are subway systems in 23 Chinese cities and other cities are either building or planning them. The most extensive subway systems are in Beijing, Shanghai, Guangzhou and Chongqing, with expanding systems in Nanjing and Chengdu. In Beijing, Shanghai and Guangzhou, you can easily take the subway from the airport into the city center and other areas. Subways are generally simple to use, safe, efficient and inexpensive.

TRAIN TRAVEL

China's train system is large, complex, convenient and cheap. You can get practically anywhere in China on a train, including Lhasa in Tibet. They are an excellent alternative to flying and allow you to experience the countryside. Train travel is divided into four classes:

Hard Seat This is generally the cheapest way to travel by train. The seats are indeed hard and the carriages can be noisy and overcrowded, but you'll get a real taste of life for ordinary people in China as this is how the majority of people travel.

Soft Seat These are the kinds of seats you would typically see on a coach

bus. They are comfortable and give you some private space. They are a great option for longer trips.

Hard Sleeper For overnight trips you will definitely want a sleeper car. Hard sleepers have six open-plan berths, three bunks on each side. There is no privacy but the beds are fairly comfortable and relatively inexpensive.

Soft Sleeper Soft sleepers have comfortable four-berth compartments and the cabin door can be closed for privacy. The beds are much larger and softer than those in hard sleepers. This is a good option for long trips, although they are quite a bit more expensive than the hard sleepers.

China's trains are numbered according to class.

G Class: Bullet Trains These are China's relatively new bullet trains. They are fast, clean and convenient. There are first-class and second-class seats on the bullet trains. G Class trains are a viable alternative to flying, without all the hassle that goes with getting to the airport early and going through security checks.

D Class: High Speed Trains These are high-speed trains that travel shorter distances during the day but

RIDE THE SHANGHAI MAGLEV TRAIN

This high-speed bullet train travels from Shanghai's Pudong International Airport to the outskirts of the city where you can transfer to one of the subway lines. The top speed is 268 mph/431 kmh.

more long-distance bus stations. There are even sleeper buses for very long trips. Buses are much cheaper than trains but they also take quite a bit longer. Long-distance bus travel is an excellent way to see the country.

TAXI TRAVEL
Every city in China has taxis. Although more expensive than subway or bus travel, taking a taxi is inexpensive and can be convenient. Most taxi drivers will not understand English but if you have your destination written in Chinese they will take you where you need to go. In some cities, such as Beijing, it is practically impossible to get a taxi during rush hour or when it is raining.

GETTING AROUND ON A BIKE
Renting or buying a bike can be an excellent way to get around in China. Vehicular traffic can be intimidating, but once you get the hang of it, a bike can be very enjoyable and convenient. Most cities have good bike lanes. Popular tourist areas and backpacker hostels typically rent bikes for a small fee.

EXPLORING ON FOOT
Depending on the city, exploring on foot is the best way to really experience a place. By going slow, you will see more and likely have a richer experience. Walking also allows you to interact directly with residents of the area. If you like street photography, this is the only way to go. One way of doing this is by taking public transportation to the cultural site or area of the city you want to see, then walk the neighborhoods in that area. You may also be able to link up walking routes between sites and enjoy the neighborhoods in between. It will give you an insight into how the Chinese live that you cannot get any other way.

Above A taxi stand in Beijing. **Right** Trolleybuses provide an important transit system mostly for locals in China's cities. **Below** Bike lanes are a boon for cyclists. Electric bicycles are increasingly popular.

may also offer longer routes, such as Beijing to Xi'an. These trains usually only have soft seats and soft sleepers and are air-conditioned.

Z Class: Non-stop Direct Express Trains
These trains usually have only one stop along a given route. They are fast, clean and efficient. Some of the trains only offer soft seats and sleepers.

T Class: Extra Fast Trains
These trains run on most railway routes and have numerous stops along the way, which makes them slower than Z Class trains. They have a wide variety of options from hard seats and sleepers to soft.

K Class: Fast Trains
These are the most popular trains in China for the majority of Chinese. There are more K trains than any other class. These trains have all categories of seats and sleepers. They are usually much more crowded and can be a bit chaotic compared to the other class trains. Most of these trains do not have air-conditioning.

BUS TRAVEL IN CHINA
Traveling by bus in Chinese cities can be challenging. They are usually very crowded and it can be difficult to learn the routes they take. But long-distance bus travel is generally comfortable and convenient. Most cities have one or

VISITING TAIWAN

Although the main focus of this book is on the mainland of China, there are two nearby areas that are uniquely Chinese—Taiwan and Hong Kong—and have the closest cultural ties to mainland China. Taiwan, in particular, a small island 110 miles (180 km) off the southeast coast of mainland China, is one of Asia's best-kept travel secrets but is now a tourism magnet for main-landers and foreigners.

Taiwan has a vibrant, capitalist, export-driven economy. The standard of living in Taiwan has risen steadily since the 1960s and it is considered a developed country. The island has a modern transportation system with high-speed rail, modern housing, an up-to-date and efficient health care system and a comfortable standard of living. The population of Taiwan is 23 million.

TAIWAN'S UNIQUE CULTURE

Although Taiwan has had more exposure to the West and has developed a modern society, the Taiwanese are generally more conservative with regard to traditional Chinese values than mainland Chinese. Taiwanese culture can best be described as the purest form of Confucianism mixed with Taoism and Buddhism, while embracing modern Japanese, Korean and American culture. It is a true hybridization of people (non-Han Chinese aboriginal tribes, native Taiwanese, Chinese immigrants from the mainland and foreigners), religions (Daoist, Buddhist, ancestral worship and Christianity), and cultures (Taiwanese, Chinese, Japanese and American).

Religious freedom has also allowed a flourishing of religious practice, from Taoism and Buddhism to a thriving Christian community. Since democratic reforms in the 1990s, Taiwan has been an open, free society. This is reflected in religious freedom, literature, film, politics and general freedom of expression.

Taiwan also has maintained use of traditional Chinese characters that have been in use for centuries in China.

While mainland China has shifted to a simplified script, it is not uncommon in Taiwan to see books printed from top to bottom and right to left in the way Chinese was traditionally printed.

TAIWAN'S CUISINE

The cuisine in Taiwan has been influenced first by Japan, then by the West. While there is plenty of traditional Chinese cuisine to be found, there are also many interesting fusion dishes among Taiwan's rich and varied street food. An example of a very popular Western-influenced Taiwan dish is Taiwan-style steak. It is usually a thin cut of beef or pork fried in a cast iron skillet, served over a heap of noodles with a peppery sauce on top. Just before it is served, an egg is cracked onto the skillet next to the steak. Another example is fried chicken. This is extremely popular in Taiwan and is served at all the night markets. It is typically either a large

boneless chicken breast pounded flat, or smaller nuggets that are breaded and deep-fried and served on a stick. It looks Western but is enhanced with Chinese seasonings and is delicious. A Japanese-

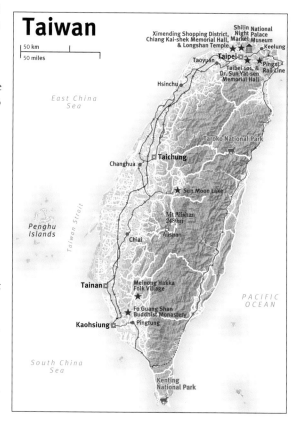

influenced popular Chinese dish is 'Tian Bu La', named after the Chinese characters for *tempura* in Japan. A uniquely Taiwanese food, it is made with fish paste shaped into various forms, deep-fried, then boiled in broth. It is then served with a sweet brown sauce. A spicy sauce can also be added. It vaguely resembles Japanese *oden* but is sweeter.

Another dish is the famous oyster omelet. This is a traditional Fujian dish that has been adapted to Taiwanese tastes. In Taiwan, the omelet, studded liberally with small local oysters, is then smothered in a sweet, sticky sauce made with sweet potato starch.

THINGS TO DO IN TAIWAN

Besides its markets and memorials, Taiwan is known for its steep mountain ranges, great beaches and stunning national parks.

Open-air Night Markets Night markets are a staple of entertainment, shopping and eating in Taiwan. Vendors set up in the evenings and sell everything from T-shirts and handbags to souvenirs and cheap knock-offs. Haggling is expected. Night markets are also full of vendors selling inexpensive Taiwanese street food. Some of the larger markets may even have a food mall with dozens of stalls selling every kind of street food imaginable. One of the bigger and more famous markets is the Shilin Night Market, adjacent to the Shilin Metro Station. The street market near the Taiwan Teacher's University, the Shida Night Market, is also a popular venue.

Ximending Shopping District Located in west Taipei, this pedestrian zone in Taiwan is considered the most fashionable and popular shopping area for locals and tourists. Somewhat similar to Shibuya in Japan, it is Taiwan's fashion center and the hub of Japanese culture in Taiwan. It is a great place to see cutting-edge fashion trends among Taiwanese youth. It is easily accessed by the Taipei metro's Ximen Station.

Taipei 101 This 101-story skyscraper in the Xinyi district of Taipei was the tallest building in the world when it was completed in 2004, but in 2010 a building in Dubai took away that honor. It is considered the tallest green building in the world because of its low environmental footprint. Built to withstand typhoons and earthquakes, the building resembles a bamboo stalk or a Chinese pagoda. The first five floors of the building are taken up by a huge high-end mall. In addition to office space, there are dozens of restaurants and clubs in the building. There is an observation deck open to the public on the 88th, 89th and 91st floors. The building also boasts the world's fastest elevator, which travels 3,281 ft (1,010 m) per minute.

National Sun Yat-sen Memorial Hall Located in Xinyi district, Taipei, this memorial pays tribute to Dr Sun Yat-sen, the founder of the Republic of China and considered the father of modern China. It was completed in 1972 and covers more than 28 acres (11 ha). It has a museum commemorating Sun's life and the revolution that he led. It also contains a multipurpose social, educational and cultural center for the public.

CHIANG KAI-SHEK MEMORIAL

THE NATIONAL PALACE MUSEUM

The National Palace Museum was originally established in 1925 as the Palace Museum in Beijing's Forbidden City. When the Nationalists were defeated in 1949, they carried hundreds of thousands of ancient Chinese art and artifacts to Taiwan, many once belonging to Chinese imperial families. The National Palace Museum, opened in 1965 in the Shilin district of Taipei, houses nearly 700,000 pieces of art, the largest collection of Chinese art in the world, including bronze vessels, porcelain, rare books and scrolls, paintings and calligraphy. Only about 1,700 pieces can be exhibited at any one time. The museum is housed in a beautiful building featuring traditional Chinese architecture and can be reached by bus or taxi.

Chiang Kai-shek Memorial Hall Opened in 1980, this is dedicated to Chiang Kai-shek who took over leadership of the Nationalist Party in 1925 when Sun Yat-sen died. He was President of the Republic of Taiwan from 1949 until his death in 1975. The immense building houses a museum, library and gift shop on the ground floor and a large memorial hall and statue of Chiang on the upper floor. The memorial is surrounded by a park and a plaza (Liberty Square) used for mass gatherings in the push for democracy in Taiwan in the 1980s and 1990s.

Pingxi Rail Line This is an 8 mile (13 km) long railway line, one of three sections of the original that remain. Old trains pass through three quaint towns—Shifen, Jingtong and Pingxi—in the Ruifang and Pingxi districts of New Taipei City. You can get off the train at each town to walk around and explore. You'll see things like an old suspension bridge, a waterfall and small, narrow streets. The Pingxi rail line can be accessed by regular train from Taipei. It is best to plan a whole day to see the sights here.

Meinong Hakka Folk Village Located in the southern Taiwan city of Kaohsiung, this is one of the best preserved traditional villages in Taiwan. It is a small farming community and the center of Hakka cultural development. A museum showcases Hakka life and culture. It is renowned for making oil paper umbrellas and is a peaceful place to walk around and spend a day.

Longshan Temple This colorful, picturesque temple is located in the Wanhua district of Taipei, surrounded by high-rise buildings. It is a quiet retreat from the hustle and bustle of Taipei. It was built in 1738 by immi-

PINGXI RAIL LINE

grants from Fujian Province. Like many temples in Taiwan, Longshan offers worshippers a mixture of Buddhist, Taoist and folk deities. It is a popular gathering place after work where you will see old and young alike burning incense and chanting prayers.

Fo Guang Shan Buddhist Monastery Located in Kaohsiung in Taiwan's far south, this is the hub of a new order of Humanistic Buddhism, an amalgam of all Eight Schools of Chinese Buddhism, founded in 1967 by Fo Guan Shan. It is also the largest charity organization in Taiwan, the International Buddhist Progress Society, which provides health care, education and poverty relief programs. The Buddha Memorial Center houses an important tooth relic of the Buddha, donated by a Tibetan lama. Temples and organizations have been established in 173 countries around the world, with more than 3,500 monks and nuns. Some parts of the monastery are open to the public to visit or worship.

KENTING NATIONAL PARK

TAROKO GORGE

NATIONAL PARKS AND OUTDOOR ACTIVITIES

Although Taiwan's cities are densely populated there are many places to get out of town and enjoy the natural beauty of the island. There are nine national parks in addition to other parks and scenic areas.

Taroko National Park This spectacular national park is located just outside the city of Hualien on Taiwan's east coast. The park is named after the Taroko Gorge, a deep and scenic gorge with walls of marble. Taroko means 'magnificent and beautiful' in the Truku language of one of Taiwan's indigenous tribes. Tourists can take a bus into the gorge, drive a car or ride a scooter or bicycle. The park begins with rugged coastal cliffs then moves through subtropical forested canyons to high elevation subalpine forests. In just 30 miles (48 km) you can travel from the coast all the way up into a mountain range at over 11,000 ft (3,353 m) high. There are waterfalls, hiking trails and caves to explore in the park. Lodging ranges from modest motels to an expensive hotel, and even a campground.

Kenting National Park This national park lies on the most southern tip of Taiwan and is famous for its beautiful beaches and lush vegetation. The small town has numerous restaurants and hotels that cater to the tourist industry. Kenting is a popular place for surfing, jet skiing, swimming or simply having fun on the beach. The area is also a tropical botanical garden with thousands of plant species, insects, birds and reptiles. It can be accessed from Taipei by high-speed rail in only 90 minutes, then a transfer bus takes you the rest of the way.

Alishan National Scenic Area A mountain resort and nature preserve in the mountains above Chiayi county in central western Taiwan, the area includes forests, waterfalls, four villages and high-altitude tea plantations. It is a popular area for hiking and mountain climbing, with the mountains averaging 8,200 ft (2,500 m). It is one of the best-known scenic spots in Taiwan.

Sun Moon Lake The largest body of water in Taiwan and one of 13 national scenic areas, Sun Moon Lake is located in Nantou county in central Taiwan. There are many hiking trails around the lake. The east side of the lake resembles a sun while the west side looks like a moon. There is a tiny island in the middle of the lake called Lalu. The area is inhabited by the Thao tribe.

Penghu Islands The Penghus form an archipelago of 64 small islands off the southwest coast of Taiwan. They are also known by their Portuguese name, the Pescadores. The islands are renowned for their beautiful beaches, temples and traditional Chinese-style houses surrounded by coral walls. The beaches are popular for all kinds of water sports. The main city in the Penghu islands is Makung, which can be reached by plane or boat from several of Taiwan's cities.

VISITING **HONG KONG**

Hong Kong, officially Hong Kong Special Administrative Region of the People's Replublic of China, is a former British colony. Located off the southern coast of China, it is a vibrant and densely populated city, a major port and global financial center, and one of the world's top tourist destinations.

A BRIEF HISTORY OF HONG KONG

Hong Kong has been called the Pearl of the Orient. It is a veritable melting pot of East and West. Up to the middle of the 19th century, Hong Kong was just a sleepy fishing village. When Britain defeated the Chinese in the First Opium War (1839–42), the area we know as Hong Kong became a British colony. Hong Kong Island was ceded outright to the British followed by the Kowloon Peninsula in 1860. In 1898, the New Territories were leased from China to the British for 99 years. Except for four years during World War II when the Japanese occupied the colony, Britain governed Hong Kong. Even though the British owned Hong Kong Island and Kowloon outright, in 1997, when the lease on the New Territories ended, it was decided to return the entire colony to the People's Republic of China.

The vast majority of Hong Kongers are Cantonese, many descended from Guangdong Province in southern China. Many of Hong Kong's residents fled the mainland in 1949 when the Communists came to power. Hong Kong Chinese are fiercely independent and proud of their Cantonese and British heritage. As in Taiwan, most people in Hong Kong prefer to distinguish themselves from mainland Chinese.

In 2008 a *Time* magazine article coined the term Nylonkong (New York, London and Hong Kong) to refer to the international nature and financial importance of the three cities in the global economy. Hong Kong truly is a major world city. As such, it has one of the highest per capita incomes in the world. It is also one of the world's most densely populated areas. Covering an area of 407 sq miles (1,054 sq km), with more than 200 islands, most of them uninhabited, Hong Kong has a population of 7.2 million. Most live in 25 sq miles (65 sq km) concentrated on Hong Kong Island, the Kowloon Peninsula and scattered towns across the New Territories.

HONG KONG'S RELATIONSHIP WITH CHINA

Since 1997, Hong Kong has been called a Special Economic Region (SAR) under the People's Republic of China. It is ruled under the principle of 'one country, two systems'. Hong Kong is exclusively in charge of internal affairs and external relations and China is responsible for its foreign affairs and defense. Although China agreed to allow Hong Kong to retain its capitalist-style governance and other institutions for a period of 50 years, and indeed much has remained the same as under British rule, some civil liberties have been curbed as the Chinese have tried to institute some forms of censorship in the media and other forms of control over Hong Kong.

Many Hong Kong citizens are deeply suspicious of the Chinese government and their plans for Hong Kong, and anti-Beijing sentiment runs high. One example is when China announced that all schools in Hong Kong would be required to provide classes in patriotism, basically mainland appreciation and extolling the benefits of one-party rule. Thousands of Hong Kong citizens took to the streets to protest what they considered an attempt at brainwashing children. The government finally backed down and scrapped the plan. More recently, thousands of pro-democarcy protestors poured into the streets of Hong Kong calling for the right to elect the city's leader in 2017, free of interference by the central government in Beijing. This kind of situation highlights the cultural, social and political gap between Hong Kong and the mainland. Compared to the mainland, Hong Kong enjoys a high degree of freedom, including a free press, the right to assemble and transparent institutions accountable to the people. These are all things that worry the government in Beijing.

HONG KONG'S UNIQUE CULTURE

Hong Kong is like no other place on earth. It is a modern, dynamic world city, with influences from both China and the West. It is a melting pot of peoples and cultures. Apart from Chinese, you will see Indian and Nepalese business people, British, American and European business people and tourists, Japanese, Vietnamese, Malaysians, Indonesians and Filipinos, and a number of other peoples. Restaurants serve every kind of food imaginable. In addition to excellent Chinese food, especially Cantonese dim sum, I've had excellent Italian and Indian food, and even Spanish tapas in Hong Kong.

This internationalization and openness to Asia and the West has created a unique culture in Hong Kong that successfully mixes the best of East and West. The education system is based on Western standards with some Chinese flavor. The population is highly educated and the people are modern and forward thinking with a clear sense of the world around them. They are Chinese in that they tend to follow a Confucian value system as in other parts of the Chinese-speaking world. Buddhism and ancestral worship are prevalent in Hong Kong but there is also a strong Christian presence of various denominations and other religions. Hong Kongers have always lived in a free society with all the benefits that this brings.

THINGS TO DO IN HONG KONG

Tsim Sha Tsui East Promenade and the Star Ferry Located at the very tip of the Kowloon Peninsula, the Tsim Sha Tsui district enjoys excellent views of Victoria Harbour. A pleasant promenade along the waterfront begins at the old Kowloon-Canton Railway clock tower and ends in Tsim Sha Tsui East area near the Hung Hom train station. Along the way is the Hong Kong Avenue of the Stars, a tribute to Hong Kong's movie stars, exceptional views of the harbor and Hong Kong Island, and at night a Symphony of Lights laser light and fireworks show.

Although a cross-harbor tunnel accommodates Hong Kong's subway system as well as cars, many people still choose to ride the Star Ferry between Kowloon and Central district on Hong Kong Island. The ferry has been in use since 1888 and is the best way to see Hong Kong's famous harbor up close.

STAR FERRY IN VICTORIA HARBOUR

VICTORIA PEAK TRAM

Victoria Peak and Tram Victoria Peak is the highest point on Hong Kong Island and offers the best views of the harbor. The fastest and most direct route is to take the tram from Central district right to the top of the peak. The tram climbs 1,300 ft (400 m) and is an enjoyable way to see the skyscrapers as you pass by. Once on top there are numerous pathways offering different views of the harbor and the skyscrapers below.

Victoria Park Located in the Causeway Bay area, Victoria Park is the largest patch of public green space on Hong Kong Island. It is named after Britain's Queen Victoria. It is a popular gathering spot in the mornings for choreographed taichi sessions and other exercise. It is also a popular spot for domestic workers (mostly Indonesians and Filipinos) to gather on their day off (Sunday) and for people celebrating the Mid-Autumn Festival to show off their lanterns. Victoria Park has also been a gathering point for Hong Kong demonstrations, many of them anti-Beijing.

Eat Dim Sum Meaning 'touch your heart', dim sum is the traditional breakfast and lunch food of the Cantonese. It consists of bite-sized servings of dumplings and other small dishes that are steamed, baked, pan-fried or deep-fried. The Cantonese in Hong Kong call going out to eat dim sum,

yum cha or 'to drink tea'. Teahouse restaurants are all over Hong Kong. They can be very large, crowded and noisy. There is no menu. Instead, women push carts through the restaurant shouting out what they are serving. A large dim sum restaurant will offer about 100 different dishes. To order, you simple motion for the lady to come over and serve the dish. By the time you are done, your table will be littered with bamboo steaming baskets and other containers, as well as teapots and teacups.

Jumbo Floating Restaurant In Aberdeen Harbour on the back side of Hong Kong Island are two floating seafood restaurants. Jumbo is the largest and looks like a cross between Beijing's Imperial Palace and a casino. It is flamboyant, kitschy and fun. There is a free ferry shuttle for diners from the pier

Steamed, baked and fried bite-sized morsels and accompanying sauces are part of the dim sum experience.

on Aberdeen Promenade. On the second floor is the Dragon Court, a fine dining restauarant serving innovative Cantonese food, or you can eat reasonably priced dim sum on the third floor.

Roof of the IFC Mall One of Hong Kong's best-kept secrets is the landscaped rooftoop picnic strip on top of the waterfront IFC (International Financial Center) Mall. It offers spectacular views of the harbor and the skyscrapers on Kowloon Peninsula. Although you can eat at several very good restaurants in the mall, you can also bring your own food and picnic on the roof garden resort-style tables and sofas, which are open to the public.

Chungking Mansions These consist of five 17-story buildings in the Tsim Sha Tsui district of Kowloon. The buildings are a maze of apartments, guest houses, Indian restaurants, souvenir shops, tailors and foreign exchange offices. They have a resident population of about 4,000, but are visited daily by about 10,000 people. Chungking Mansions is a prime example of globalization with 120 different nationalities walking through the place on a yearly basis. Most of those who work there are South Asian or African. It is considered the unofficial African quarter of Hong Kong. It's a fun place to wander around, shop and pick up a good plate of curry.

Left The skyline of Hong Kong is considered one of the best in the world, with the surrounding mountains and Victoria Harbour complementing its 8,000 high-rise buildings.
Below Jumbo Floating Restaurant, one of the world's largest of its type, is a popular seafood dining spot in Aberdeen Harbour. It has featured in many Jackie Chan and other movies.

Temple Street Night Market

The Temple Street Night Market, located in central Kowloon, is one of the liveliest street bazaars in Kong Kong. It is the place to go for cheap clothes, trinkets, pirated CDs and DVDs, fake label designer goods, shoes, cookware and just about anything else. It is also a great place to try Hong Kong's street food sold from food stalls on wheels, and to see fortune-tellers, herbalists and, occasionally, some free open-air Cantonese opera performances. The market is cut in two by the Tin Hau Temple complex where you can see worshippers and lots of incense smoke.

Wong Tai Sin Temple This is a popular and active Taoist temple in the northern part of Kowloon below Lion Rock. Wong Tai Sin or 'Great Immortal Wong' is a popular deity said to have the power of healing. This temple was built in 1921 and is a busy working temple visited by all walks of Hong Kong society. It is a colorful explosion of red pillars, roofs, latticework, flowers, incense and worshippers.

Po Lin Buddhist Monastery and Tian Tan Buddha This huge monastery, a major center of Buddhism in Hong Kong, is on Lantau Island, also the location of Hong Kong's international airport. It was built in 1924. On the hill above the monastery is the Tian Tan Buddha, also known as the Big Buddha, a seated representation of the Buddha that is 112 ft (34 m) high, completed in 1993. Walking paths lead up to and around the Buddha. Inside the Buddha is a large bell that is controlled by computer and rings 108 times a day to symbolize the escape from the 108 troubles of mankind.

The most scenic way to get to the monastery is to take the Tung Chung rail line to Tung Chung. From there take the Ngong Ping 360 25-minute aerial tram across the bay and up to the Ngong Ping village, which is a five-minute walk to Po Lin Monastery. The tram offers excellent views of Lantau Island, the airport and other neighboring islands and bays.

Tai O Fishing Village Home to the Tanka people, Tai O village is located on the western side of Lantau Island. It was once an important trading and fishing port with China. Salt and fish are the main exports. Although the village is in decline, except for tourism, some of the older residents still raise ducks, sell fish and make the celebrated shrimp paste and salted fish that you will see and smell all over the village. It's a popular place for locals to buy both fresh and dried seafood. Some of the original stilt houses built over the waterway are still standing. This is a good place to get a feel for Hong Kong's past.

Cheung Chau Island This is a small island 6.2 miles (10 km) off the coast of Hong Kong Island and can be reached by ferry. It is a dumbbell-shaped island with about 20,000 residents living in the middle of the island where it is flat. It is a bustling fishing port that was settled back in the Ming Dynasty (1368–1644). It is known for good seafood restaurants, clean beaches, hiking trails and a laid-back vibe. It is a pleasant way to escape the hustle and bustle of Hong Kong for a day.

JUMBO FLOATING RESTAURANT

Shutterstock.com; **75 top, left below** © Li Lin/Dreamstime.com; **75 bottom, right** © Hanhua/Dreamstime.com; **75 bottom, left** © Dean Groom/flickr.com; **76 top** © Jorisvo/istockphoto.com; **77 middle, left** © Sunflowerey/Shutterstock.com; **77 bottom** © whaihs/123rf.com; **78 top** © Sean Pavone/Dreamstime.com; **79 top** © leungchopan/Shutterstock.com; **79 left, above** © TonyV3112/Shutterstock.com; **79 bottom** © Stuart Jenner/Dreamstime.com; **80/81top** © XiXinXing/Shutterstock.com; **80 bottom** © Rawpixelimages/Dreamstime.com; **81 top** © imtmphoto/Shutterstock.com; **81 left, below** © Shannon Fagan/Dreamstime.com; **83 top** © Operation Shooting/Shutterstock.com; **83 bottom** © li jianbing/Shutterstock.com; **84 top, right** © Maomaotou/Dreamstime.com; **84 middle, left** © Rafael Ben-ari/Dreamstime.com; **84 bottom** © Tsangming Chang/Dreamstime.com; **85 above** © Hupeng/Dreamstime.com; **85 below** © Huating/Dreamstime.com; **86 top** © Lovephoto227/Dreamstime.com; **86 bottom** © Ilya Terentyev/istockphoto.com; **88 bottom** © Tom Wang/Dreamstime.com; **90 below** © lzf/Shutterstock.com; **92 top** © Denis Makarenko/Dreamstime.com; **92 left, above** © Li Lin/Dreamstime.com; **92 bottom, inset** © tc397/istockphoto.com; **92/93 bottom, middle** © Korkusung/Shutterstock.com; **93 top** © Grosremy/Dreamstime.com; **93 top, inset; 98 top, right** lzf/istockphoto.com; **93 right, above** © John Anderson/Dreamstime.com; **93 bottom, inset** © TonyV3112/Shutterstock.com; **93 right, below; 110 bottom** © EdStock/istockphoto.com; **94 top** © Hupeng/Dreamstime.com; **94 bottom** © luxizeng/istockphoto.com; **95 left, above** © Fotokon/Shutterstock.com; **96 top, left** © HongChan001/Dreamstime.com; **96 top, right** © Daniel Budiman/Dreamstime.com; **96 bottom** © Szefei/Dreamstime.com; **97 above** © windmoon/Shutterstock.com; **97 below** © Petegar/istockphoto.com; **98 top, left** © zhang bo/istockphoto.com; **98 top, middle** © BreatheFitness/istockphoto.com; **98 top, right** © lzf/istockphoto.com; **99 top** © Jjspring/Dreamstime.com; **99 left, below** © Maocheng/Dreamstime.com; **100 top** © peng wu/istockphoto.com; **100 bottom** © foomtsuruhashi/flickr.com; **101 top** © Song Heming/Dreamstime.com; **102 top, left** © DFree/Shutterstock.com; **103 top** © Li Lin/Dreamstime.com; **104 bottom** © Dk88888/Dreamstime.com; **105 top, left** © Kevin_Hsieh/Shutterstock.com; **105 bottom** © Katerina Kousalova/Dreamstime.com; **106 top, left** © Xi Zhang/Dreamstime.com; **110 top, left** © EdStock/istockphoto.com; **110 top, right** © Denis Makarenko/istockphoto.com; **110 bottom** © EdStock/istockphoto.com; **111 top, left** © Denis Makarenko/Dreamstime.com; **112 bottom** © Anton_Ivanov/Shutterstock.com; **114 right, below** © Erinpackardphotography/Dreamstime.com; **116 top** © Hung Chung Chih/Shutterstock.com; **116 left, bottom** © Yong hian Lim/Dreamstime.com; **116/117 bottom, middle** © Xianghong Wu/Dreamstime.com; **117 left, top** © Hupeng/Dreamstime.com; **117 left, middle** © Markandcressie/Dreamstime.com; **117 top, inset** © Linqong/Dreamstime.com; **117 right** © Mike K./Dreamstime.com; **118 top** © 1828858957/Shutterstock.com; **119 top** © Frenta/Dreamstime.com; **119 bottom** © Xi Zhang/Dreamstime.com; **120 above** © Songquan Deng/Shutterstock.com; **120 below** © Hupeng/Dreamstime.com; **120/121 top, middle** © Photo168/Dreamstime.com; **121 top, right** © Atosan/Dreamstime.com; **122 top, left** © Rivercc/Dreamstime.com; **122 top, right** © Wing Travelling/Dreamstime.com; **122 bottom** © Andres Garcia Martin /Dreamstime.com; **123 top, left** © Frenta/Dreamstime.com; **123 top, right** © Tempestz/Dreamstime.com; **124 top** © Hxdylzj/Dreamstime.com; **125 top** © Luq1/Dreamstime.com; **125 left** © Xing Wang/Dreamstime.com; **125 bottom** © Hung Chung Chih /Shutterstock.com; **126 top, right** © beibaoke/Shutterstock.com; **126 middle, right** © Anita Kuipers/Dreamstime.com; **126 bottom, above** © beibaoke/Shutterstock.com; **126 bottom, below** © beibaoke/Shutterstock.com; **127 top, middle** © beibaoke/Shutterstock.com; **127 top, left** © Trial/Shutterstock.com; **127 right, middle** © Daniel Prudek/Shutterstock.com; **127 bottom, left** © lkoimages/Shutterstock.com; **127 bottom, right** © Vadim Petrakov/Shutterstock.com; **128 middle** © Galyna Andrushko/Shutterstock.com; **128 bottom, left** © Udompeter/Shutterstock.com; **128 bottom, right** © Vladimir Melnik/Shutterstock.com; **129 top, left** © Chun Guo/Dreamstime.com; **129 top right** © Lin Gang/Dreamstime.com; **129 top, middle** © Littlewormy/Dreamstime.com; **130 top, left** © Mayinxi/Dreamstime; **130 top, right** © John Mccabe/Dreamstime.com; **130 bottom** © Xankee/Dreamstime.com; **131 top, left** © 栋田/Dreamstime.com; **131 top, right** © Cons972/Dreamstime.com; **131 right, middle** © The Curious Travelers/Shutterstock.com; **132 top** © GuoZhongHua/Shutterstock.com; **132 bottom** © Jackmalipan/Dreamstime.com; **133 top** © Pindiyath100/Dreamstime.com; **134 top** © Outcast85/Dreamstime.com; **135 top** © gracethang2/Shutterstock.com; **135 middle, right; 116 left, middle** © Lcc54613/Dreamstime.com; **135 right** © LIU, CHIN-CHENG/Shutterstock.com; **136 top** © Superjoseph/Dreamstime.com; **136 bottom** © fototrav/istockphoto.com; **137 top** © Uwe Halstenbach/istockphoto.com; **138 top** © StargazeStudio/Dreamstime.com; **139 top** © Iakov Kalinin/Shutterstock.com; **139 middle** © Meccasky/Dreamstime.com; **140 top, left** © Typhoonski/Dreamstime,com; **140 top, right** © Leung Cho Pan/Dreamstime.com; **141 top** © Twickey/Dreamstime.com; **141 bottom** © Pindiyath100/Dreamstime.com; **144 top, left** © Anton_Ivanov/Shutterstock.com; **144 top, right** © Derrick Neill/Dreamstime.com; **144 middle, right** © Hupeng/Dreamstime.com; **144 middle, bottom** © byvalet/Shutterstock.com; **144 bottom, left above** © Rudra Narayan Mitra/Dreamstime.com; **144 bottom, left below** © Piccaya/Dreamstime.com; **inside back cover 1st row, right** © Hupeng/Dreamstime.com; **2nd row, middle** © chungking/Shutterstock.com; **2nd row, right** © Rafael Ben-ari/Dreamstime.com; **3rd row, left** © Kanok Sulaiman/Shutterstock.com; **3rd row, middle left** © DFree / Shutterstock.com; **4th row, far left** © Bobby Brill/Dreamstime.com; **4th row, left** Maran Garai/Shutterstock.com; **4th row, right** © Pak To Tam/Dreamstime.com

The images in the following pages are in the public domain and have been made available through the generosity of the following sources in Wikimedia Commons and Wikipedia

https://commons.wikimedia.org/: **9 bottom, inset**; **10 top, right**; **10 bottom, right** Yuan, Zhongyi; **11 bottom, left** Hannah~commonswiki; **11 bottom, middle** Tokyo National Museum; **11 bottom, right**; **12 top** Portal, Jane (Ed.); **13 above** Tang Li Xian Mu Bi Hua (1974); **13 below** Richard M. Barnhart; **14 top**; **14 middle**; **14 bottom** Library of Congress; **15 bottom** The Grosvenor House Antiques Fair; **16 top** Chinese archives; **16 middle** US National Archives; **17 top, left** www.fordlibrarymuseum.gov; **28 bottom** www.epochtimes.com; **43 bottom** Gavatron at English Wikipedia; **65 top, left** www.voachinese.com; **82 bottom, left** Kantgrad; **82 bottom, right inset** Wuhan University; **82 bottom, right** Zhangmoon618; **101 bottom**; **102 top, right** Totoiverson; **102 bottom** flic.kr/p/vjWPhr; **103 bottom** Flickr; **105 top, right** Mk2010; **107 bottom, left** http//comic.people; **114 left** www.flickr.com; **114 right, above** http: cctvnews.cntv.cn;

en.wikipedia files:

107 bottom, right Art by Alfonso Wong; **109 top, left** www.imdb.com; **109 top, middle** www.movieposterdb.com; **109 top, right** Sevilledade; **109 bottom, above** www.posteritati.com; **109 bottom below** www.movieposterdb.com; **110/111 middle** http: chinesemov.com; **111 top, right** © 2005 Columbia Pictures; **111 bottom** Siam Zone; **112 top, left**; **112, top middle**; **112/113 top, middle** http: movie.mtime.com; **113 top, right** http: movie.douban.com; **112 middle, right** http: movie.douban.com; **113 middle, left** MoviePosterDB.com; **115 top** http: mgsrc.baidu.com; **115 bottom** source: http://v.qq.com

ACKNOWLEDGMENTS

My students over the years have been a constant source of inspiration and are the ones that motivated the writing of this book. It really was for them, particularly my Flagship students, that I wrote this book in an attempt to help them better prepare for and succeed in China-related careers.

My former student, colleague and content advisor Michael Paul provided valuable assistance in the research that went into this book. He reviewed and edited each section of the book and provided valuable comments and recommendations. His practical advice and ideas were greatly appreciated. He was also a great traveling companion on several trips to China. I appreciate his friendship and assistance.

I am grateful to several of my colleagues at Brigham Young University for their input and advice on various sections of this book, particularly Shu-pei Wang, Rachel Yu Liu, Xinyi Wu and Rita Chen.

Finally, a big thanks to my wife and kids for always being there for me and supporting me in my career and my travels in China.

ABOUT TUTTLE
BOOKS TO SPAN THE EAST AND WEST

Our core mission at Tuttle Publishing is to create books which bring people together one page at a time. Tuttle was founded in 1832 in the small New England town of Rutland, Vermont (USA). Our fundamental values remain as strong today as they were then—to publish best-in-class books informing the English-speaking world about the countries and peoples of Asia. The world has become a smaller place today and Asia's economic, cultural and political influence has expanded, yet the need for meaningful dialogue and information about this diverse region has never been greater. Since 1948, Tuttle has been a leader in publishing books on the cultures, arts, cuisines, languages and literatures of Asia. Our authors and photographers have won numerous awards and Tuttle has published thousands of books on subjects ranging from martial arts to paper crafts. We welcome you to explore the wealth of information available on Asia at www.tuttlepublishing.com